This thought-provoking colle of
union with Christ from exegeti 's.
It is foundational in the New is
the essence of the *ordo salutis*. -
pastors who contribute to this ... contours of
the concept, reminding us that participation in Jesus Christ is no mere
academic consideration, but stands guard over every spiritual blessing
enjoyed by the redeemed soul. They also help us see that while a simple
phrase like 'union with Christ' can engage the deepest thinking and
even stir up controversy in the church, it represents a motif which
permeates Scripture and which, when considered in the Bible's own
light, leads to a life dedicated to the Saviour. This is a welcome addition
to the literature on the subject.

IAIN D CAMPBELL
Point Free Church of Scotland, Isle of Lewis, UK

In
Christ Alone

Edited by
STEPHEN CLARK AND MATTHEW EVANS

affinity
gospel churches in partnership

Ɽ**ENTOR**

Copyright © Affinity 2016

ISBN 978-1-78191-770-1

Published in 2016
in the
Mentor Imprint
by
Christian Focus Publications Ltd,
Geanies House, Fearn, Ross-shire
IV20 1TW, Scotland
www.christianfocus.com

Cover design by Daniel van Straaten

Printed by Bell and Bain, Glasgow

CONTENTS

PREFACE

The substance of chapters 1 to 6 of the present volume was presented at the 2015 Affinity Theological Study Conference at The King's Centre, Northampton. The theme of the conference was 'Union With Christ'. This theme was chosen by the organising committee because it is a subject that is so important to biblical Christianity but is one which has not received the attention which it once commanded in the church of Jesus Christ. In recent years there has been the beginning of a healthy recovery of this doctrine. For this reason, it was felt that it would be good to explore the subject in some depth.

All the speakers either have been or are involved in training men for gospel ministry and been involved in gospel ministry themselves. This was a fundamental criterion for inviting them to address the conference because of the conviction of the organising committee that the truth which we study must be related to real church life. The choice of particular speakers was determined by their evangelical commitment and their giftedness in the particular aspect of union with Christ which they were to address. Cor Bennema pursued doctoral studies in the Gospel of

John and has published a number of works on this Gospel. Tim Ward is involved in training men in a Bible-teaching ministry and has given considerable thought to Paul's letter to the Galatians. Robert Letham, who lectures in the same institution as Cor Bennema – Wales Evangelical School of Theology, in South Wales – did doctoral studies in John Calvin and has also published a book on the theme of union with Christ, while John Fesko, from the USA, is involved in training men for gospel ministry and has published material on John Owen. David McKay is in pastoral ministry and theological education in Northern Ireland, while Paul Wells was similarly occupied for many years in Provence in France. Both of these men have ministered, therefore, and trained men for ministry, in areas where Roman Catholicism has had a considerable presence, and where clarity upon the doctrines of justification and sanctification is especially important.

Inevitably a conference has to be selective in those aspects of a subject which are to be addressed. The organising committee was firmly committed to beginning with biblical teaching before going on to consider historical material. Papers five and six then sought to consider how aspects of this subject should be 'systematised'. The Johannine literature (excluding the book of Revelation) and the writings of Paul (dealt with through the letter to the Galatians) would prove a fruitful source of biblical material. The names of John Calvin and John Owen shine in the theological firmament, and their contributions to this area of truth are of considerable significance. Too frequently the doctrines of justification and sanctification have been considered apart from the doctrine of union with Christ, which is not at all how the New Testament approaches things.

The only material not presented at the conference is the final chapter, which I have written. A word of explanation will be in order as to the purpose of this chapter. Inevitably the papers on the biblical material were specialised, being confined to two biblical authors, both of whom wrote New Testament books. It is necessary, however, to see how the doctrine of union with

Christ – as, indeed, how any doctrine – is to be found in all the Scriptures and develops throughout the Bible. In other words, the hiatus or gap between the study of isolated biblical material and the construction of systematic theology needs to be filled with a *biblical theological* approach, which traces a theme through the whole Bible. The last chapter seeks to do this, by finding the doctrine in germinal or embryonic form in Genesis chapter 3, and then developed throughout the whole of the Bible. Furthermore, the papers delivered at the conference inevitably raised a whole range of questions, some concerning the nature of biblical interpretation and others of a more systematic theological nature. I have sought to address some of these issues, sometimes in the main text and sometimes in extended footnotes. I hope I have shed light upon these issues rather than added to confusion. Whether I have succeeded in this, I leave the reader to judge. Finally, it is important that this teaching be applied to the needs of God's people today, and the experiential implications of union with Christ needed some exploration. This I seek to do towards the end of the chapter I have written. Like the other contributors to this volume, I am engaged both in gospel ministry as the pastor of a church, and in training men for gospel ministry, my particular field of instruction being that of systematic theology or Christian doctrine.

It is the prayer of the organising committee and of all the contributors that this book will shed light in the minds, produce warmth in the hearts, and lead to practical godliness in the lives of all who read it. *Soli Deo Gloria.*

Stephen Clark

Chair of the Affinity Theological Study Conference

LIST OF ABBREVIATIONS

ANE   Ancient Near East(ern)
CO   Calvini Opera [quae supersunt Omnia]
JETS   Journal of the Evangelical Theology Society
JPT(SS)   Journal of Pentecostal Theology (Supplement Series)
OS   Opera Selecta (John Calvin)
PL   Patrologia Cursus Completus: Series Latina (ed. P. Migne).
SJT   Scottish Journal of Theology
WTJ   Westminster Theological Journal

Bibles

AV   Authorised Version (King James Bible)
ESV   English Standard Version
NASB   New American Standard Bible
NIV   New International Version

LIST OF CONTRIBUTORS

Cornelis Bennema Senior Lecturer in New Testament at Union School of Theology (www.ust.ac.uk)

Stephen Clark Minister of Freeschool Court Evangelical Church, Bridgend; Lecturer in Systematic Theology, London Theological Seminary, and on the Theological Training Course of the Evangelical Movement of Wales of which he is Principal and Director

John Fesko Professor of Systematic and Historical Theology, Westminster Seminary, California

Robert Letham Professor of Systematic and Historical Theology, Union School of Theology

David McKay 'Professor of Systematic Theology, Ethics and Apologetics, Reformed Theological College, Belfast, and minister of Shaftesbury Square Reformed Presbyterian Church, Belfast

Tim Ward Associate Director, PT Cornhill Training Course

Paul Wells Faculté Jean Calvin, Aix-en-Provence, France and Extraordinary Professor at North-West University, South Africa

CHAPTER ONE

'Union with Christ' in the Johannine Writings

CORNELIS BENNEMA

1. Introduction

Paul is probably best known for his phrase 'in Christ' to depict the believer's union with Christ, but John also has a great deal to say on this topic in both his Gospel and the Letters. As we examine the Johannine literature, the text confronts us with various questions: What reality does our union with Christ indicate? Is our union with Christ secure or can it be broken? What does union with Christ look like in daily life? In order to answer these questions, I adopt a bottom-up, text-centred approach for two reasons. First, the phrase 'union with Christ' does not occur in the Johannine literature – it is a concept – so we must examine the Johannine text to find out what language John uses to convey this concept (sections 2-3). Second, once we know what to look for in the Johannine text and where, we can examine the key passages in order to understand the nature and mechanics of 'union with Christ' (sections 4-7).

2. John's Language for 'Union with Christ'

The phrase 'union with Christ' does not occur in any of the Johannine writings. Instead, it is a concept. However, if we wish to speak legitimately of a Johannine concept of union with Christ, rather than importing a foreign concept into the text, we must show that such a concept is rooted in real words in the Johannine writings. Hence, we must first think about the language or literal terms John uses that gives rise to this concept. The questions that I will address in this section are: What language or linguistic expressions does John use to indicate the concept 'union with Christ'? Which of these expressions are most common to convey this concept? In which parts of the Johannine literature does this concept occur most? In short, when we want to speak of 'union with Christ' in the Johannine writings, *what should we look for and where?*

In this section, I will outline five Johannine linguistic expressions that convey the idea of 'union with Christ', and in section 3, I will analyse the data. In sections 4-7, I will examine the key passages in order to explain the concept of union with Christ.[1]

2.1 Oneness

John 10:16 I have other sheep that do not belong to this fold. I must bring them also, and they will listen to my voice. So there will be <u>one flock, one shepherd</u>.

John 10:16 καὶ ἄλλα πρόβατα ἔχω ἃ οὐκ ἔστιν ἐκ τῆς αὐλῆς ταύτης· κἀκεῖνα δεῖ με ἀγαγεῖν καὶ τῆς φωνῆς μου ἀκούσουσιν, καὶ γενήσονται <u>μία ποίμνη, εἷς ποιμήν</u>.

*****

John 10:30 The Father and I <u>are one</u>.

John 10:30 ἐγὼ καὶ ὁ πατὴρ <u>ἕν ἐσμεν</u>.

*****

John 11:51-52 He did not say this on his own, but being high priest that year he prophesied that Jesus was about to die for the

---

1.   The translation is from the NRSV with the occasional, altered translation shown in italics. The Greek text is that of Nestle-Aland, 28ᵗʰ edition.

nation, [52]and not for the nation only, but <u>to gather into one</u> the dispersed children of God.

John 11:51-52 τοῦτο δὲ ἀφ' ἑαυτοῦ οὐκ εἶπεν, ἀλλὰ ἀρχιερεὺς ὢν τοῦ ἐνιαυτοῦ ἐκείνου ἐπροφήτευσεν ὅτι ἔμελλεν Ἰησοῦς ἀποθνῄσκειν ὑπὲρ τοῦ ἔθνους, καὶ οὐχ ὑπὲρ τοῦ ἔθνους μόνον ἀλλ' ἵνα καὶ τὰ τέκνα τοῦ θεοῦ τὰ διεσκορπισμένα <u>συναγάγῃ εἰς ἕν</u>.

*****

John 17:11 And now I am no longer in the world, but they are in the world, and I am coming to you. Holy Father, protect them in your name that you have given me, <u>so that they may be one, as we are one</u>.

John 17:11 καὶ οὐκέτι εἰμὶ ἐν τῷ κόσμῳ, καὶ αὐτοὶ ἐν τῷ κόσμῳ εἰσίν, κἀγὼ πρὸς σὲ ἔρχομαι. πάτερ ἅγιε, τήρησον αὐτοὺς ἐν τῷ ὀνόματί σου ᾧ δέδωκάς μοι, <u>ἵνα ὦσιν ἓν καθὼς ἡμεῖς</u>.

*****

John 17:20-23 I ask not only on behalf of these, but also on behalf of those who will believe in me through their word, [21] <u>that they may all be one</u>... [22] The glory that you have given me I have given them, <u>so that they may be one, as we are one</u>, [23] I in them and you in me, <u>that they may become completely one</u>.

John 17:20-23 Οὐ περὶ τούτων δὲ ἐρωτῶ μόνον, ἀλλὰ καὶ περὶ τῶν πιστευόντων διὰ τοῦ λόγου αὐτῶν εἰς ἐμέ, [21] <u>ἵνα πάντες ἓν ὦσιν</u>... [22] κἀγὼ τὴν δόξαν ἣν δέδωκάς μοι δέδωκα αὐτοῖς, <u>ἵνα ὦσιν ἓν καθὼς ἡμεῖς ἕν</u>· [23] ἐγὼ ἐν αὐτοῖς καὶ σὺ ἐν ἐμοί, <u>ἵνα ὦσιν τετελειωμένοι εἰς ἕν</u>.

2.2 Indwelling/Abiding

There is a significant semantic overlap between the expressions 'to be in' and 'to remain in', suggesting that they denote the same reality, namely that of indwelling or abiding.

John 6:56 Those who eat my flesh and drink my blood <u>abide in me, and I in them.</u>

John 6:56 ὁ τρώγων μου τὴν σάρκα καὶ πίνων μου τὸ αἷμα <u>ἐν ἐμοὶ μένει κἀγὼ ἐν αὐτῷ.</u>

*****

John 8:31 Then Jesus said to the Jews who had believed in him, 'If you <u>*remain* in my word</u>, you are truly my disciples'.

John 8:31 ἔλεγεν οὖν ὁ Ἰησοῦς πρὸς τοὺς πεπιστευκότας αὐτῷ Ἰουδαίους· ἐὰν ὑμεῖς <u>μείνητε ἐν τῷ λόγῳ</u> τῷ ἐμῷ, ἀληθῶς μαθηταί μού ἐστε

*****

John 8:35 <u>The slave does not have a permanent place in</u> the household; <u>the son has a place</u> there forever.

John 8:35 <u>ὁ δὲ δοῦλος οὐ μένει ἐν τῇ οἰκίᾳ</u> εἰς τὸν αἰῶνα, <u>ὁ υἱὸς μένει</u> εἰς τὸν αἰῶνα.

*****

John 10:38 But if I do them [the works of my Father], even though you do not believe me, believe the works, so that you may know and understand that <u>the Father is in me and I am in the Father.</u>

John 10:38 εἰ δὲ ποιῶ, κἂν ἐμοὶ μὴ πιστεύητε, τοῖς ἔργοις πιστεύετε, ἵνα γνῶτε καὶ γινώσκητε ὅτι <u>ἐν ἐμοὶ ὁ πατὴρ κἀγὼ ἐν τῷ πατρί.</u>

*****

John 14:2-3 In my Father's house there are many <u>dwelling places.</u> If it were not so, would I have told you that I go to prepare a place for you? [3]And if I go and prepare a place for you, I will come again and will take you to myself, so that where I am, there you may be also.

John 14:2-3 ἐν τῇ οἰκίᾳ τοῦ πατρός μου <u>μοναὶ</u> πολλαί εἰσιν· εἰ δὲ μή, εἶπον ἂν ὑμῖν ὅτι πορεύομαι ἑτοιμάσαι τόπον ὑμῖν; καὶ ἐὰν πορευθῶ καὶ ἑτοιμάσω τόπον ὑμῖν, πάλιν ἔρχομαι καὶ παραλήμψομαι ὑμᾶς πρὸς ἐμαυτόν, ἵνα ὅπου εἰμὶ ἐγὼ καὶ ὑμεῖς ἦτε.

*****

John 14:10-11 Do you not believe that <u>I am in the Father and the Father is in me</u>? The words that I say to you I do not speak on my own; but <u>the Father who dwells in me</u> does his works. [11] Believe me that <u>I am in the Father and the Father is in me</u>; but if you do not, then believe me because of the works themselves.

John 14:10-11 οὐ πιστεύεις ὅτι <u>ἐγὼ ἐν τῷ πατρὶ καὶ ὁ πατὴρ ἐν ἐμοί ἐστιν</u>; τὰ ῥήματα ἃ ἐγὼ λέγω ὑμῖν ἀπ' ἐμαυτοῦ οὐ λαλῶ, <u>ὁ δὲ πατὴρ ἐν ἐμοὶ μένων</u> ποιεῖ τὰ ἔργα αὐτοῦ. [11] πιστεύετέ μοι ὅτι <u>ἐγὼ ἐν τῷ πατρὶ καὶ ὁ πατὴρ ἐν ἐμοί</u>· εἰ δὲ μή, διὰ τὰ ἔργα αὐτὰ πιστεύετε.

*****

John 14:17 This is the Spirit of truth, whom the world cannot receive, because it neither sees him nor knows him. You know him, because <u>he abides with you,</u> and <u>he will be in you.</u>

John 14:17 τὸ πνεῦμα τῆς ἀληθείας, ὃ ὁ κόσμος οὐ δύναται λαβεῖν, ὅτι οὐ θεωρεῖ αὐτὸ οὐδὲ γινώσκει· ὑμεῖς γινώσκετε αὐτό, ὅτι <u>παρ' ὑμῖν μένει</u> καὶ <u>ἐν ὑμῖν ἔσται</u>.

*****

John 14:20 On that day you will know that <u>I am in my Father, and you in me, and I in you.</u>

John 14:20 ἐν ἐκείνῃ τῇ ἡμέρᾳ γνώσεσθε ὑμεῖς ὅτι <u>ἐγὼ ἐν τῷ πατρί μου καὶ ὑμεῖς ἐν ἐμοὶ κἀγὼ ἐν ὑμῖν</u>.

*****

John 14:23 Jesus answered him, 'Those who love me will keep my word, and my Father will love them, and <u>we will</u> come to them and <u>make our home with them.</u>'

John 14:23 ἀπεκρίθη Ἰησοῦς καὶ εἶπεν αὐτῷ· ἐάν τις ἀγαπᾷ με τὸν λόγον μου τηρήσει, καὶ ὁ πατήρ μου ἀγαπήσει αὐτὸν καὶ πρὸς αὐτὸν ἐλευσόμεθα καὶ <u>μονὴν παρ᾽ αὐτῷ ποιησόμεθα</u>.

*****

John 15:4-10 <u>Abide in me as I abide in you</u>. Just as the branch cannot bear fruit by itself unless it abides in the vine, neither can you unless you abide in me. [5] I am the vine, you are the branches. <u>Those who abide in me and I in them</u> bear much fruit, because apart from me you can do nothing. [6] Whoever does not abide in me is thrown away like a branch and withers; such branches are gathered, thrown into the fire, and burned. [7] <u>If you abide in me, and my words abide in you</u>, ask for whatever you wish, and it will be done for you. [8] My Father is glorified by this, that you bear much fruit and become my disciples.

[9] As the Father has loved me, so I have loved you; <u>abide in my love</u>. [10] If you keep my commandments, <u>you will abide in my love</u>, just as I have kept my Father's commandments and abide in his love.

<u>John</u> **15:4-10** <u>μείνατε ἐν ἐμοί, κἀγὼ ἐν ὑμῖν</u>. καθὼς τὸ κλῆμα οὐ δύναται καρπὸν φέρειν ἀφ᾽ ἑαυτοῦ ἐὰν μὴ μένη ἐν τῇ ἀμπέλῳ, οὕτως οὐδὲ ὑμεῖς ἐὰν μὴ ἐν ἐμοὶ μένητε. [5] ἐγώ εἰμι ἡ ἄμπελος, ὑμεῖς τὰ κλήματα. <u>ὁ μένων ἐν ἐμοὶ κἀγὼ ἐν αὐτῷ</u> οὗτος φέρει καρπὸν πολύν, ὅτι χωρὶς ἐμοῦ οὐ δύνασθε ποιεῖν οὐδέν. [6] ἐὰν μή τις μένη ἐν ἐμοί, ἐβλήθη ἔξω ὡς τὸ κλῆμα καὶ ἐξηράνθη καὶ συνάγουσιν αὐτὰ καὶ εἰς τὸ πῦρ βάλλουσιν καὶ καίεται. [7] <u>ἐὰν μείνητε ἐν ἐμοὶ καὶ τὰ ῥήματά μου ἐν ὑμῖν μείνη</u>, ὃ ἐὰν θέλητε αἰτήσασθε, καὶ γενήσεται ὑμῖν. [8] ἐν τούτῳ ἐδοξάσθη ὁ πατήρ μου, ἵνα καρπὸν πολὺν φέρητε καὶ γένησθε ἐμοὶ μαθηταί. [9] Καθὼς ἠγάπησέν με ὁ πατήρ, κἀγὼ ὑμᾶς ἠγάπησα· <u>μείνατε ἐν τῇ ἀγάπῃ τῇ ἐμῇ</u>. [10] ἐὰν τὰς ἐντολάς μου τηρήσητε, <u>μενεῖτε ἐν τῇ ἀγάπῃ μου</u>, καθὼς ἐγὼ τὰς ἐντολὰς τοῦ πατρός μου τετήρηκα καὶ μένω αὐτοῦ ἐν τῇ ἀγάπῃ.

*****

John 16:33 I have said this to you, so that <u>in me</u> you may have peace. In the world you face persecution. But take courage; I have conquered the world!

John 16:33 ταῦτα λελάληκα ὑμῖν ἵνα <u>ἐν ἐμοὶ</u> εἰρήνην ἔχητε. ἐν τῷ κόσμῳ θλῖψιν ἔχετε· ἀλλὰ θαρσεῖτε, ἐγὼ νενίκηκα τὸν κόσμον.

*****

John 17:21, 23a <u>As you, Father, are in me and I am in you, may they also be in us</u>, so that the world may believe that you have sent me… [23]<u>I in them and you in me</u>, that they may become completely one,

John 17:21, 23a <u>καθὼς σύ, πάτερ, ἐν ἐμοὶ κἀγὼ ἐν σοί, ἵνα καὶ αὐτοὶ ἐν ἡμῖν ὦσιν</u>, ἵνα ὁ κόσμος πιστεύῃ ὅτι σύ με ἀπέστειλας… <u>ἐγὼ ἐν αὐτοῖς καὶ σὺ ἐν ἐμοί</u>, ἵνα ὦσιν τετελειωμένοι εἰς ἕν,

*****

1 John 2:6 whoever says, '<u>I abide in him</u>', ought to walk just as he walked.

1 John 2:6 ὁ λέγων <u>ἐν αὐτῷ μένειν</u> ὀφείλει καθὼς ἐκεῖνος περιεπάτησεν καὶ αὐτὸς [οὕτως] περιπατεῖν.

*****

1 John 2:24, 27-28 Let what you heard from the beginning abide in you. If what you heard from the beginning abides in you, then <u>you will abide in the Son and in the Father</u> … [27]As for you, <u>the anointing that you received from him abides in you</u>, and so you do not need anyone to teach you. But as his anointing teaches you about all things, and is true and is not a lie, and just as it has taught you, abide in him. [28] And now, little children, <u>abide in him</u>, so that when he is revealed we may have confidence and not be put to shame before him at his coming.

1 John 2:24, 27-28 ὑμεῖς ὃ ἠκούσατε ἀπ᾽ ἀρχῆς, ἐν ὑμῖν μενέτω. ἐὰν ἐν ὑμῖν μείνῃ ὃ ἀπ᾽ ἀρχῆς ἠκούσατε, καὶ <u>ὑμεῖς ἐν τῷ υἱῷ καὶ ἐν τῷ πατρὶ μενεῖτε</u>… καὶ ὑμεῖς <u>τὸ χρῖσμα ὃ ἐλάβετε ἀπ᾽ αὐτοῦ, μένει ἐν ὑμῖν</u> καὶ οὐ χρείαν ἔχετε ἵνα τις διδάσκῃ ὑμᾶς, ἀλλ᾽ ὡς τὸ αὐτοῦ χρῖσμα διδάσκει ὑμᾶς περὶ πάντων καὶ ἀληθές ἐστιν καὶ οὐκ ἔστιν ψεῦδος, καὶ καθὼς ἐδίδαξεν ὑμᾶς, μένετε ἐν αὐτῷ. [28] Καὶ νῦν, τεκνία, <u>μένετε ἐν αὐτῷ</u>, ἵνα ἐὰν φανερωθῇ σχῶμεν παρρησίαν καὶ μὴ αἰσχυνθῶμεν ἀπ᾽ αὐτοῦ ἐν τῇ παρουσίᾳ αὐτοῦ.

*****

1 John 3:6 <u>No one who abides in him sins</u>; no one who sins has either seen him or known him.

1 John 3:6 <u>πᾶς ὁ ἐν αὐτῷ μένων οὐχ ἁμαρτάνει·</u> πᾶς ὁ ἁμαρτάνων οὐχ ἑώρακεν αὐτὸν οὐδὲ ἔγνωκεν αὐτόν.

*****

1 John 3:24 <u>All who obey his commandments abide in him, and he abides in them.</u> And by this we know that he abides in us, by the Spirit that he has given us.

1 John 3:24 καὶ <u>ὁ τηρῶν τὰς ἐντολὰς αὐτοῦ ἐν αὐτῷ μένει καὶ αὐτὸς ἐν αὐτῷ·</u> καὶ ἐν τούτῳ γινώσκομεν ὅτι μένει ἐν ἡμῖν, ἐκ τοῦ πνεύματος οὗ ἡμῖν ἔδωκεν.

*****

1 John 4:12-16 No one has ever seen God; if we love one another, <u>God lives in us,</u> and his love is perfected in us. [13] By this we know that <u>we abide in him and he in us</u>, because he has given us of his Spirit. [14] And we have seen and do testify that the Father has sent his Son as the Saviour of the world. [15] <u>God abides in those who confess that Jesus is the Son of God, and they abide in God.</u> [16] So we have known and believe the love that God has for us. God is love, and <u>those who abide in love abide in God, and God abides in them.</u>

1 John 4:12-16 θεὸν οὐδεὶς πώποτε τεθέαται. ἐὰν ἀγαπῶμεν ἀλλήλους, <u>ὁ θεὸς ἐν ἡμῖν μένει</u> καὶ ἡ ἀγάπη αὐτοῦ ἐν ἡμῖν τετελειωμένη ἐστίν. [13] Ἐν τούτῳ γινώσκομεν ὅτι <u>ἐν αὐτῷ μένομεν καὶ αὐτὸς ἐν ἡμῖν</u>, ὅτι ἐκ τοῦ πνεύματος αὐτοῦ δέδωκεν ἡμῖν. [14] καὶ ἡμεῖς τεθεάμεθα καὶ μαρτυροῦμεν ὅτι ὁ πατὴρ ἀπέσταλκεν τὸν υἱὸν σωτῆρα τοῦ κόσμου. [15] <u>Ὃς ἐὰν ὁμολογήσῃ ὅτι Ἰησοῦς ἐστιν ὁ υἱὸς τοῦ θεοῦ, ὁ θεὸς ἐν αὐτῷ μένει καὶ αὐτὸς ἐν τῷ θεῷ.</u> [16] καὶ ἡμεῖς ἐγνώκαμεν καὶ πεπιστεύκαμεν τὴν ἀγάπην ἣν ἔχει ὁ θεὸς ἐν ἡμῖν. Ὁ θεὸς ἀγάπη ἐστίν, καὶ ὁ μένων ἐν τῇ ἀγάπῃ ἐν τῷ θεῷ μένει καὶ ὁ θεὸς ἐν αὐτῷ μένει.

*****

2 John 1:9 Everyone who does not abide in the teaching of Christ, but goes beyond it, does not have God; whoever abides in the teaching has both the Father and the Son.

2 John 1:9 Πᾶς ὁ προάγων καὶ μὴ μένων ἐν τῇ διδαχῇ τοῦ Χριστοῦ θεὸν οὐκ ἔχει· ὁ μένων ἐν τῇ διδαχῇ, οὗτος καὶ τὸν πατέρα καὶ τὸν υἱὸν ἔχει.

2.3 Intimacy

John 1:18 No one has ever seen God. It is God the only Son, who is close to the Father's heart, who has made him known.

John 1:18 Θεὸν οὐδεὶς ἑώρακεν πώποτε· μονογενὴς θεὸς ὁ ὢν εἰς τὸν κόλπον τοῦ πατρὸς ἐκεῖνος ἐξηγήσατο.

*****

John 13:23 One of his disciples – the one whom Jesus loved – was reclining next to him;

John 13:23 ἦν ἀνακείμενος εἷς ἐκ τῶν μαθητῶν αὐτοῦ ἐν τῷ κόλπῳ τοῦ Ἰησοῦ, ὃν ἠγάπα ὁ Ἰησοῦς.

2.4 Participation

1 John 1:3, 6-7 We declare to you what we have seen and heard so that you also may have fellowship with us; and truly our fellowship is with the Father and with his Son Jesus Christ. ... [6] If we say that we have fellowship with him while we are walking in darkness, we lie and do not do what is true; [7] but if we walk in the light as he himself is in the light, we have fellowship with one another, and the blood of Jesus his Son cleanses us from all sin.

1 John 1:3, 6-7 ὃ ἑωράκαμεν καὶ ἀκηκόαμεν, ἀπαγγέλλομεν καὶ ὑμῖν, ἵνα <u>καὶ ὑμεῖς κοινωνίαν ἔχητε μεθ᾽ ἡμῶν. καὶ ἡ κοινωνία δὲ ἡ ἡμετέρα μετὰ τοῦ πατρὸς καὶ μετὰ τοῦ υἱοῦ αὐτοῦ Ἰησοῦ Χριστοῦ.</u> ⁶ Ἐὰν εἴπωμεν ὅτι <u>κοινωνίαν ἔχομεν μετ᾽ αὐτοῦ</u> καὶ ἐν τῷ σκότει περιπατῶμεν, ψευδόμεθα καὶ οὐ ποιοῦμεν τὴν ἀλήθειαν· ⁷ ἐὰν δὲ ἐν τῷ φωτὶ περιπατῶμεν ὡς αὐτός ἐστιν ἐν τῷ φωτί, <u>κοινωνίαν ἔχομεν μετ᾽ ἀλλήλων</u> καὶ τὸ αἷμα Ἰησοῦ τοῦ υἱοῦ αὐτοῦ καθαρίζει ἡμᾶς ἀπὸ πάσης ἁμαρτίας.

2.5 Friendship and Family

John 15:13-15 No one has greater love than this, to lay down one's life for one's friends. ¹⁴ <u>You are my friends</u> if you do what I command you. ¹⁵ I do not call you servants any longer, because the servant does not know what the master is doing; but <u>I have called you friends</u>, because I have made known to you everything that I have heard from my Father.

John 15:13-15 μείζονα ταύτης ἀγάπην οὐδεὶς ἔχει, ἵνα τις τὴν ψυχὴν αὐτοῦ θῇ ὑπὲρ τῶν φίλων αὐτοῦ. ¹⁴ <u>ὑμεῖς φίλοι μού ἐστε</u> ἐὰν ποιῆτε ἃ ἐγὼ ἐντέλλομαι ὑμῖν. ¹⁵ οὐκέτι λέγω ὑμᾶς δούλους, ὅτι ὁ δοῦλος οὐκ οἶδεν τί ποιεῖ αὐτοῦ ὁ κύριος· <u>ὑμᾶς δὲ εἴρηκα φίλους</u>, ὅτι πάντα ἃ ἤκουσα παρὰ τοῦ πατρός μου ἐγνώρισα ὑμῖν.

*****

John 20:17 Jesus said to her, 'Do not hold on to me, because I have not yet ascended to the Father. But go to <u>my brothers</u> and say to them, "I am ascending to <u>my Father and your Father, to my God and your God</u>".'

John 20:17 λέγει αὐτῇ Ἰησοῦς· μή μου ἅπτου, οὔπω γὰρ ἀναβέβηκα πρὸς τὸν πατέρα· πορεύου δὲ πρὸς <u>τοὺς ἀδελφούς μου</u> καὶ εἰπὲ αὐτοῖς· ἀναβαίνω πρὸς <u>τὸν πατέρα μου καὶ πατέρα ὑμῶν καὶ θεόν μου καὶ θεὸν ὑμῶν.</u>

3. Analysis of the Data

Having outlined the language that John uses to present the concept 'union with Christ', we must analyse the data. I present a basic statistical analysis of the data in the form of (i) a table that shows the total occurrences of each linguistic expression in the Johannine writings, and (ii) a chart that shows where the concept 'union with Christ' occurs in the Johannine writings.

	Occurrences
Oneness	7
Indwelling/Abiding	31
Intimacy	2
Participation	3
Friendship, Family	3
	—
Total	46

Spread of Expressions Communicating 'Union with Christ'

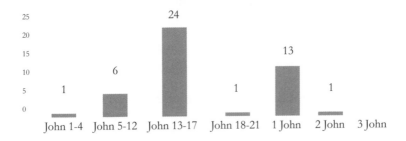

Based on this statistical analysis, I make three inferences:

1. From the table of occurrences, I infer that the language of oneness and indwelling/abiding makes up 83 per cent of the concept 'union with Christ'.

2. From the chart of occurrences across the Johannine literature, I deduce that 80 per cent of occurrences that express the concept 'union with Christ' occur in John 13-17 and 1 John, which contains essentially didactic or paraenetic material.

3. The dominant linguistic expressions that indicate the concept
    'union with Christ' (indwelling/abiding and oneness) occur
    primarily in those parts of the Johannine literature that
    contain the highest density of references to 'union with
    Christ' (John 13-17; 1 John).

This logically leads to the conclusion that *the Johannine concept
'union with Christ' is primarily indicated by the language of indwelling/
abiding and oneness, and concentrated in the didactic material of John 13-
17 and 1 John.* This leads to the next step of examining the key
passages in order to determine the nature and mechanics of the
believer's union with Christ. I have selected four passages – John
14 on indwelling/abiding, John 15 on indwelling/abiding, John
17 on oneness and indwelling/abiding, 1 John on indwelling/
abiding – and raised one major issue in each passage in order to
make the analysis feasible.

4. The Mysterious and Mystical Union in John 14

Main Issue

What is the nature of our union with Christ?
Is it a relational or ontological union?

Usually, 14:2-3 is taken to mean an eschatological, heavenly abode
where believers will be re-united with Jesus after death.[2] In light
of John's realised eschatology, however, I contend that 14:2-3
refers to Jesus' preparing a place for believers in God's family
through His death and resurrection.[3] Let me explain. The terms
οἶκός and οἰκία can mean 'house' or 'household'. While οἶκός
(τοῦ πατρός μου) in 2:16 refers to God's house, that is the temple,
οἰκία in 4:53 and 8:35 refers respectively to the royal official's
household and to God's household or family where 'sons'/
believers have a permanent place. Hence, the context must decide

---

2. e.g., Steven M. Bryan, 'The Eschatological Temple in John 14', *Bulletin for Biblical Research* 15 (2005), pp. 187–98. The majority of commentators take this view.

3. cf. Mary L. Coloe, *Dwelling in the Household of God: Johannine Ecclesiology and Spirituality* (Collegeville: Liturgical Press 2007), pp. 108–12, 145–8.

whether οἶκός/οἰκία refers to a physical structure (abode) or to a social unit (family). Related to this is the issue of the referent of Jesus' going (in order to prepare a place for His followers) and of His coming back (to gather His followers to Himself). On the view that 14:2-3 alludes to the believer's place in heaven, Jesus' departure and return would refer to the Ascension and Parousia, while a reference to the believer's place in God's family on earth implies that Jesus' departure and return refer to the crucifixion and resurrection.

I suggest that οἰκία (τοῦ πατρός μου) in 14:2 refers to God's household/family rather than house/heaven for various reasons. First, the term μονή ('dwelling place') occurs in the Johannine literature only in 14:2 and in 14:23, and the close proximity of the two occurrences suggests a similar referent. In the latter verse, Jesus promises that He and the Father will make their μονή with believers, which refers to an imminent reality because Jesus' return to His disciples in 14:18-19 most likely refers to the resurrection rather than the Parousia. Besides, this divine indwelling most likely occurs by means of the coming Spirit (14:16-17). In which case, Jesus' enigmatic saying in 14:3 that He is leaving to prepare a place for His followers and will return to take them with Him is probably a reference to the cross and resurrection. Indeed, the phrase 'I will take you to myself' in 14:3 echoes 'I will draw all people to myself' in 12:32.[4] At the cross, Jesus prepares a permanent place for His followers, and after the resurrection, He can gather His followers into God's family. Therefore, only after the resurrection, Jesus can call them, for the first time, 'brothers' (20:17) and give them the Spirit to seal their family membership (20:22).[5] In sum, the expression that believers will be in the same place where Jesus is (14:3),

---

4. The phrase 'to myself' (πρὸς ἐμαυτόν) only occurs in these two verses in John.

5. For this interpretation of 20:22, see Cornelis Bennema, 'The Giving of the Spirit in John 19–20: Another Round', in I. Howard Marshall, Volker Rabens and Cornelis Bennema (eds.), *The Spirit and Christ in the New Testament and Christian Theology: Essays in Honor of Max Turner* (Grand Rapids: Eerdmans 2012), pp. 86–104.

most likely refers to their being part of God's family (cf. 17:24, where Jesus desires the same for future believers). Jesus' death at the cross and His resurrection enable His followers to reside in the divine household in union with the Son and the Father. This implies that 'union with Christ' is a soteriological concept because it refers to a place in God's family and the provision for this occurs at the cross.[6]

I seek to probe further into the issue of *how* the Father and Son indwell the believer. First, we must observe the instrumentality of the Spirit in mediating or facilitating the divine presence to the believer. The context of 14:16-23 points to the post-Easter reality of the Father and Son indwelling the believer *by means of* the indwelling Spirit (cf. 14:17, 'the Spirit παρ' ὑμῖν μένει καὶ ἐν ὑμῖν ἔσται'). Thus, the believer is united with the Father and Son through the Spirit. Second, we must determine the nature of John's language to designate this divine-human union. Should we understand the idea that the Father and Son indwell the believer through the Spirit as literal or metaphorical (that is, nonliteral)? On the one hand, it seems absurd to take this in a literal sense as if the Father and Son can be physically located in a believer when cut open. On the other hand, the idea of divine indwelling is probably not so ethereal or intangible to reject a literal sense entirely. Using different categories, we may ask whether John's concept of indwelling/abiding is relational or ontological language. I contend that it is both. This needs explanation.

In older theories, a phrase is either literal or metaphorical. Lest I be misunderstood, the distinction is not between literal=real and metaphorical=unreal. Literal and metaphorical language are simply two different linguistic ways to speak of reality. While we would immediately sense that John's indwelling language cannot be literal – no one expects to find Jesus physically in us – the inference that

---

6.   If 14:2–3 refers to the believer's place in heaven after the Parousia, 'union with Christ' would be an eschatological concept.

it must therefore be metaphorical is not exactly accurate, however. Noting the problems with the literal/metaphorical binary that scholars typically use, David Aaron suggests a 'continuum of meaning' with *degrees* of figurative language or metaphoricalness – ranging from literal meaning to ascription to weakly figurative to strongly figurative to nonsense.[7] For example, to understand Jesus' assertion to be 'the bread of life' as literal would be absurd, and hence it is a strong metaphorical phrase. However, an expression such as Jesus abiding or being 'in' the believer is somewhat more ambiguous. While no one expects to find Jesus physically in us, the phrase is not so ambiguous or absurd as to reject a literal sense entirely and demand a metaphorical sense. Using Aaron's meaning continuum, I put the metaphorical strength of the Father and Son 'indwelling' the believer as 'weakly figurative' or 'quasi-literal'. While the believer may not be indwelled by God ontologically (the believer does not share the divine essence), a divine indwelling in terms of an intimate relationship with God through the Spirit can still be viewed in a quasi-literal or mystical sphere. Although the 'indwelling' of the Father and Son through the Spirit should probably be interpreted primarily in relational rather than ontological categories, we cannot equate relational with metaphorical and ontological with literal. It is not inconceivable to perceive the Spirit indwelling the believer at a literal level; it probably has a literal sense of an intimate relationship without demanding the same literalness as possessing a physical object. For example, to say 'I have the Spirit' would not be very different from saying, 'I have a spouse' or 'I have colleagues'. Although I do not have the Spirit, my spouse or colleagues as I possess, for example, a key, there is nonetheless a literal sense to my relationship

---

7.   David H. Aaron, *Biblical Ambiguities: Metaphor, Semantics and Divine Imagery* (Leiden: Brill 2001), chs 2–6 (see esp. the diagram on p. 112).

with them. Using the category of relational ontology (over against substance ontology), I suggest that John has in mind a *mystical union* between the believer and God.[8]

5. Nurturing Union in John 15

Main Issue
Can our union with Christ be broken? If so, how?

In the parable of the vine and the branches, Jesus introduces Himself as 'the true vine'. In the Old Testament, the vine was a symbol for Israel, but sadly, she failed to bear the fruit that was expected of her (Ps. 80:8-16; Isa. 5:1-10; Jer. 2:21-2; Ezek. 15:1-8; 19:10-14; Hos. 10:1; 14:7). In contrast to Israel in the Old Testament, Jesus, as the new and true Israel, will fulfil her divine purpose. Our focus, however, is the two kinds of branches that are depicted in the parable – fruitless and fruitful ones. In the role of vinedresser, the Father removes every branch that does not bear fruit and prunes every branch that does bear fruit so that it may bear more fruit (15:1-2). Both verbs 'to remove' and 'to prune' are related in the Greek (αἴρειν and καθαίρειν respectively), and in both instances there is an element of taking away.[9] However, while pruning is a partial taking away to increase

---

8.   The Eastern Orthodox Church also advocates the concept of relational ontology. John D. Zizioulas, for example, fervently argues for an understanding of God as 'persons in communion'. He is influenced by the Cappadocian father St Basil the Great, who preferred to speak about God using the ontological category of communion (κοινωνία) rather than that of substance (οὐσία): 'The *nature* of God is communion' (*Being as Communion: Studies in Personhood and the Church* [New York: St Vladimir's Seminary Press 1985], p. 134). Similarly, P. M. Collins remarks regarding the Cappadocian fathers' understanding of the Godhead: 'The communion of the Godhead is therefore understood in terms of an identity of *ousia*, which is differentiated among the three persons. The *koinōnia* of the persons is the shared common *ousia*' (*Trinitarian Theology: West and East. Karl Barth, the Cappadocian Fathers, and John Zizioulas* [New York: Oxford University Press 2001], p. 165). See also Clark H. Pinnock, *Flame of Love: A Theology of the Holy Spirit* (Downers Grove: InterVarsity Press 1996), ch. 1; Jürgen Moltmann, *The Spirit of Life: A Universal Affirmation* (Minneapolis: Fortress Press 1992), p. 309.

9.   Although αἴρειν can also mean 'to lift up', in view of 15:6 the meaning in 15:2 is most likely 'to remove'.

the branch's fruitfulness, the removal of the fruitless branch is a permanent taking away implying destruction (cf. 15:6).

Almost before the disciples can wonder whether they are fruitless branches, Jesus assures them that they are already clean because of His word (15:3). The Greek verb for 'to prune' (15:2) can also mean 'to cleanse', and the associated adjective is intentionally used in 15:3 to translate 'clean'. Hence, God is 'pruning', that is cleansing or purifying, the disciples so that they can bear much fruit. Jesus' assertion that the disciples are already clean echoes His words in 13:10, but He now clarifies *how* they have become clean: through His word or teaching (cf. 4:10, 14; 6:63; 17:17). The picture that emerges is that God continuously cleanses believers through His word, mediated through Jesus' teaching (3:34), in order to increase their fruitfulness and make them better disciples. Jesus' insistence on the mutual indwelling between Him and His disciples (15:4) is simple to understand when we bear in mind the metaphor of the vine and the branches: just as a branch cannot bear fruit by itself unless it remains in the vine, so disciples cannot bear fruit unless they abide in Jesus. Union with Jesus, then, is not an option but an absolute necessity, and the bearing of fruit is the inevitable outcome or demonstration of this union.

The consequence of not abiding in Jesus is vividly described in 15:6, creating a sombre and scary picture. The one who does not remain in Jesus will be thrown away like the branch and wither (15:6a). The comparative use of 'like' may be a reference to 15:2: the disciple who does not remain in Jesus and hence does not bear fruit will be thrown away and dry up spiritually, just as a fruitless branch is removed from the vine and withers. Such branches are gathered, thrown into the fire and burned (15:6b). This is how most English translations, such as the NRSV and NIV, render 15:6b, but the literal translation goes: 'They gather them [the withered branches] together, throw them into the fire and they are burned.' This raises some questions. Who gathers these 'disciples' who fail to abide in Jesus? And when does this gathering and throwing into the fire take place? The KJV says that 'men' gather these fruitless people, but there is nothing in the text to warrant such a translation. I suggest that we may have an allusion to the events described in Mark 13:27 and Matthew 13:40-3; 24:31, speaking of the gathering of the elect by the angels at the Parousia. John may be referring to the same event but only describing the fate of the unfaithful (cf. Matt. 24:51; 25:30-2, 41; Rev. 20:15). In this case, *angels* will gather the 'withered branches' at the final day of judgment.

This interpretation still leaves us with a disturbing question. Who are these fruitless branches broken off from the vine? It is probably not a picture of believers who struggle with sin, lest most of us qualify and texts such as 1 John 1:5-10 become meaningless. Instead, I suggest that 15:2a, 6 speaks of *defection* or *apostasy*. I speak of defection when a believer wilfully abandons or rejects his or her allegiance to Jesus, and of apostasy when a believer defects *and* joins the opposition. Since the text speaks of a branch being removed and of discontinuing its abiding in the vine, it is clear that prior to this the branch was attached to the vine. Hence, the situation of 15:2a, 6 does not refer to unbelievers but applies to those who once belonged, or claimed to belong, to Jesus. In the Johannine writings, we can identify at least four such persons or groups: (i) Judas; (ii) the defecting disciples in 6:60-6; (iii) the nine disciples who seem to have deserted Jesus at his arrest (16:32; 18:15; cf. Mark 14:50) and then later Peter who defected (18:15-27), although only temporarily; (iv) the antichrists in 1 John.

According to the Johannine account, Judas is a branch that does not bear fruit and has to be removed. John 13 describes the tragic downfall of Judas. Having come under the influence of the devil (13:2) and being unaffected by Jesus' cleansing word (13:10-11), Judas eventually rejects Jesus' last attempt for restoration and is being indwelled by the devil (13:27-30). Judas becomes an apostate by allowing his union with Jesus to be broken and to start a union with the devil; from being a disciple of Jesus to a disciple of the devil.[10] In his first Epistle, John indicates that his church might have been troubled by defection or apostasy (1 John 2:18-27). The so-called 'antichrists' – those who 'belonged' but had left – may have been 'false believers'. The apparent possibility of a broken union with Christ is not only disturbing but also in tension with other Johannine texts that seem to deny such possibility. In 10:28-9, Jesus asserts regarding His sheep: 'I give them eternal life, and they will never perish. No one will snatch them out of my hand. What my Father has given me is greater than all else, and no one can snatch it out of the Father's hand.' Indeed, John 17:12 informs us that Jesus has successfully kept all the disciples secure – *except* (εἰ μή) the 'son of hell', that is Judas.[11] Thus, the *norm* is that Jesus protects the believer's union with Him, and only in *exceptional* circumstances can such union be broken. Although defection/apostasy, as an intentional abandoning of the faith, indicates a chilling reality, this is perhaps not a possibility for the elect but only for the non-elect. As John Calvin maintains, apostasy is impossible for the elect; apostates never truly belonged, never were part of God's elect.[12]

---

10. While we should not take Peter's denial of his allegiance to Jesus lightly, this is an act of defection (of which restoration is possible, as John 21 shows) rather than apostasy (Peter never shows allegiance to the devil).

11. It is unnecessary to read a doctrine of predestination into Judas's life, as some English translations do ('the one destined to be lost' [NRSV]; 'the one doomed to destruction' [NIV]). The Greek text speaks of 'the son of destruction' and James V. Brownson argues that the Greek term ἀπώλεια ('destruction') probably stands for the Hebrew *Abaddon*, a term used for hell (Prov. 15:11; 27:20; 1QH 3:16, 19, 32) or hell personified – the devil (Job 28:22), ('Neutralizing the Intimate Enemy: The Portrayal of Judas in the Fourth Gospel', *Society of Biblical Literature Seminar Papers* 31, [1992], pp. 49–60). This reference to Judas as 'son of destruction/hell' corresponds to the earlier description of Judas as 'devil' (6:70–1). Thus, Jesus' reference to Judas in 17:12 as 'son of destruction' implies that Judas is an agent of the devil, in that he belongs to the devil and acts like him. Whether Judas was (pre)destined for destruction was probably not an issue for John. The fact that Judas' betrayal fulfils Scripture was already indicated in 13:18, which probably alludes to Psalm 41:9, where David speaks of being betrayed by an intimate friend whom he trusted and had table-fellowship with.

12. cf. John Calvin, *Calvin's Commentaries: The Gospel according to St. John 11–21 and the First Epistle of John*, ed. T. H. L. Parker (Edinburgh: Saint Andrew Press 1961), pp. 94–6.

The fruitless branches that God removes in 15:2 may thus refer to branches that *claim* to belong but do not truly belong because if they truly belonged they would have produced fruit. In addition to Judas and the antichrists in the Johannine church, the 'disciples' in 6:60-66 may also be such fruitless branches in that their defection seems to indicate that they never truly belonged. If these 'disciples' continue in their non-attachment to Christ, they will, according to 15:6, wither and (at the Parousia) be thrown into hell. While defection and apostasy seem to apply to those who belonged to Jesus, who were attached to the vine, at another level defection and apostasy can only be committed by those who never truly belonged. At least, this is implied by 1 John 2:19: 'They went out *from us* but they were *not from us*; for if they had been *from us*, they would have remained *with us*. But [this occurred] to show/reveal that all were *not from us*.' The phrase 'to be from us' (εἶναι ἐξ ἡμῶν) is an expression of origin and belonging. Their departure shows that they do not belong, and vice versa, those who truly belong will stay (the so-called 'perseverance of the saints').

We must nevertheless be careful to observe what John says and what he does *not* say. He does not say that those who abide in Jesus will never, or can never, leave. He does not claim to have known that people would leave Jesus; he only *observes*. Elsewhere John indicates that no one can come to Jesus unless the Father draws/ gives that person to Jesus and that no one can snatch the believer out of Jesus' hand. So, when we observe that someone comes to Jesus, we can infer that this is the result of a divine act; we cannot conclude that those who have not come to Jesus never will or that those who have come to Jesus truly belong and will never defect. Hence, *if something happens, we can infer something; if nothing has happened, we cannot infer anything.* From a human perspective, defection or apostasy is the movement from belonging to not belonging; the falling away from faith. From a divine perspective, these defectors or apostates never truly belonged; they never were part of the elect. We can only draw conclusions when something happens: when someone comes to faith, we infer that the Spirit has been at work (3:8); when people defect and never return, we infer that they never truly belonged (hence, we may only conclude this at the Parousia); when people defect and return, we infer that they have backslidden (cf. Peter's temporary defection). From a human perspective, Judas 'belonged' to Jesus and hence could betray Him, but from a divine perspective, he never truly belonged and hence is (characterised as) a devil (6:71).

In sum, the urge for believers to continue their union with Christ is the exhortation to continue in salvation or the Christian life. Whilst believers should not be afraid that they can 'loose' this union or 'fall off' the vine – the Spirit is given to secure this union and Jesus will keep them secure till the end – it is not entirely impossible to think of situations where 'believers' no longer want this union and reject it, but these may not have been true believers. This reality is probably only known to God.

6. Identity Formation through Sharing in the Divine Union in John 17

Main Issue
How does union with Christ shape our identity?

John 17:11, 20-3 is dominated by the existential language 'to be one' and 'to be in', which relates to the issue of identity. John 17 records Jesus' last communication with His Father before His arrest and death, and we naturally expect only the most urgent matters to be on Jesus' mind. Among these, the singular idea of oneness/unity-indwelling seems of utmost importance (17:21a and 17:23a show that 'to be one' is virtually synonymous or semantically overlapping with 'to be in'). Jesus expresses a burning desire for oneness/unity among His followers – both present (17:11) and future (17:20-3). The comparative conjunction 'just as' (καθώς) in 17:11, 21-3 indicates that the oneness/unity among believers is rooted in or derived from the oneness/unity that exists between the Father and Son. But why is this the most pressing issue for Jesus? I can think of two reasons. First, the concept of oneness/unity goes to the heart of who God is and who believers are because their identities are being shaped as they share in the divine identity. Second, unity among believers constitutes a testimony that may lead others to belief (17:21, 23; cf. 13:35). I will elaborate on the first reason.

Identity has to do with who one is – a notion of self (personhood), or the set of qualities, values, characteristics and behaviour that distinguishes a person from others. The essential dynamic or identity of God is best captured by the concept of communion. The literal term κοινωνία occurs only in 1 John 1:3-7, to denote the communion that exists between the Father and Son, in which the believer partakes.[13] The concept of communion, however, is widespread in the Johannine literature through the concepts of oneness/unity and indwelling. The oneness/unity that exists between the Father and Son is the template for the oneness/unity among believers in the divine family (17:11, 21-3; cf. 10:30). Similarly, just as the Father and Son indwell each other, so they indwell the believer (17:21-3).[14] John 17:21-3 clarifies that 'to be one' and 'to be in' are synonymous existential concepts – to be 'one' with the Father and Son *is* to be 'in' them. While this is primarily functional or relational language for the intimate relationship between the Father, Son and believer, an

---

13. Max Turner explains that John's usage of κοινωνία as 'personal fellowship with someone' is rather unique in the New Testament. While κοινωνία usually refers to participation, for the first time here the Bible speaks of a divine-human κοινωνία. The use of μετά indicates that believers are partners *with* the Father and Son. Κοινωνία with the Father and the Son therefore means 'the mutual sharing of believers in a personal *communion* with the Father and the Son'. 1 John thus gives κοινωνία a theocentric dimension and introduces the idea of personal fellowship with God ('The Churches of the Johannine Letters as Communities of "Trinitarian" *Koinōnia*', in W. Ma and R. P. Menzies (eds.), *The Spirit and Spirituality: Essays in Honour of Russell P. Spittler*, Journal of Pentecostal Theology Supplement 24 (London: T & T Clark 2004), pp. 53–5).

14. The Spirit will also indwell the believer (John 14:17; 1 John 2:27). In fact, the Father and Son will indwell the believer by means of the Spirit (John 14:23).

ontological dimension cannot be ruled out.[15] It is unlikely, on Aaron's continuum of meaning, that the terms 'to be one' and 'to be in' literally mean believers are divine (a form of theosis or deification) or that the Father, Son, and believer are identical or physically inside one another.[16] However, it is equally unlikely that these terms are such strong metaphorical assertions that they only denote closeness of relationship. Instead, I suggest that this language is 'ascriptive' or 'quasi-literal,' indicating a mystical, divine communion that affects the believer at every level (see also the discussion in section 4). Essentially, it would be safe to conclude that communion (fellowship, oneness, unity, indwelling) appears to be the most significant identity marker of the divine family (cf. n. 8).

As I explained above, the essential aspect of the divine identity is communion and when we examine the Johannine writings we find that this communion is primarily characterised or constituted by life/ζωή (5:21, 26), love (3:35; 5:20; 14:31; 15:9), truth/knowledge (8:55; 10:15; 14:6; 17:17) and honour/glory (17:1-5).[17] This relationship of life, love, truth and honour between the Father and Son is not exclusive; believers are drawn and participate in this saving relationship through a birth 'from above'. Believers do not so much possess this divine identity as they participate or share in it by virtue of their union with God. As believers share in the divine identity of a perpetual

15. Contra Jan G. van der Watt, who takes such language as purely functional and does not allow for a reference to a mystical union: *Family of the King: Dynamics of Metaphor in the Gospel according to John* (BINS 47; Leiden: Brill 2000), pp. 289–90).

16. John's 'oneness' language with reference to people does certainly not refer to a hypostatic union. Only the incarnate Son, truly human and truly divine, represents a hypostatic union of two natures. The 'oneness' language does not refer to ontology/substance because then the believer would share the divine essence and cross the creator/creation divide. John is also not speaking of the Father and Son sharing the same divine essence – these are concepts developed by the later church.

17. cf. Cornelis Bennema, 'Christ, the Spirit and the Knowledge of God: A Study in Johannine Epistemology', in Mary Healy and Robin Parry (eds.), *The Bible and Epistemology: Biblical Soundings on the Knowledge of God* (Milton Keynes: Paternoster 2007), p. 120.

communion of life, love, truth and honour, it is natural that this communion affects the believers and transforms them in their thinking and behaviour. Thus, the believers' identity is shaped along the lines of the divine identity because their sharing in the divine identity has a transformative effect.

It must be noted that the Christian identity is not so much an individual or psychological identity but a *collectivist identity*, where the individual's identity is embedded in a larger group.[18] The New Testament employs various concepts to articulate this group-oriented Christian identity, such as 'the body of Christ', 'in Christ', 'church', 'believers', 'God's family' and 'flock'. In effect, the Christian identity is the shared understanding of who a person is as part of a group or community that considers itself in union with Christ. The Christian identity is created and shaped in union with the Father and Son.

7. Union with God and Godly Behaviour in 1 John

Main Issue

How does union with Christ shape our behaviour?

Besides the few references to communion (κοινωνία) in 1 John (see section 6), the rest of the language in 1 John regarding 'union with Christ' refers to the idea of indwelling (1 John 2:6, 24-8; 3:6, 24; 4:12-16; see section 2). The dominant idea in these texts is that the believers' union with Christ not only shapes their identity but also their behaviour. John stresses the reciprocity that exists between the mutual indwelling of God and believers and their behaviour. In 1 John 2:6, for example, John stresses that those who claim to abide in God should 'walk' (περιπατεῖν), that is behave, like Him. In 1 John 2:27, John indicates that the 'abiding anointing' instructs believers in 'all things', which most probably refers to the Spirit's didactic function (John 14:26; 16:12-15). Then, in 1 John 3:6, John explains that those who abide in God do not

---

18. For the concept of a collectivist identity, see Bruce J. Malina, *The New Testament World: Insights from Cultural Anthropology*, 3rd edn. (Louisville: WJK 2001), pp. 60–7.

sin. What is probably in view here is not that believers should be sinless or perfect (lest 1 John 1:5-10 becomes redundant) but that their lives are not to be controlled or dominated by sin. 1 John 3:24 and 4:12 show the reciprocity of the relationship between union and behaviour: the believers' union with God should result in proper behaviour, and vice versa, proper behaviour (the keeping of God's commandments, specifically to love one another) demonstrates their union with Him.

Thus, the believers' inclusion in the divine identity necessarily precipitates transformational behaviour in that they are expected to behave according to the divine family code. Believers (should) behave like children of God because that is who they are. So, believers should love God and one another because love has become part of their identity. Believers should testify to the truth because they have knowledge of and belong to the truth. The believers' ongoing access to the divine reality results in a growing awareness of who God is, what He does, and what He expects from people. This increased knowledge of the truth should motivate believers to demonstrate and propagate the truth, that is, the divine reality. At the same time, behaviour is also transformative – right behaviour affirms, strengthens and probably even shapes one's identity. The believers' continuous acts of discipleship (behaviour), such as believing, loving, following, abiding, obedience, serving and testifying, authenticate and shape the family bond between the believer, God and fellow-believers (identity). These acts of discipleship are tangible expressions of acceptable family behaviour, which reveal the believers' identity (they are God's children because they behave as such), ensure they remain in the divine family and enhance their honour. Thus, there is a reciprocal, transformative dynamic between identity and behaviour; each has the potential to shape the other.

8. Conclusion

Based on an analysis of the Johannine text, I concluded that the concept 'union with Christ' is expressed primarily by the ideas of indwelling/abiding and oneness in John 13-17 and 1 John. A brief examination of key passages led to the following findings: Using the category of relational ontology, I suggested that the believer being 'indwelled' by the Father and Son through the Spirit refers to a mystical or quasi-literal union (John 14). While the norm is that believers bear fruit in their lives and that Jesus keeps them secure, in exceptional cases defection or apostasy can occur – perhaps indicating that such 'broken-off believers' never truly belonged (John 15). Union with Christ implies sharing in who He is (identity) and becoming like Him (transformation) (John 17). Vice versa, union with Christ also shapes the believers' conduct – they are to behave like Him (1 John). In fact, there is a reciprocal relationship between identity and behaviour; both shape each other.

QUESTIONS FOR DISCUSSION

1. How do you understand John's language of 'oneness' and 'indwelling'? What kind of reality does the believer's union with Christ refer to according to John?

2. Do you think the believer's union with Christ can be broken – temporarily or permanently, in the present or only at the end – and how?

3. How, in what ways, does our union with Christ affect and transform us?

4. How does this union benefit us?

5. What are the practical and pastoral implications of John's presentation of the believer's union with Christ?

6. What does the believer's union with Christ look like in daily life according to John?

CHAPTER TWO

The Union of the Believer with Christ in Paul

TIM WARD

1. Introduction

J. I. Packer has written: 'For Paul union with Christ is not fancy but fact – the basic fact, indeed, in Christianity; and the doctrine of imputed righteousness is simply Paul's exposition of the forensic aspect of it.'[1] Two significant claims are being made here. The first is to do with the importance of union within Paul's understanding of Christian faith: that it is so central as to warrant being called for him 'the basic fact' of Christianity. The second claim concerns the relation of union with Christ to justification as traditionally understood: for Paul, according to Packer, justification is the articulation of a particular aspect of union. Both of these viewpoints have been widely held, although they have not always been on the surface of evangelical convictions and preaching.

A short paper like this on a topic as broad as the union of the believer with Christ in Paul inevitably has to choose a rather limited focus if it is to say anything substantial, to avoid giving

---

1. Quoted in Marcus Peter Johnson, *One With Christ: An Evangelical Theology of Salvation* (Wheaton: Crossway 2013), pp. 110–11.

an unsatisfactorily thin overview of a large swathe of material. Therefore it is on these two claims and the place of union with Christ in Paul that I will focus. I am offering here what I trust is a little illuminating depth with wide implications on a couple of central questions, as opposed to aiming for breadth on a whole variety of issues.

A further methodological issue needs to be noted. A difficulty arises materially from the ways in which Paul speaks of union and in which he deploys the topic. From one perspective, the theme of the union of the believer with Christ is ubiquitous in Paul, as countless writers on Paul observe.[2] For example, he uses the crucial little phrase *en Christo* seventy or eighty times.[3] Of course the theme of union is not restricted simply to usages of that particular phrase. It crops up regularly, expressed in other terms, both as a theme in its own right and as fundamental support and background argumentation for a wide variety of other themes.

However, from another perspective union with Christ has not always proved easy to spot in Paul. I think here particularly of evangelical writing and piety, which is often said to have inadvertently found ways of filtering union out of its reading and use of Paul, or at least of not tuning fully into it. Despite evangelicalism's strong focus on Paul, the doctrine of the union of the believer with Christ in his writings has at times been somewhat hidden in plain sight. As is often pointed out, an unfortunate division has widely been made (or assumed) between two soteriological categories – the forensic/legal, and the relational/transformative – and this division has loomed rather too large. The forensic/legal has received rather more

---

2. James Dunn gives a helpfully concise history of the rise to prominence in Pauline studies of the themes of union with and participation in Christ (James D. G. Dunn, *The Theology of Paul the Apostle* [Grand Rapids: Eerdmans 1998], pp. 90–6).

3   Seventy-three times according to Constantine R. Campbell (*Paul and Union with Christ: An Exegetical and Theological Study* [Grand Rapids: Zondervan 2012], p. 67), who is counting only uses of the precise phrase en Christo, and eighty-three times according to Dunn (*The Theology of Paul,* p. 396), who seems to be including very closely related phrases such as 'in the Lord Jesus Christ'.

attention from evangelicals than the relational/transformative, such that 'the preaching of the gospel' has often come to be understood to refer simply to the proclamation and explanation of the forensic, with the relational regarded as a subsequent component of Christian discipleship and life. Thus when language of 'gospel' is found in Paul, the assumption is made that it refers without remainder to Christ's forensic work, with a consequent strong focus on forgiveness as the chief associated benefit. Further, as is also often pointed out, closely related to this has been an emphasis on the crucifixion as doing the bulk of the soteriological spade-work, with a resultant thinning down of what Paul is taken to have to say of the resurrection's contribution to salvation. In fact, though, as Richard Gaffin has laboured to demonstrate, a good case can be made for seeing the believer's union with Christ in His resurrection as the very heart of Paul's theology of salvation.[4]

In light of these issues here is how I will proceed. I will begin with a brief look at some of the lie of the land as set out for us in two recent works; it is important to take note of this, as works on union with Christ, especially as found in Paul, are appearing quite thick and fast. I will then take the bulk of my time to work through one particular letter – Galatians – with a focus on the way in which themes of union unfold through that letter and how they function within its developing argument. Inevitably this narrows the scope of our study to a great degree. However, I trust that the gains will outweigh the losses, as I aim to open up a little the particular ways in which, through the shape and flow of the arguments of one of Paul's more influential letters, it is true to say that union is both a 'basic fact' and also the core reality of which justification (and other things) is an aspect. It is one thing – and a helpful thing – to assert that union is 'basic' to

---

4.   '[T]he central soteriological reality [in Paul's theology] is union with the exalted Christ by Spirit-created faith.' (Richard B. Gaffin, Jr., *By Faith, Not By Sight: Paul and the Order of Salvation* [Phillipsburg: Presbyterian & Reformed 2013], p. 49. See also his *Resurrection and Redemption: A Study in Paul's Soteriology* [Phillipsburg: Presbyterian & Reformed 1987]).

Paul and at the core of his view of salvation, and to line up a large number of texts to make one's case. It is another thing to look a little more deeply at the particular ways in which union can be said to function as basic and core within an extended argument of Paul's, and it is here that I hope to shed some light. Within this there will be some small scope as we go for noting occasionally how other Pauline letters expand on or nuance themes that we observe in Galatians.

2. Two recent works on union with Christ in Paul

Constantine Campbell's *Paul and Union with Christ: An Exegetical and Theological Study*[5] is a remarkable piece of work for which we should be very grateful to the author. In the long exegetical section (and to me this is the really admirable piece of work) he fills two hundred pages with a treatment of every single usage by Paul of the key phrases *en Christo*, *eis Christon*, *syn Christo* and *dia Christou* (in, to/towards, with and through Christ). He then devotes a further sixty pages to texts in Paul which do not use any of those explicit 'Christ' phrases but which contain metaphors that are clearly related to union – body of Christ, temple and building, marriage, new clothing, and verbs of 'putting on' or 'being clothed'. It is an impressive and exhaustive compendium, particularly in his discussion of the 'Christ' phrases, which has the potential to serve the on-going discussion very well for a long time to come. There are many excellent exegetical insights to be gleaned along the way.

The theological section is, perhaps inevitably, somewhat briefer and a bit thinner, although not without stimulating conclusions. Among these, for our purposes, two particular conclusions stand out. As regards the task of defining union, Campbell suggests that we need not just one term but four if we are to express the breadth of what we find in Paul: the word union itself, to express the mutual indwelling of the believer and Christ; participation, for the believer's sharing in the events experienced by Christ;

---

5.   Grand Rapids: Zondervan 2012.

identification, for the sense in which the believer is now in the realm of Christ, rather than in the realm of Adam and sin and death; and (fourthly) incorporation, to capture the sense of now being a member of Christ's body.[6] Some may want to haggle over precise terms and nuances, but the breadth of terminology seems necessary if we are to capture the scope and depth of what we inevitably call, for the sake of brevity, 'union'. In what follows I will often speak of 'union and participation', to capture something of this breadth.

Campbell also addresses, secondly, the place of union within the structure of Paul's thought, and here he wants to be careful with his terminology. He does not think that it is accurate to speak of union as the central concern of Paul's thought. After all, he counts only thirty-two places in which he thinks Paul addresses union directly. Instead he prefers to conceive of union as the 'webbing' that holds everything else together: 'Every Pauline theme and pastoral concern ultimately coheres with the whole through their common bond – union with Christ.'[7] We will see some evidence to support this way of understanding union in Paul, I will argue, in Galatians.

Still more recent is Grant Macaskill's *Union with Christ in the New Testament*.[8] Although it ranges more widely than just Paul, inevitably the apostle occupies a great deal of his attention. Macaskill's particular contribution for our concerns is his extended and careful argument that union with Christ in the New Testament functions as the fulfilment of Old Testament covenantal themes. Within those covenantal themes, he argues, lies the basic notion of God's presence with His people, and that is a theme which finds its most profound fulfilment in the New

---

6.   Campbell, *Paul and Union with Christ*, p. 413.

7.   Campbell, *Paul and Union with Christ*, p. 441. Richard Gaffin concludes similarly: Paul's theology does not have a 'centre', he says, if by that is meant a single concept from which his other concerns can all be deduced; but it does have a 'centre' in the more straightforward sense that there are plainly some matters that are more important to him than others (Gaffin, *By Faith, Not By Sight*, p. 24).

8.   Oxford: Oxford University Press 2013.

Testament in the union of the believer with Christ. Moreover, covenant provides a framework in which an individual can function representatively, with his narrative being ascribed to others, and Macaskill makes much use of Isaiah's Servant Songs as crucial background for union in the NT. Thus two themes arise in the Old Testament, says Macaskill: the restoration of the presence of divine glory among God's people, and 'the narrative of an individual who will, in himself, break the pattern of sin and failure'. The question of how these two themes come together in the New Testament defines for us, says Macaskill, 'the question of participation'.[9]

He therefore provides a significant biblical context in which to anchor Paul's use of the theme of union. Many think that one of the several reasons why union is a topic which has sometimes been hidden in plain sight in evangelicalism is that it seems, loosely, too 'mystical'. Indeed, contemporary evangelicals are sometimes taken aback to discover that some of their forebears were not averse to speaking explicitly of a mystical union with Christ. However, the biblical-theological background which Macaskill proposes alleviates the concern somewhat. Paul, along with other New Testament writers, is not giving legitimacy to ill-defined hyper-spirituality. Instead, when speaking of union, he is choosing a particularly powerful way of expressing the fulfilment of rather clear and well-defined Old Testament themes, which themselves are solidly grounded in historical revelation and reality.

To give one of Macaskill's examples: in Ephesians chapters 1 and 2, and also in 1 Corinthians chapters 3, 6, 10 and 12, we find coming together two notions about the church: that it is the body of Christ, and (partly in the background of this) that it is the temple of God. The linkage of body-imagery and temple-imagery anchors the former solidly in the rich Old Testament background of the latter. This linkage, Macaskill argues, is 'core to

---

9.   Macaskill, *Union with Christ in the New Testament*, p. 127. It is certainly possible, I think, to question the legitimacy of certain aspects of the interpretative background that Macaskill proposes for New Testament texts; nevertheless his overall point remains sound.

the New Testament theologies of participation'. [10] He concludes: 'To be united to Jesus, to be in him, is to be in the covenant through his representative headship.'[11] We will find some of this covenant background, too, expressed in Galatians, in which – to make a broad observation – significant themes of union and participation in Christ in chapter 2, and then again in chapters 5 and 6, surround covenantal arguments about Abraham and law in chapters 3 and 4, which are themselves regularly described in terms of union and participation.

3. Union with Christ in Galatians

As already stated, my aim here is to argue that the theme of union runs right through the bloodstream of Galatians, and to pick away a little at the particular ways in which it does so. In thinking of union in this way I am in agreement with Constantine Campbell, not wanting to argue that union is the central concern of Galatians, such that Paul, if asked to summarise the content of his letter in three English words, would have said 'union with Christ'. Rather, union provides the webbing (to use Campbell's image) or runs through the bloodstream (to use mine) that gives life to and connects the most explicit central concerns of the letter.

Galatians has of course been the site of some of the fiercest battles over the interpretation of Paul, and this remains the case. My observations, if valid, will inevitably have implications for some of these debates. It is not, though, my aim in this paper to mount arguments about such implications. I will therefore try to avoid getting caught in the cross-fire from such disputes since, though strongly related to my focus, they are not strictly our concern for now.

Resurrection and crucifixion
Galatians has a strikingly matching set of references to crucifixion and resurrection at its beginning and end. The letter opens with,

---

10. Macaskill, *Union with Christ in the New Testament*, p. 170.

11. Ibid., p. 298.

'Paul, an apostle – sent not from men nor by a man, but by Jesus Christ and God the Father *who raised him from the dead*' (1:1).[12] Then immediately following the wishing of grace and peace to the recipients from the Father and from Christ comes this description of Christ: 'who gave himself for our sins to rescue us from the present evil age' (1:4).[13] Thus Paul opens with reference to the resurrection followed closely by crucifixion, with both understood as events in the career of Jesus Christ – the former straightforwardly as an act of the Father with regard to the Christ, and the latter as an act of Christ with effect on believers.

Crucifixion and resurrection recur at the end, the former explicitly and the latter implicitly. Crucifixion comes first. 'May I never boast', says Paul in 6:14, 'except in the cross of our Lord Jesus Christ, through which the world has been crucified to me, and I to the world.' And then immediately follows this: 'Neither circumcision nor uncircumcision means anything; what counts is the new creation' (6:15). In light of the whole letter, language of 'new creation' is best taken as a strong allusion to resurrection. Of course it is true that in Galatians the cross itself is seen as bringing to an end the old era, and doing so in a way that deeply affects the believer in Christ, as just noted in 6:14 and first brought to light in 2:19-20. However, 6:15b contains an allusion to more than just the effect of crucifixion with Christ. In 2:20 Paul refers specifically to the life that follows crucifixion with Christ in terms of the Christ who is now alive living 'in me'. The presence of the resurrected Christ in the believer is what constitutes the reality of the believer's new life beyond his death with Christ. It is this new reality, with its allusions specifically to the believer's union with Christ in His resurrection, which Paul has in mind in his use of the phrase 'the new creation'.

---

12. This and subsequent biblical quotations in this chapter are taken from the New International Version (NIV) 2011 unless otherwise indicated.

13. This way of describing the effect of the crucifixion seems to be at the heart of Paul's way of expressing himself, since the same phrase appears in the important passage 1 Corinthians. 15:3ff., which is a summary of the gospel that Paul saw himself as passing on.

We therefore find strong references/allusions to crucifixion and resurrection at both the opening and closing of the letter. However, by the end two things have changed with regard to the opening. First, the order is reversed: resurrection-crucifixion at the beginning, and crucifixion-resurrection at the end. In light of what we will see as we progress through the letter, it is unlikely to be insignificant that here resurrection (as it were) encloses crucifixion, linking the two strongly together. The most obvious change from opening to closing, however, is that the opening sense of these things as events in the life of Christ that are outside believers and work an effect on them, has changed by the end into language of the believer's participation in those events. The ending speaks of the believer's crucifixion to the world and the world's to him through the cross of Christ, and of the believer's existence now in 'the new creation'.

The situation addressed in Galatians is one in which the objective events of cross and resurrection are not in question. Most directly in question, however, are what Paul takes to be the implications of the believer's personal identification with those events. Indeed we can rightly describe the most fundamental purpose running through Galatians as Paul's attempt to persuade those who already assent to the brute facts of resurrection and crucifixion and see some significance in them, as set out in the opening, that they must also come to be convinced of the believer's participation in those events. This is especially so of the theological, ecclesiological and ethical implications of that participation, as set out by the end. If the former assent stops short of the latter conviction and practices, the stakes are very high: at least in Galatia, the outcome was what Paul calls 'a different gospel – which is really no gospel at all' (1:6-7). Participation and union with Christ therefore fall within the bounds of Paul's understanding of the 'gospel of Christ', at least as he uses that term in this letter.

Paul's response to Peter in Antioch, 2:11-21

The second half of chapter 1 and all of chapter 2 are taken up with autobiographical material. This long section in Galatians has a number of clear purposes within the overall intention of the letter. In particular, Paul seems to present himself implicitly as an exemplary pattern which the Galatian believers ought to follow in their own circumstances. He tells them that he himself did not give in to pressure to have Titus circumcised, 'so that the truth of the gospel might be preserved for you' (2:5). Through this letter he is urging them not to give in to the same pressure to seek circumcision that is now coming on them, in order that the truth of the gospel that he fought to preserve for them might now be preserved in them. The climax comes with the final three verses of chapter 2 (vv. 19-21):

> For through the law I died to the law so that I might live for God. I have been crucified with Christ and I no longer live, but Christ lives in me. The life I now live in the body, I live by faith in the Son of God, who loved me and gave himself for me. I do not set aside the grace of God, for if righteousness could be gained through the law, Christ died for nothing!

We have already noted that crucifixion (explicitly) and resurrection (strongly implied) come together in 2:20, and this for the first time in the letter since the opening of 1:1-4. This suggests that 2:19-21 forms a significant climax thus far in Galatians. Further evidence for this understanding of the rhetorical function of 2:19-21 is found in their placement at the end of Paul's response to Peter concerning his actions in Antioch.[14]

The basic link between crucifixion and resurrection in 2:20 ought to be noted. Being crucified with Christ is a death which is necessary in order for the resurrected Christ to come and live within the believer.[15] Crucifixion with Christ is viewed here as a past

---

14. Interpreters differ as to whether 2:19–21 form part of Paul's summary of what he said to Peter when he confronted him over his withdrawal from table-fellowship with Gentiles, or whether they constitute his later reflection on that event. For our purposes it matters little, since at the very least these final verses of chapter 2 bring Paul's argument against Peter's actions to a climax, even if they do not report what he said to Peter on that occasion.

15. What Paul says of himself in the first person in 2:19–21 must be intended to refer not just to a purely personal experience of his, but to be instead a personalised way of asserting what is true of every believer. The location of these verses in the climax of his response to Peter's breaking of table-fellowship with Gentile believers makes that plain.

event which makes possible – clears the space for, we may say – the on-going indwelling of the resurrected Christ in the believer. This makes some sense of the juxtaposition of crucifixion and resurrection which we noted at the letter's opening and closing.

There seems to be a clear structural link between vv. 19 and 20. It makes best sense to think of each half of v. 19 as taken up again and given appropriate theological support in each half of v. 20. Thus the claim that 'through the law I died to the law' is supported by the statement that 'I have been crucified with Christ and I no longer live.' Next the statement in v. 19b that 'I died to the law so that I might live for God' is picked up and supported by the statement that Christ now lives in the believer, and that life lived in the flesh in the present is life that is lived by faith in the Son of God who gave Himself out of love. Paul's purpose in all this is to round off his demonstration of why Peter was wrong to withdraw from table-fellowship with Gentiles. In order to do so he makes a radical statement about the non-claim of the law on believers, grounded in their union with Christ in His past death and in His on-going resurrected life.

There is a significant pastoral use of union with Christ here. Of course there is disagreement among evangelicals over the precise situation that the letter is addressing, that is, the particular view of the law with regard to Gentile believers that Peter in Antioch had been temporarily pressured into adopting. According to one view, Peter had been persuaded to regard uncircumcised Gentiles as simply cut off from membership of the covenant people, whatever they may have professed about Christ. This view regards the primary focus of Galatians as a whole as being on the assertion of justification by faith, as traditionally understood. If that view is taken to be correct, it is noteworthy that Paul thinks of the believer's co-crucifixion with Christ and the risen Christ's presence in the believer as significant arguments in response to a misunderstanding of justification by faith.

According to another view of Galatians, however, Peter had come to act as if uncircumcised Gentiles in Christ were in a perilous situation with regard to being found to be justified in

Christ on the last day, lacking a commitment to torah that would keep them secure in Christ and safeguarded from the realities of 'the present evil age' while continuing in some sense to live in it. If this is right, then Paul's appeal to union at this point in Galatians has even wider pastoral reach. Past union with Christ in His crucifixion and present union with Christ in His resurrection become foundational realities which the believer needs to remain aware of in order to anchor in secure ground the whole of what Paul calls 'the life I now live in the body'. It is ground that is both objective and external to the believer, but also by virtue of God's action in those external events of cross and resurrection it is ground that is subjective and internal, in the sense that the believer has been united to Christ in death and resurrection.

An additional perspective on resurrection with Christ can be noted here, as found elsewhere in Paul. At the beginning of Colossians 3 he speaks of resurrection with Christ as a past event: 'you have been raised with Christ' (3:1). That past event, though, serves as the reason for consciously living in on-going union with Christ in His resurrected life: 'Since you have been raised with Christ, set your hearts on things above, where Christ is' (v. 1). And where Christ is, is also now, mysteriously, where we are; and who Christ is, is also now who we are: 'For you died, and your life is now hidden with Christ in God. When Christ, who is your life, appears, then you also will appear with him in glory' (vv. 3-4). This is given in Colossians as the basis for rigorous ethical obedience: 'Put to death, therefore, whatever belongs to your earthly nature' (v. 5). What we find in Colossians 3:1ff in condensed form is a line of argument that is broadly similar in structure to the more extended argument of Galatians (to anticipate a little the line we will continue to trace through Galatians): the theme of Christ's indwelling of the believer, which in Galatians comes to be expressed in terms of the Spirit, will lead to the ethical injunctions of chapters 5 and 6. The same is also true of Romans, where participation with Christ in His death and resurrection forms the explicit basis of strong moral instruction (6:1-14); effectively the same theological basis and ethical reality recur in Romans 8, but now expressed, as in Galatians, in terms of the Spirit.

The second half of Galatians 2 has proved to be the site of many battles over justification and related concepts. N. T. Wright has found 2:16 to be especially significant, taking it, on the basis of an early date for Galatians, to be Paul's first extant use of the language of justification. In particular, much has been built on the observation that this language is used here by Paul with the purpose of resolving an issue of Jew-Gentile social relationships within the emerging Christian church, leading to a general conclusion that language of justification is primarily to do with issues of belonging and relationship. I mention this not in order to wade into such contentious territory, but to raise two observations. First, that Paul's use of justification language in order to begin to deal with Peter's actions at Antioch is no valid argument that this language is primarily to do with issues like those at Antioch. It is perfectly possible to deal with the Antioch situation by appealing to an implication of justification language which itself has a different primary concern in view.[16]

Second, and more importantly for our concerns, it must be significant that Paul brings his response to Peter to a climax not with language of justification on its own but also with language of participation in Christ and of union with Him. He anticipates that, of course, with the earlier reference to himself and Peter as Jews who have sought 'to be justified in Christ' (2:17). In particular, in the climax that is 2:19-21, the verbs are participatory in sense – 'crucified with', and 'Christ lives in me'. This is a noticeable shift from the earlier prominence of the verb 'justify'.

Implicit here in the shape of Paul's argument at the close of chapter 2 is a point made by a number of recent writers, and indeed exemplified in the quote from J. I. Packer with which I began: justification language in Scripture is best understood as a vital but

---

16. As Douglas Moo neatly puts it, Wright here 'illegitimately privileges context over semantics'. (Douglas J. Moo, *Galatians*, Baker Exegetical Commentary on the New Testament [Grand Rapids: Baker 2013], p. 4).

also particular aspect of union with Christ. Kevin Vanhoozer, in something of a *tour de force*, has made this point with regard to N. T. Wright in particular, rather tellingly to my mind, arguing in effect that greater use of the Reformed doctrine of union with Christ could allow Wright's overall project on Paul to retain a great deal that Wright holds dear without needing to jettison – or at least to appear to many readers to jettison – some of the concerns traditionally addressed by appeal to justification. Vanhoozer recommends that the notion of adoption is especially useful here, since it rather pertinently includes both judicial and relational aspects. Greater use of the doctrine of adoption, he argues, would prevent the judicial and relational aspects of salvation in Paul being played off rather needlessly and inappropriately against each other.[17] We will come to adoption shortly within Galatians, in chapter 4.

Of course it is true that in the final phrases of Galatians 2 language of justification/ righteousness, which was prominent in verses 16-17, recurs, this time as a noun: 'if righteousness (*dikaiosune*) could be gained through the law, Christ died for nothing' (2:21b). Recent evangelical commentators tend to think that *dikaiosune* here is to be understood forensically, because of the clearly forensic sense of the cognate verb in vv. 16-17. However, there has been some dissent, with a case being made that by 2:21 the word has come contextually to take on additional tones of righteous living, in light of the theme of the life lived in faith which has just been raised in 2:20 and which will later become prominent in chapters 5 and 6.[18]

---

17. Kevin J. Vanhoozer, 'Wrighting the Wrongs of the Reformation? The State of the Union with Christ in St. Paul and Protestant Soteriology', in Nicholas Perrin and Richard B. Hays, (eds.) *Jesus, Paul and the People of God: A Theological Dialogue with N. T. Wright* (Downers Grove: InterVarsity Press 2011), pp. 235–59. James Dunn provides a rather clear example of a statement which sets the participatory aspects of Christ's sacrifice over against the judicial: the obvious outworking of Paul's theology of sacrifice, he says, 'would be in terms of the sinner sharing in Christ's death (and resurrection), rather than in a judicial verdict pronounced on the basis of Jesus' sacrificial death.' (Dunn, *The Theology of Paul*, pp. 90–1).

18. For the view that *dikaiosune* in 2:21 is purely forensic, see Moo, *Galatians*, p. 173 n.18; Thomas R. Schreiner, *Galatians*, Zondervan Exegetical Commentary on the New Testament (Grand Rapids: Zondervan 2010), p. 174. For a demurral see Longenecker, who summarises the verse as saying: 'for neither status nor lifestyle does the Christian depend on the law' (Richard N. Longenecker, *Galatians*, Word Biblical Commentary, vol. 41 [Dallas: Word Books 1990], p. 95).

Whatever view one takes on the particular question of the precise sense to be ascribed to 'righteousness' in 2:21, it is important that the crucial function of 2:19-20 in the rhetorical climax of Paul's argument, with its strong themes of union, not be set aside. It seems likely that 2:21 as a whole is to be understood as a summary of the entire argument from 2:15 onwards, up to and including v. 20. It would seem to run counter to the grain of Paul's argument to isolate the clearly forensic sense of vv. 15-16 as the only truly significant argument running through the section, with the result that v. 20, while acknowledged, is treated as effectively incidental to Paul's argument. As we have seen, its occurrence at this point in Paul's response to Peter and its bringing together of the opening themes of resurrection and crucifixion – along with what we will come to see is its role as a fountain-head of a great deal that will be central later in the letter – all serve to suggest it as integral to the case that Paul is building.

Beyond the complex question of the interpretation of particular occurrences of righteousness language in Paul, my primary point here is to highlight Galatians 2:19-21 as an instance in which Paul's strong language of the believer's participation in and union with Christ is not in effect an additional theological aside, included to bolster a more central argument that focuses purely on judicial righteousness and for which it is ultimately not strictly necessary. Instead, it is at the heart of his response to Peter, being strongly intertwined with his arguments about judicial righteousness in vv. 16-17. What we must further take account of, as we proceed, is that participation and union, along with strongly associated language of Spirit, will come to loom rather larger in Galatians than language primarily of judicial standing before God.

Chapters 3 and 4: Spirit, law and covenant

Chapter 3 opens with a shift of both tone and language, as Paul berates the Galatians for their foolishness and introduces language of Spirit which will recur several times again at the end of the

letter. It is important that our understanding of his statement in
3:1 – 'before your very eyes Jesus Christ was clearly portrayed as
crucified' – is controlled by its context in Galatians. The nature
of the crucifixion referred to here must be taken to include both
what he has just said about the cross, that is that believers have
been included in Christ's crucifixion and that consequently Christ
has come to live in them, as well as the wide-ranging effect of
the cross set out in introductory fashion in 1:4. This goes against
a tendency sometimes found, at least in popular handling of this
text, to regard this reference to the cross as alluding only to the
judicial theme of 2:16-17. Instead Paul is carrying over themes
of union from chapter 2 into the beginning of chapter 3. This
makes explicable the otherwise rather jarring shift from crucifixion
in 3:1 to Spirit in 3:2. The reception of the Spirit referred to in
3:2 is another way of speaking of the life of Christ in the believer
set out in 2:20. This functional equivalence of the indwelling of
Christ and of the Spirit in the believer is found elsewhere in Paul,
of course. Romans 8:9-10 provides a particularly clear example,
where Paul speaks of the Spirit of God living in believers, and
then in the next breath of Christ living in them.

To anticipate a little where this will lead us when we come to
the end of Galatians, this virtual identification of Christ living
in believers and believers receiving the Spirit forms a link which
chapter 5 and the first half of chapter 6 will build on in an ethical
direction. In pastoral terms, that helps to say something provisional
about the purpose of 5:1–6:10 within the letter as a whole. It is not
very satisfactory to think that Paul decides to conclude the letter
by heading off the potential misunderstanding that justification
by faith and not by works opens the door to libertarian living. It
makes rather more integrated sense of Galatians as a whole to
think of chapters 5 and 6 as making clear that the righteous life
which must be lived, if a claim to stand right before God is to
be taken seriously, is to be sought and will prosper only in and
through the indwelling Spirit, and not at all in the torah to which
the agitators of the Galatian church are encouraging the believers

to look. The link between 2:20 and 3:2, between union with Christ and Spirit, suggests that the final two chapters of the letter are intended to be an exposition of the theological significance and ethical power of union with Christ in His death and resurrection, set in contrast to the kind of ethical life governed by torah which the Galatian believers are being tempted with. More on this will follow when we come to chapter 5.

Back in chapter 3, we find a further intertwining of judicial and participatory themes in vv. 13 and 14. Christ's bearing of the judicial curse of the law for the purpose of redeeming sinners is clearly expressed in v. 13. Verse 14 then sets out a purpose of the redemption achieved in that way: 'He redeemed us in order that the blessing given to Abraham might come to the Gentiles through Christ (*en Christo*), so that by faith we might receive the promise of the Spirit.'

There are a couple of features of this verse that are relevant to our concerns. First is the question of the translation of *en Christo*, which pertains to the coming now to the Gentiles of the blessing given to Abraham. It is just possible that it has a purely instrumental sense, as suggested by the NIV's translation 'through Christ'. However the translation 'in Christ' (as in ESV), understood to have the sense of 'by virtue of their union with Christ', seems more likely. There is a lexical reason for this, since Paul wrote *en* when he could have used *dia*. There are also two contextual indicators. The theme of union with Christ seems to continue strongly in the background, marked by the reference to Gentile reception of the Spirit, with all the connotations of union that that already carries by this point in Galatians. In addition, instrumentality *is* referred to in the verse, but it comes at the end (at least in the Greek) and with regard to faith, through which (*dia* this time) the promised Spirit is received. If this is the right way to understand *en Christo* in v. 14 – or even if it be granted that Paul has this sense at least partly in view – then the logic of vv. 13 and 14 is this: Christ's death, understood judicially with regard to His bearing of the curse of the law, occurred in order that Gentiles might receive the

Spirit in union with Christ alone (and not by uniting themselves to torah in any sense), through the instrumentality of their faith alone (and not by virtue of any acts of torah observance). This being so, it is right to think of 3:13-14 as linking together rather clearly the judicial and participatory themes which have already been set alongside each other in 2:15-21, and now with a logical relationship between them made more explicit.

Secondly, we can recall Grant Macaskill's contention that union with Christ has covenant themes as its primary biblical explanatory background. That is indeed what we see here. Talk of 'the blessing given to Abraham' is explicitly covenantal. That blessing appears in 3:14 to be equated with the giving of the Spirit, or it may instead be that the blessing is that of judicial standing before God (see 3:6), now marked by reception of the Spirit. However that may be, covenant themes from the OT are taken to find their fulfilment in being 'in Christ'. Gentiles are explicitly said to receive this covenantal blessing only 'in Christ'. Indeed all are implicitly said to do so, which is probably what the shift from 'the Gentiles' to 'we' (presumably now all Christians, both Jew and Gentile) at the end of v. 14 is subtly intended to indicate.

In the following section of chapter 3, vv. 15-22, the theme of covenant continues, now with Christ's covenantal headship coming to the fore. Crucially for us, this does not represent a move into a new topic but is explicatory of vv. 13-14, as the opening of v. 15 makes clear ('Brothers and sisters, let me take an example . . .'). Paul here interprets the Old Testament concept of Abraham's seed as referring ultimately to a single individual, 'one person, who is Christ' (v. 16). Paul's train of thought here provides an example of Macaskill's notion that to be in Christ is to be in the covenant through Christ's representative headship. The consistency of these themes running through this section of Galatians is clear in the interim summary given in 3:22b (what was promised is given through faith in Jesus Christ, and is given to all who believe), which is a slightly abbreviated repetition of 3:14. The argument is progressing, but it does so partly by way of recapitulations that have language of union at their heart.

I suggest that it is noteworthy that the most obvious fountainhead of these themes in Galatians is 2:20. This makes it likely that concentration on the notions of faith in Christ and believing, such as we find in the repetition in 3:22b, is intended to call to mind what is said about faith back in 2:20, which set faith squarely in the context of life lived in union with Christ, just as much as it should call to mind what was said of faith as the means of justification itself in 2:16-17. If there is some truth in this suggestion, then it seems that however necessary it is (and it is vital!) to make a clear doctrinal distinction between the forensic ground of justification by faith and the actual ethical transformation of the believer in Christ, it is important not to read that distinction too quickly into our exegesis and also our preaching of the workings of Paul's rather rich forms of argumentation in Galatians.

From 3:23 onwards language of children, heirs and adoption comes to the forefront. A similar pattern to one observed previously is evident early in this section. Verses 24 and 25 speak straightforwardly of the faith by which believers are justified as now having come. Then, rather as we saw in 3:14, a consequence is said to follow which is expressed in rich language and imagery of union: 'So (*gar*) in (*en*) Christ Jesus you are all children of God through faith, for all of you who were baptised into Christ have clothed yourselves with Christ' (3:26-7). The second clause there introduced by 'for' (again *gar*, v. 27) gives an additional basis for the assertion of believers as being children of God in Christ Jesus (v. 26). Therefore it appears that the statement about adoption in v. 26 ('in Christ Jesus you are all children of God through faith') is both preceded and followed by supporting statements, the former speaking of justification and the latter of a double image of union with Christ. Thus again we find an extraordinarily close intertwining of these two themes in Paul's soteriological logic. Adoption in Christ as something of a climax is grounded quite tightly in 3:24-7 in both forensic and participatory realities. That is entirely fitting, of course, since adoption by its very nature brings the two together in a unified concept. What we have noticed here within the structure of Paul's argumentation in Galatians 3 with regard to his running together of the forensic and the participatory is evident in a number of other places too. Texts which express this include Romans 8:1; 1 Corinthians 1:30; Philippians 3:8-10.

It is important to see that the following much-quoted v. 28 – 'There is neither Jew nor Gentile, neither slave nor free, nor is there male nor female, for you are all one in Christ Jesus' – begins by alluding back to the confrontation with Peter over Jew-Gentile relations among believers, grounding and summarising Paul's argument against Peter in the phrase 'in Christ Jesus'. Therefore this latter phrase may well be intended as a concise summary of 2:20. Verse 28 then continues by expanding the reach of the union-with-Christ argument that Paul raised against Peter to include further kinds of human division.

Hinted at also in 3:28-9 is the nature of the church in relation to union with Christ. Whatever other effects Peter's actions in Antioch implied, they most certainly brought a social rupture into what ought to have been a unified church community. Elsewhere Paul will make a great deal of the corporate church's existence being in Christ, to such an extent that the church seems even to be equated with Christ (e.g., Eph. 1:22). He will expand especially on the unity of Jew and Gentile believers in Christ in strong terms in Ephesians: 'His purpose was to create in himself one new humanity out of the two, thus making peace, and in one body to reconcile both of them to God through the cross, by which he put to death their hostility' (Eph. 2:15b-16). This statement is something of a development of the point made in Galatians 3:28 with regard to Peter's behaviour in Antioch.[19]

---

19. Somewhat speculatively, I wonder if one reason for wariness towards union with Christ in some evangelical circles, or at least relative ignorance of it, is its connection in Paul with his ecclesiological language of Christ's body. Or, to put the same thing another way round, it may not be a coincidence that historically the branches of evangelicalism which have been more comfortable with giving a central place to union with Christ have often been those which have also had a more readily expressed, self-conscious and full-orbed ecclesiology at the heart of their sense of self-identity. A similar point could be made, with ramifications that go far beyond the concerns of this paper, with regard to baptism and the Lord's Supper.

The conclusion to the section provided in 3:29 ties together themes that have now been running for a while – union (or better participation, since it is literally, 'if you are of Christ'), and covenant ('you are Abraham's seed' and 'according to the promise') – with the recently introduced notion of being a child who has the right to inherit.

I trust that a key thrust of my argument is clear through these textual details. Most would acknowledge that as Paul's argument unfolds through Galatians, language and imagery of union in and participation with Christ are retained persistently. My argument is that more than that must be said. In particular, Paul weaves such language and imagery very directly into various topics as he comes to deal with them, which in chapters 3 and 4 are particularly believers' relationship to the law, their relationship to the covenant with Abraham and his seed, and also their status as children who have the rights of inheritance. As each of these topics is dealt with, it appears that Paul brings his argument in relation to it to a climax or summary by expressing it in terms explicitly of union and participation in Christ. I offer these observations of Galatians chapters 3 and 4 as examples, running over a number of paragraphs of Paul's writing, to support Campbell's understanding of union as that concept in Paul which most consistently serves to link coherently together his most central topics.

To be clear, I do not intend in the least to airbrush out of Galatians its strong judicial themes and prominent language of justification. My aim is to highlight a rather more neglected theme in the letter, and to show at the very least how utterly integral it is, in remarkably inextricable ways, to Paul's overall argument and to his deployment of concepts of justification – along with law, covenant and adoption.

Paul's drawing together of law, union and Spirit to articulate the believer's identity as a child and heir of God culminates in 4:4-6. In v. 6 the previous implicit linkage of 'Christ lives in me' with the Galatians' reception of the Spirit is made explicit, and now becomes a mark of adoption by God: 'Because you are his sons, God sent the Spirit of his Son into our hearts.' Also evident here is the fact that believers' identity as adopted sons of God is by virtue of who they are in the One who is uniquely and eternally the Son. Any tendency to let union with Christ slide towards a blurring of humanity into the being of God is firmly resisted here.

These verses hark back to previous themes of union in other ways, too. There seems to be a similar logic in 4:4-5 to that which we noticed in 3:13-14. There Christ's relation to the law in His death was the focus, bearing its curse; here in 4:4 His relation to the law is expressed again, but more broadly now, specifically in relation to His birth and implicitly to His entire earthly existence: 'born of a woman, born under law'. In 3:14 we saw that Christ's becoming a curse was with the purpose of redemption, so that Gentiles too could be *in Christ*, and so receive the Spirit by faith. In chapter 4, in rather similar terms, Christ's coming under the law is said again to have the purpose of redeeming, indeed redeeming us for an adoption which, as we have just seen, is additionally said to be possible and real only because of our *sharing* in Christ's own Sonship. A repeated pattern of soteriological thought, with union at its heart, is evident.

One further reference should be noted in chapter 4. In 4:8-20 Paul reverts to personal appeal, somewhat in the vein of 3:1-5. As that appeal comes to a crescendo, language of union recurs (perhaps not now surprisingly so), but in a form which is new in Galatians: 'My dear children, for whom I am again in the pains of childbirth *until Christ is formed in you* . . .' (4:19; expressed strikingly in the Greek word order as 'until is formed Christ in you'). The new element here is the sense in which the indwelling of Christ in believers is not yet complete, which is not something we would have expected in light of 2:20 and 3:2. Earlier we noted that Paul is capable of expressing union with Christ in His resurrection in both past and future senses. We see here that the same is the case with the indwelling of Christ in believers.[20]

Chapters 5 and 6: Spirit, love and new creation

Galatians 5:5 can rightly be regarded as somewhat programmatic for the letter as a whole: 'For through the Spirit we eagerly await by faith the righteousness for which we hope.' In light of the reference to justification in the previous verse it seems certain that 'righteousness' in 5:5 is to be understood forensically. However, it is also the case, crucially, that v. 5 has a forward-looking dimension, speaking of a righteousness that believers hope for. Douglas Moo treats this as an example of what he takes to be the typical sense of righteousness language in Galatians – namely, that it refers to the Galatians remaining securely in their right standing before the Lord, with a view all the way forward to (in Moo's phrase) 'ultimate justification' on the last day.[21]

Significant for us is that the security of that standing is said here by Paul to be found 'through the Spirit . . . by faith', and therefore, by implication, not through torah. These phrases are likely to be the trigger for the reappearance of union with Christ in the next verse, v. 6 ('for in Christ Jesus neither circumcision nor uncircumcision has any value'), since we have often seen how closely those three concepts (Spirit, faith and union) function together in Galatians. The thing that Paul goes on in 5:6b to

---

20. Gaffin makes much of there being in Paul future elements also to union with Christ in His death (Phil. 3:10) and adoption (Rom. 8:23), along with (more controversially) justification, for which he appeals especially to Galatians 5:5. He insists that this view of justification falls within Reformed orthodoxy, albeit as a minority form of expression, and does not at all undermine the doctrine of a discrete act of judicial declaration by the Lord of believers' right standing with Him (Gaffin, *Resurrection and Redemption*, pp. 133–4). A little more on this will follow below.

21. Moo, *Galatians*, pp. 61–2. He insists that this in no way adds the life lived by a believer to the basis on which he has the status of right standing before God (Douglas J. Moo, 'Justification in Galatians', in Andreas J. Köstenberger and Robert W. Yarbrough (eds.) *Understanding the Times: New Testament Studies in the Twenty-First Century*, Festschrift D. A. Carson [Wheaton, Illinois: Crossway 2011], pp. 160–95, at 186–95).

say does count – meaning, count as the right means by which to remain securely in a right standing with God to the final judgment – is 'faith expressing itself through love'.

In 5:11 it is most probably the case that Paul is responding to an accusation that his approach with regard to circumcision is inconsistent: he has urged on Galatians the danger of seeking it, whereas (so his opponents say) in Jewish contexts he happily allows it. Significant for us is that Paul defends himself by saying that if he were guilty of this charge then the 'the offence of the cross' would have been abolished. In the immediate context Paul has previously referred to circumcision as being of no account, as we have seen, because of believers being 'in Christ'. In 5:6 and 11 language of the offence of the cross is therefore closely paralleled with the notion of being 'in Christ Jesus'. As we have noted before, the roots of this bringing together of cross and union within Galatians are to be traced back to the crucial function of 2:20. This suggests that the offence of the cross that Paul has in mind in 5:11 is not only its declaration that human works can never bring about right standing before God – although he most definitely has nothing less than that in mind. Yet he has an additional offence of the cross in mind: its implication that human works, exemplified in the Galatian situation by circumcision, are of no value or account in demonstrating that one is remaining securely in right standing before God, since such works are not of faith (cf. 3:12, 'the law is not of faith'), and therefore by definition are not acts performed out of the new life that the believer now lives in Christ by faith – a life that the believer now lives only because he has first been crucified with Christ. Nor, we might add, do such works find their natural expression in love, which according to 5:5 is what does count. It may well be that in this reference to love Paul is still partly harking back to Peter's withdrawal from table-fellowship with Gentiles in Antioch, since that action demonstrated a lack of love towards fellow-believers in Christ.

In the section 5:13–6:11 Paul turns to ethical injunctions about life in the Spirit: 'So I say, live by the Spirit' (5:16). It ought to be difficult, by this point in Galatians, for the reader to hear these words as something less than or different from a concise command to put into action the already existing reality of Christ living in them, which itself has come about only because of their co-crucifixion with Christ. Indeed, that background theme from 2:20 is made explicit in relation to the ethical focus of this section when just a little later, having described the fruit of the Spirit, Paul says: 'Those who belong to Christ Jesus [literally: who are of Christ Jesus] have crucified the flesh with its passions and desires' (5:24). Something rather more is going on here than the erection of a barrier to libertarian conclusions being wrongly drawn from the truth of justification by faith. Paul is recalling the co-crucifixion of 2:20 and its link with Spirit-reception in 3:2, and expressing the natural ethical and transformational aspect of that reality. Transformation by the indwelling Spirit results from identifying oneself with Christ in the event of crucifixion.

Paul returns to this notion of his experiential participation in crucifixion in his final explicit mention of the cross in Galatians, in 6:14. This is the third time in the letter he has related the believer's action and experience directly to the cross (cf. 2:20; 5:24). The verse summarises the epochal effect of the cross, already adumbrated at the outset in 1:4, but now expressed in terms which make clear that those effects come about only to the extent that the believer is a participant with Christ in His death, and is united with Him in His resurrection (as the subsequent v. 15 will make clear) by virtue of the risen Christ's indwelling of him.

The section 5:13–6:18 is therefore more substantially and more integrally a climax of Galatians than is sometimes realised. This is not to argue, for example, that 'Spirit' is the real concern of the letter rather than justification. Instead, 5:13–6:18 forms the ultimate climax of all that Paul would want to say to Peter about the implications of his actions in Antioch. Peter had been persuaded to put one model of Christian life into action. It failed to express love to every kind of person who is in Christ by faith. More significantly, it implicitly denied that faith is sufficient for right standing with God. As part of this crucial denial, it further implied that torah needs to be added to faith in Christ if the believer is to remain confident in his right standing before the Lord.

Paul rejects that version of Christian thought and life. He does so by beginning with what would have been assented to on all sides: the events of Christ's death for sin and His being raised by the Father. He proceeds by raising a number of topics – most significantly justification, along with law, Abraham and covenant, adoption, the kind of life that pleases God and befits belonging to Him – and expresses each of these, especially in summary form and often linked together, in terms of the believer's participation in and union with Christ in resurrection and (especially) crucifixion. These expressions often occur as the conclusions to particular sub-sections.

It is therefore not that union with Christ can be said to be the central concern of Galatians. However, it is the one theme which provides the terms in which every significant central concern is consistently expressed throughout the letter. It is also the theme which is deployed most regularly at those moments when a particular point is being summarised, and which is most regularly carried forward to provide a link to the introduction of subsequent themes.

4. Conclusion

Of much that could be said in addition to the foregoing, two final points can be made – the first theological, the second pastoral.

First, Paul's use of union with Christ is profoundly interwoven into the warp and woof of Galatians, and this in two particular ways. He regularly expresses the letter's central concepts in terms of union. He also regularly brings his argument against Peter in Antioch and the agitators in Galatia to a climax by clustering together different kinds of language of union with Christ. This suggests that questions about Paul which think in terms of his relative emphasis on participatory categories over against other categories, such as the judicial, are often already insufficiently sensitive to the way in which the apostle thought. The kinds of questions which arise out of some hotly debated theological topics might be good theological questions, but as applied directly to Galatians they may not be questions to which the letter in itself is explicitly designed to give clear answers. Exegetical categories and theological ones do not always overlap exactly, although the same vocabulary might be used for both.

Second, Paul resorts to union with Christ in order to set the Galatians straight on quite a range of issues, even within a short letter, that are ultimately pastoral ones. These include: the ground of the believer's right standing before God; the nature of solid confidence that believers are remaining in right standing before God; the seriousness of the breaking of table-fellowship within the church; the significance of believers' initial reception of the Spirit; the source of the growth of righteous living within the believer. In light of this, it may be true to say that we do not fully grasp Paul's convictions about the union of the believer with Christ unless we consciously apply those same convictions to similar real-life struggles in faith and life, as he did, both in ourselves and in the lives of others.[22]

QUESTIONS FOR DISCUSSION

1. Do you think that what Paul says about union has been underplayed in evangelical understandings of Paul, or not? Why?

2. In those areas where evangelical understanding of union with Christ in Paul has been weak, what have the effects of that been, both in theology and Christian discipleship?

3. What do you make of the case that has been outlined about union with Christ in Galatians?

---

22. I am grateful to my colleague Dr Jonathan Griffiths for his insightful comments on an earlier draft of this paper.

4. How do other letters of Paul expand, nuance or qualify what Galatians says about union?

5. How much does what Paul says about union with Christ in Galatians already figure in your own preaching, teaching and pastoral ministry?

6. In particular, how can the purposes for which Paul uses union with Christ in Galatians shape our own pastoral ministry and preaching?

CHAPTER THREE

'Union with Christ' in the Theology of John Calvin

ROBERT LETHAM

1. The centrality of union with Christ

For Calvin, union with Christ is right at the heart of the Christian doctrine of salvation.[2] He wrote: 'For we await salvation from

---

1. All citations from the Bible are in citations of Calvin, not taken directly from any English version. The only exception is where I cite 2 Peter 1:4 which is my translation and taken from the Nestle-Aland text, 28th edition.

2. John Fesko argues strongly against making Calvin the benchmark against which all subsequent Reformed theology is to be measured; he was one of many voices. See J. V. Fesko, *Beyond Calvin: Union with Christ and Justification in Early Modern Reformed Theology (1517–1700)* (Göttingen: Vandenhoeck & Ruprecht 2012). In this he is correct, as I have written elsewhere; see Robert W. A. Letham, 'Faith and Assurance in Reformed Theology: Zwingli to the Synod of Dort', 2 vols, Ph.D. unpublished thesis (University of Aberdeen, 1979); Robert Letham, 'Faith and Assurance in Early Calvinism: A Model of Continuity and Diversity', in W. Fred Graham (ed.), *Later Calvinism: International Perspectives*, (Kirksville, Missouri: Sixteenth Century Journal Publishers 1994), pp. 55–84. However, it would be amiss to go to the opposite extreme and discount Calvin. He was clearly considered by his contemporaries to be *primus inter pares*. The reception of his writings in the following generations demonstrates his stature; see Andrew Pettegree, 'The Reception of Calvinism in Britain', in Wilhelm H. Neuser and Brian G. Armstrong (eds.), *Calvinus Sincerioris Religionis Vindex: Calvin as the Protector of the Purer Religion* (Kirksville: Sixteenth Century Journal Publishers, 1997), pp. 267–89, esp. 280–2, 289, who confirms from English and continental publishers' book lists, theological works published

him not because he appears to us afar off, but because he makes us, engrafted into his body, participants not only in all his benefits but also in himself.'[3] Indeed, 'as long as Christ remains outside of us, and we are separated from him, all that he has suffered and done for the salvation of the human race remains useless and of no value to us.'[4] As a consequence, 'Christ, having been made ours, makes us sharers with him in the gifts with which he has been endowed. We do not, therefore, contemplate him outside ourselves from afar in order that his righteousness may be imputed to us but because we put on Christ and are engrafted into his body – in short, because he deigns to make us one with him.'[5] Indeed, 'all that he [Christ] possesses is nothing to us until we grow into one body with him.'[6] In his commentary on Ephesians, Calvin goes so far as to affirm that Christ does not consider Himself to be complete apart from union with us. 'It is the highest honour of the church that in some sense the Son of God considered himself imperfect unless he was united to us.'[7] This theme was present ever since the 1539 edition of the *Institutes* where he says, 'he benefits only those whose Head he is ... who ... have put on him.'[8] In summary, Garcia comments that 'it is widely agreed that union with Christ is of fundamental

---

in English, and books bequeathed in Cambridge wills 'the preeminent position of Calvin as the dominant theological influence in Elizabethan England', easily outstripping all competitors from whatever source.

3.   John Calvin, *Institutes of the Christian Religion*. Trans. Ford Lewis Battles;; ed. John T. McNeill (Philadelphia: Westminster Press 1960), 3:2:24.

4.   Calvin, *Institutes*, 3:1:1.

5.   Calvin, *Institutes*, 3:11:10.

6.   Calvin, *Institutes*, 3:1:1.

7.   My translation. See John Calvin, *Calvin's Commentaries: The Epistles of Paul to the Galatians, Ephesians, Philippians and Colossians*. Trans. T. H. L. Parker (Grand Rapids: Eerdmans 1965), p. 138; 'Hic vero summus honor est ecclesiae, quod se Filius Dei quodammodo imperfectum reputat, nisi nobis sit coniunctus.' John Calvin, *Commentarii in Pauli Epistolas, Ioannis Calvini Opera Exegetica* (Genève: Librairie Droz 1992), p. 176.

8.   Calvin, *Institutes* (1539), 3:1:3, in John Calvin, *Opera Selecta*, ed. Petrus Barth; (Munich: Chr. Kaiser 1936), 4:5.

importance for Calvin's soteriology."[9] He considers that the extent to which the theme pervades Calvin's *Commentary on Romans* is 'astonishing'.[10]

2. The *nature* of union with Christ

What does Calvin mean by union with Christ? This topic is a notoriously difficult theme to grasp as, to a large extent, it transcends our capacities. As we shall see, Calvin too considers that it surpasses his understanding. In order for us to get a broad view of how he approaches the subject we will start by referring to his correspondence with Pietro Martire Vermigli in 1555.[11]

This exchange was opened by Vermigli, who wrote to Calvin on 8 March 1555, on 'the communion we have with the body of Christ and the substance of his nature' (*de communione quam habemus cum corpore Christi atque substantia ipsius naturae*),[12] since it is a matter of great importance that the manner of our union with Christ be understood.[13] Vermigli wrote that the chief benefit of the incarnation is that Christ has chosen to communicate with us in His flesh and blood so that we become partakers of these. This incarnational union is common and weak (*communis admodum haec esset et debilis*) since in this sense Christ is in communion with the whole human race.

Vermigli then moves on to describe a second form of communion, which is peculiar to the elect. By faith the elect believe in Christ and are not only pardoned for sin and reconciled to God – which is a true and solid *ratio* for justification – but by the power of the Holy Spirit their flesh and blood are made

---

9.   Mark Garcia, *Life in Christ: Union with Christ and Twofold Grace in Calvin's Theology* (Milton Keynes: Paternoster 2008), p. 34.

10. Mark Garcia, *Life in Christ*, p. 93.

11. Vermigli's letter to Calvin of 8 March is found in John Calvin, *Opera quae supersunt Omnia*, Guilielmus Baum, Eduardus Cunitz, and Eduardus Reiss (eds.) (Brunswick: C. A. Schwetschke and Son 1863–1900), 15:492–7, hereafter CO. Calvin's reply, dated 8 August, is in CO, 15:722–5.

12. English citations from this correspondence are my translation.

13. CO, 15:494.

capable of an immortal nature and are increasingly conformed to Christ (*qua nostra quoque corpora, caro, sanguis et natura immortalitatis capacia fiunt, et Christiformia [ut ita dixerim] indies magis ac magis evadunt.*) The substance of their nature is unchanged but they share in the spiritual gifts and properties He bestows. According to Vermigli, we therefore have two communions with Christ – one is natural from birth through our parents, while the other consists in justification and renewal by the Spirit of Christ *quo ab ipsa regeneratione ad speciem eius gloriae innovamur.*[14]

However, there is also a third form of union, between the above two, Vermigli claims. This is the *fons et origo* of spiritual likeness with Christ and occurs immediately we believe that Christ Himself is our head and we are His members. In this, the Spirit flows from Christ, the head, and animates the members. Here Vermigli uses the analogy of the body, with the heart central from which come the veins and arteries. So Christ, when we are first converted (*dum convertimur*) efficaciously joins us to Him. This is that hidden communion (*illa est arcana communio qua illi dicimur inseri*), by which we become flesh of His flesh, and bone of His bones, as the apostle says, while our bodies are on earth, and Christ's is in heaven, seated and reigning with the Father. Faith, the word of God and the sacraments are the primary means by which He feeds and assimilates His members through the Spirit. However, this union does not mean we are united with Christ in the same *hypostasis*.[15] Various scholars have termed the latter two aspects of union spiritual and mystical respectively.[16]

Calvin, in his reply, dated 8 August, expresses his agreement and adds comments of his own. He refers only briefly to the communion achieved in the incarnation, writing more on the third form of union by which Christ makes us coalesce in

---

14. CO, 15:494.

15. CO, 15:495.

16. Mark Garcia, *Life in Christ*, pp. 273–86; J. V. Fesko, *Beyond Calvin: Union with Christ and Justification in Early Modern Reformed Theology* (1517–1700) (Göttingen: Vandenhoeck & Ruprecht 2012), pp. 88–206.

one body with Him (*in unum cum ipso corpus coalescimus*), which some scholars call mystical.[17] In this, he says, we are made His members and life flows to us from Him the head (*nos fieri eius membra, et vitam ab eo non secus atque a capite in nos defluere*). We only benefit from Christ's sacrifice if we are one with Him. (*Neque enim aliter nos Deo mortis suae sacrificio reconcilat, nisi quia noster est ac nos unum cum ipso.*) The terms 'society' and 'fellowship' are too weak to express the unity by which the son of God unites us in His body and communicates all that is His, for it is a sacred unity 'by which the Son of God engrafts us into one body and communicates to us all his things. So we drink life from his flesh and blood, so that it is not inappropriately called nourishment.'[18] The Spirit makes Christ dwell in us. Calvin precludes a mixture of substances (*crassis interea commentis de substantiae commixtione aditum praecludo*) for it is enough that Christ is in heavenly glory and life flows to us from Him. He opposes as absurd the idea that we become one essence with Christ. He recognises that it is beyond his understanding.[19]

Calvin then discusses the second aspect mentioned by Vermigli. After Christ by the inward power of the Spirit joins us to Himself and unites us to His body, the power of the Spirit is manifest in His gifts.[20]

Hence, for Calvin and Vermigli there are three aspects to union with Christ. First, there is Christ's union with us in His incarnation. This is His assumption of human nature. It is the foundation of the union with Christ that believers have, but of itself it does not effect salvation.

Second is the union effected by the Holy Spirit in which all who believe are made members of the body of Christ and

---

17. CO, 15:722–3.

18. 'Neque vero nomen consortii vel societatis mentem eius satis exprimere videtur, sed mihi sacram illam unitatem designat, qua filius Dei nos in corpus suum inserit, et nobiscum sua omnia communicat.' ibid.

19. 'Quomodo id fiat, intelligentiae meae modulo longe altius esse fateor.' CO, 15:723.

20. ibid.

become bone of His bone, flesh of His flesh. In this, the life of Christ flows to us as from the head to the body. This is a mystery that transcends our abilities to understand, let alone describe. Third, there is an aspect of union consisting of justification and in the power of the Spirit being made known in the gifts Christ gives to His body.

So for Calvin Christ's union with us in the incarnation is the foundation for our union with Him, both now and in the eternal future: 'our common nature with Christ is the pledge of our fellowship with the Son of God; and clothed with our flesh he vanquished death and sin together that the victory and triumph might be ours.'[21] On the other hand, this is a weak union in the sense that it is not by itself redemptive.[22] However, it is central to redemption, not merely as its *sine qua non* but also because redemption takes place in Christ. Thus, Christ is prior to His benefits, since 'we cannot possess the good things of our Lord Jesus Christ to take any profit from them, unless we first enjoy him.'[23]

Yet we must be joined to Christ by the Spirit. As in Tony Lane's vivid analogy, electricity lines may go past a house but to benefit from the electricity supply the house must be connected to the lines.[24] As Calvin puts it, 'First, we must understand that as long as Christ remains outside of us, and we are separated from him, all that he has suffered and done for the salvation of the human race remains useless and of no value for us.'[25] There are two linked realities here. Without the electricity surging through the grid, the house could have no benefit, even if the wires were connected. If Christ were not incarnate and had not, in our flesh, rendered satisfaction to God's justice on the cross, there would

21. Calvin, *Institutes*, 2:12:3.

22. Calvin, *Institutes*, 3:1:1.

23. John Calvin, *Sermons on the Epistle to the Ephesians* (1577; repr., Edinburgh: Banner of Truth 1973), p. 403.

24. Anthony N. S. Lane, *Justification by Faith in Catholic-Protestant Dialogue: An Evangelical Assessment* (London: T & T Clark 2002), p. 23.

25. Calvin, *Institutes*, 3:1:1.

be nothing to deliver us from sin and the just and holy wrath of God. It is in addition to this that the linkage to the grid is possible. In the next sentence to the one cited above Calvin states

> Therefore, to share with us what he has received from the Father, he had to become ours and to dwell within us. For this reason, he is called 'our Head' [Eph. 4:15], and 'the first-born among many brethren' [Rom. 8:29]. We also, in turn, are said to be 'engrafted into him' [Rom. 11:17], and 'to put on Christ' [Gal. 3:27]; for, as I have said, all that he possesses is nothing to us until we grow into one body with him. It is true that we obtain this by faith. Yet since we see that not all indiscriminately embrace that communion with Christ which is offered in the gospel, reason itself teaches us to climb higher and to examine into the secret energy of the Spirit, by which we come to enjoy Christ and all his benefits.[26]

Both the incarnate Son and the Holy Spirit together, distinctly but indivisibly, bring about our union with Christ. Union itself consists in both a right status before God in justification and a communion with Christ that transforms us. As Lane remarks, 'faith is effective not in itself but because it unites us to Christ. Justification is by faith alone not because of what faith merits or *achieves* but because of what it *receives*.'[27]

3. Union with Christ and the *ordo salutis*

Claims have been made that, for Calvin, union with Christ was the organising principle of his whole doctrine of salvation. From this it has been argued that he was indifferent as to the relative priority of justification and sanctification.[28] However, Richard Muller has convincingly demonstrated that Calvin, in his *Institutes*, in treating sanctification before justification in Book Three is simply following the order of teaching in Paul's Letter to

---

26. Calvin, *Institutes*, 3:1:1.

27. Lane, *Justification*, p. 26.

28. Richard B. Gaffin, Jr., 'Biblical Theology and the Westminster Standards', *WTJ* 65 (2003), pp. 176–7.

the Romans, which provided the basis for his ordering of topics in the *Institutes* from the 1539 edition onwards, largely following Melanchthon.[29] In doing this, in the 1559 edition he had already considered justification in Book Two. It follows that the order of his treatment of topics in Book Three does not disclose any particular set of priorities in his theology. The *ordo salutis* was not a huge issue at the time Calvin wrote, although he considered the outworking of salvation to be ordered and sequential.[30] He set out to present an orderly account of salvation and, beyond that, of the whole gamut of the Christian faith. A number of arrangements can be proposed to describe this – Calvin's own structuring of the late edition of his *Institutes* around the knowledge of God and a loose connection to the Apostles' Creed comes closest to reality – but none are entirely satisfactory. They seem to be later impositions. Furthermore, the idea of a central organising principle only arose in nineteenth-century German scholarship; it is anachronistic to look for it three hundred years earlier.[31]

As Wenger argues, union with Christ cannot be said to *control* Calvin's soteriology. Still less does it determine the relative order of priority of justification and sanctification in his thought. There is plenty of evidence in the 1559 *Institutes* itself indicating that he shared the views of the later Reformed that justification was foundational. He regards it as 'the main hinge on which religion turns' since it is necessary as a foundation on which to establish our salvation and build piety towards God.[32] He repeatedly stresses its basic importance for salvation, the Christian life

---

29.   Richard A. Muller, *The Unaccommodated Calvin: Studies in the Foundation of a Theological Tradition*, (New York: Oxford University Press 2000), pp. 118–30.

30.   As Muller notes, 'The order of *loci* identified by Melanchthon in Paul's Epistle to the Romans thus established a standard for the organization of Protestant theology.' Muller, *The Unaccommodated Calvin*, p. 129.

31.   Thomas L. Wenger, 'The New Perspective on Calvin: Responding to Recent Calvin Interpretations', *JETS* 50 (2007), pp. 311–28.

32.   Calvin, *Institutes*, 3:11:1.

and assurance of salvation.[33] In his *Reply to Sadoleto*, he insists, 'wherever the knowledge of it is taken away, the glory of Christ is extinguished, the Church destroyed, and the hope of salvation utterly overthrown.'[34] Yet there can be no question but that union with Christ had for Calvin a prominent place, relating to the application of redemption from election to glorification. While, correctly, he does not consider Calvin to have had a 'central dogma', Todd Billings nevertheless agrees that 'participation', 'union', 'engrafting', and 'adoption' are central images for Calvin's conception of what it means to be 'in Christ'.[35]

3.1 Union with Christ and election

For Calvin, union with Christ has regard to the eternal determination of God in which He established our salvation. Assurance of election is to be sought in Christ precisely because we were chosen in Christ before the foundation of the world. Any attempt on our part to probe the mysteries of election is in vain, for it is beyond us. However, God has revealed Himself in His Son, in whom we have salvation.

> Accordingly, those whom God has adopted as his sons are said to have been chosen not in themselves but in his Christ [Eph. 1:4] for unless he could love them in him, he could not honour them with the inheritance of his Kingdom if they had not previously become partakers of him. But if we have been chosen in him, we shall not find assurance of our election in ourselves; and not even in God the Father, if we conceive him as severed from his Son. Christ, then, is the mirror wherein we must, and without self-deception may, contemplate our own election. For since it is into his body the Father has destined those to be engrafted whom he has willed from eternity to be his own, that he may hold as sons all whom he acknowledges

33. Calvin, *Institutes*, 3:11:6, 11; 3:13:5.

34. John Calvin, 'Reply to Sadolet', in Henry Beveridge and Jules Bonnet (eds.), *Selected Works of John Calvin: Tracts and Letters*, (Grand Rapids: Baker 1983), 1:41.

35. J. Todd Billings, *Calvin, Participation, and the Gift: The Activity of Believers in Union with Christ* (Oxford: Oxford University Press 2007), p. 19.

to be among his members, we have a sufficiently clear and firm testimony that we have been inscribed in the book of life [cf. Rev. 21:27] if we are in communion with Christ.[36]

Calvin considers that election in Christ has definite practical implications. We can have assurance of our election in this life if we are in communion with Christ since we were elected in union with Him. Faith in Christ here and now mirrors the eternal electing purpose of God, since the latter was undertaken with Christ as our head. Calvin considers that Christ 'claims for himself, in common with the Father, the right to choose'.[37] Furthermore, following Augustine, he talks of Christ as the first of the elect, since He Himself was chosen to the office of mediator. He is 'the clearest light of predestination and grace', appointed mediator solely by God's good pleasure.[38] The Father has gathered us together in Christ the head and joined us to Himself 'by an indissoluble bond'. So the members of Christ 'engrafted to their head... are never cut off from salvation'.[39] Election cannot be properly conceived in separation from Christ.

3.2 Union with Christ and justification

Calvin's understanding of the relationship between union and justification is seen in clear relief in his controversy with Andreas Osiander (1496-1552), controversial within the Lutheran communion, who held that justification consists in our participation in the divine righteousness of Christ. Consequently we become righteous ourselves. This was a construction set in opposition to an alien righteousness of Christ by imputation.[40] In effect, Osiander made infused righteousness the basis of justification and, by introducing the good works of believers into the equation, confused justification and sanctification.

---

36.   Calvin, *Institutes*, 3:24:5.
37.   Calvin, *Institutes*, 3:22:7.
38.   Calvin, *Institutes*, 3:24:5.
39.   Calvin, *Institutes*, 3:21:7.
40.   Mark Garcia, *Life in Christ*, pp. 204–5.

Calvin could say, in connection with Osiander's claim that we are justified by the divine righteousness of Christ, 'he has clearly expressed himself as not content with that righteousness which has been acquired for us by Christ's obedience and sacrificial death, but pretends that we are substantially righteous in God by the infusion both of his essence and of his quality'.[41] Underlying Osiander's Christological confusion at this point was the Lutheran view of the *communicatio idiomatum*. This construction held that the characteristics of Christ's divine nature were communicated to His humanity. It was a departure from the classic Christology in which characteristics of the natures of Christ are predicable of His person.

In refutation, Calvin insisted that justification is forensic, involving the imputation of Christ's righteousness. In turn, sanctification consists of ethical transformation by the Holy Spirit. 'To be justified means something different from being made new creatures.'[42] However, both are received in union with Christ. While some scholars have argued strongly against a forensic doctrine of union with Christ in Calvin,[43] it is clearly present in his doctrine of justification and so too as a vital element of union.

> Therefore, we explain justification simply as the acceptance with which God receives us into favour as righteous men. And we say that it consists in the remission of sins and the imputation of Christ's righteousness.[44]

Moreover, Calvin insists that *the obedience of the incarnate* Christ secures our justification. He took Adam's place in obeying the Father, presenting our flesh as satisfaction to the judgment of

---

41. Calvin, *Institutes*, 3:11:5.

42. Calvin, *Institutes*, 3:11:6.

43. James B. Torrance, 'Covenant or Contract? A Study of the Background of Worship in Seventeenth-Century Scotland', *SJT* 23 (1970), pp. 51–76; Julie Canlis, *Calvin's Ladder: A Spiritual Theology of Ascent and Ascension* (Grand Rapids: Eerdmans 2010), pp. 105–8.

44. Calvin, *Institutes*, 3:11:2.

God, paying the penalty we had deserved.[45] Osiander's teaching
that Christ's divine righteousness justifies implied that justification
was achieved by the whole Trinity.[46] Osiander interpreted union
in an ontological manner; Calvin pointed to the Spirit as the bond
of union, so preserving the distinction between justification and
sanctification.[47]

So, contrary to Osiander, this union does not consist in
participation in Christ's divine nature but union with His *person*
by the Holy Spirit.

> Therefore, that joining together of Head and members, that
> indwelling of Christ in our hearts – in short, that mystical union
> – are accorded by us the highest degree of importance, so that
> Christ, having been made ours, makes us sharers with him in the
> gifts with which he has been endowed. We do not, therefore,
> contemplate him outside ourselves from afar in order that his
> righteousness may be imputed to us but because we put on
> Christ and are engrafted into his body – in short, because he
> deigns to make us one with him. For this reason, we glory that
> we have fellowship of righteousness with him.[48]

Calvin is not saying that we are justified on the grounds of the
mystical union Christ establishes, His indwelling in our hearts.
Rather, the two are inseparable but distinct. Both stem from
union, justification from our being united to Christ in what He
has done for us in taking Adam's place, the indwelling and the
gifts from our union with Him in what He does in us. From
another angle, in his Commentary on 1 Corinthians 1:30, Calvin
remarks on the distinction as well as simultaneity of justification
and sanctification. It is impossible to be justified through faith
apart from renewal to a holy life. They are distinguishable but
yet 'those gifts of grace go together as if tied by an inseparable

---

45. Calvin, *Institutes*, 2:12:3.

46. Calvin, *Institutes*, 3:11:8.

47. Calvin, *Institutes*, 3:11:6.

48. Calvin, *Institutes*, 3:11:10. For an extensive study on Calvin's teaching on union
    with Christ, see Mark Garcia, *Life in Christ*.

bond, so that if anyone tries to separate them, he is, in a sense, tearing Christ to pieces.'[49] Tony Lane has compared them to two legs of a pair of trousers.[50] Paul, Calvin states, ascribes to Christ alone the fulfilment of all – righteousness, holiness, wisdom, and redemption. Mark Garcia considers that for Calvin 'the two basic saving events (justification and sanctification) are distinct and yet inseparable precisely because of a reality still more basic or fundamental: the believer's Spirit-effected *unio cum Christo*. This model, which will be called Calvin's *unio Christo – duplex gratia* soteriology, is a prominent feature in Calvin's theology.'[51]

Michael Horton has a different argument. He agrees that with Calvin union with Christ embraces both forensic and renovative aspects of salvation. However, in developing his own exposition of union, based in part on his understanding of Calvin, his language is at times confusing. It seems to many who have read him that he considers justification to have priority to union itself.[52] We stress again that Horton is stating his own position but nevertheless this emerges from an interpretation of Calvin. He writes of Calvin, 'Forensic justification through faith alone is the fountain of union with Christ in all its renewing aspects.'[53] Again, he thinks that in classic Reformed theology, Calvin included,

---

49. 'Unde etiam colligimus, non posse nos gratis iustificari sola fide, quin simul sancte vivamus. Istae enim gratiae quasi individuo nexu cohaerent: ut qui eas separare nititur, Christum quodammodo discerpat. Proinde, qui per Christum gratuita Dei bonitate iustificari quaerit, cogitet fieri hoc non posse simul in sanctificationem eum apprehendat, hoc est, eius spiritu renascatur in vitae innocentiam & puritatem.' John Calvin, *Commentarii in Priorem Epistolam Pauli ad Corinthios* (Strassburg: Per Wendelium Ribelium 1546), 32a-b; John Calvin, *Calvin's Commentaries: The First Epistle of Paul the Apostle to the Corinthians*. Trans. John W. Fraser; (Grand Rapids: Eerdmans 1960).

50. Lane, *Justification*, p. 18.

51. Mark Garcia, *Life in Christ*, pp. 2–3.

52. For example, Richard B. Gaffin, Jr., 'Covenant and Salvation: A Review Article', *Ordained Servant* (March 2009), accessible online at http://www.opc.org/os.html?article_id=141

53. Michael S. Horton, *Covenant and Salvation: Union with Christ* (Louisville: Westminster John Knox Press 2007), p. 143.

'the act of justification is logically prior to union'.[54] He argues that Calvin makes justification 'that which brings everything else (again, the whole process of inward renewal) in its wake.' In turn, Horton wants to see justification as the 'forensic, declarative, covenantal Word that simultaneously creates the new status *and* the new being of those who are in Christ.'[55] In effect justification is, for Horton, an illocutionary and perlocutionary speech-act by which God effects what He declares, and so implements faith, union with Christ, regeneration and so forth.

On the surface, Horton seems to imply that God's speech-act of justification brings about faith, which would be more a case of justification by decree. It also suggests that justification effects union with Christ, which in turn would mean that justification occurs outside union. This is not to be found in Calvin. The fact that justification is 'the main hinge on which religion turns'[56] is different than its being the ground of, or prior to, union.

Notwithstanding, Horton could also mean that the forensic aspects of union have priority in relation to the transformative ones, and so be reserving 'union' for the latter. The reference above to justification as the fountain of 'union with Christ in all its renewing aspects' would suggest this. In so doing, he would be comparing justification with renewal but reserving the term 'union' for the latter. If so, he has a strong case, provided that the two dimensions are understood to be inseparable. Did Calvin regard our transformation by the Spirit as based on a right relation with God? Yes. Did he think our relation to God in justification was grounded on the work of the Spirit within us? No, it was due to the imputation of the righteousness of Christ. Moreover, our good works he saw as accepted by God on that basis as well. The misleading part is that Horton had already referred to union with Christ, in itself and in Calvin, as embracing both forensic and transformative aspects.

---

54. Horton, *Covenant and Salvation*, p. 147.

55. Horton, *Covenant and Salvation*, p. 201.

56. Calvin, *Institutes*, 3:11:1.

In contrast, Richard B. Gaffin, Jr. points to the order Calvin adopts in the 1559 *Institutes*, where he treats sanctification *before* justification. From this he concludes that for Calvin the order between them is indifferent and so either can be regarded as prior. Lee Gatiss agrees.[57] Gaffin has been misled by the sequence of the 1559 edition, missing the point that Calvin, from the 1539 edition onwards, followed what he regarded as the order of teaching in Paul's Letter to the Romans and did not intend to provide an *ordo salutis*.[58] As Lane remarks, in the 1559 *Institutes*, Calvin considered regeneration and sanctification first 'in order to make it clear that we cannot have justification without sanctification'[59] so as to rebut the charges of the Roman church that the Protestants were undermining good works by their teaching of justification by faith alone. In fact, Calvin considered both to be distinct but inseparable, and to flow from union with Christ; ' . . .as Christ cannot be torn into parts, so these two which we perceive in him together and conjointly are inseparable – namely, righteousness and sanctification.' He writes that while Paul 'clearly indicates that to be justified means something different from being made new creatures' they are as inseparable, and as distinct, as light and heat.[60] This argues against indifference on the part of Calvin and points to a clear commitment to inseparability and distinction. If we ask about the relationship between justification and sanctification – allowing that they are inseparable – it can certainly be argued that Calvin gives justification a priority. Justification is 'the main hinge on which religion turns'.[61]

As a sequel, integral to the classic Reformed doctrine of justification was the imputation of the righteousness of Christ.

---

57. Gaffin, Jr., 'Westminster Standards'; Lee Gatiss, 'The Inexhaustible Fountain of All Good Things: Union with Christ in Calvin on Ephesians', *Themelios* 34, no. 2 (2009).

58. Muller, *The Unaccommodated Calvin*, pp. 118–38; Wenger, 'The New Perspective on Calvin'.

59. Lane, *Justification*, p. 23.

60. Calvin, *Institutes*, 3:11:6.

61. Calvin, *Institutes*, 3:11:1.

While a minority, even a century later, were reluctant to include the active obedience of Christ in the justificatory imputation the clear consensus was that, in addition to His atoning sufferings for our disobedience, Christ's perfect obedience to the law is imputed or reckoned to us in justification and that this occurs in union with Christ, imputation and union being compatible, not contradictory.[62]

3.3 Union with Christ and sanctification

Calvin stresses in his *Letter to Sadoleto* that Christ 'has been given to us for our justification and our sanctification'.[63] Garcia points to Calvin's comments on Romans where, in the Argumentum, he insists that 'we cannot receive righteousness in Christ without at the same time laying hold of sanctification' (*non posse nos iustitiam in Christo percipere, quin simul sanctificationem apprehendamus*) and also 'no one can put on the righteousness of Christ without regeneration'.[64] Calvin repeats and expands on this in his comments on chapter 6, where Paul treats baptism as the sign of union with Christ.[65] Thus, 'the secret union (*arcanam coniunctionem*)' is the way by which Christ's power is transferred to us, for 'as the graft has the same life or death as the tree into which it is engrafted, so it is reasonable that we should be as much partakers of the life as of the death of Christ.'[66] Not only do we 'derive the strength and sap of the life which flows from Christ, but we also pass from our nature into his (*sed in eius naturam ex nostra demigramus*).'[67] It is in union with Christ that both justification and sanctification are

---

62. Robert Letham, *The Westminster Assembly: Reading Its Theology in Historical Context* (Phillipsburg: Presbyterian & Reformed 2009), pp. 250–64.

63. Calvin, 'Reply', 1:43.

64. Mark Garcia, *Life in Christ*, pp. 96–7; John Calvin, *Calvin's Commentaries: The Epistles of Paul the Apostle to the Romans and to the Thessalonians*. Trans. Ross MacKenzie (1960; repr., Grand Rapids: Eerdmans 1973), p. 8; John Calvin, *Commentarius in Epistolam Pauli ad Romanos, Ioannis Calvini Opera Omnia* (Genève: Librairie Droz 1999), p. 9.

65. Mark Garcia, *Life in Christ*, p. 97.

66. Calvin, *Romans and Thessalonians*, p. 124; Calvin, *ad Romanos*, p. 120.

67. Calvin, *Romans and Thessalonians*, p. 124; Calvin, *ad Romanos*, p. 121

located, specifically in the distinction but inseparability of the death and resurrection of Christ.[68] Behind this is the basic axiom of the inseparable works of the Trinity; Christ and the Spirit, while distinguished, cannot be divided, neither can Their actions be separated. While justification has a theological priority, it is not related to sanctification as cause to effect by Calvin but both are distinct but inseparable effects, or aspects, of union with Christ.[69] Hence, commenting on John 17:19, he states

> It is because he consecrated himself to the Father that his holiness might come to us. For as the blessing is spread to the whole harvest from the first-fruits, so God's Spirit cleanses us by the holiness of Christ and makes us partakers of it. And not by imputation alone, for in that respect he is said to have been made to us righteousness (1 Cor. 1:30); but he is also said to have been made to us sanctification, because he has, so to say, presented us to his Father in his own person (*in sua persona*) that we may be renewed to true holiness by his Spirit.[70]

Calvin's characteristic idea is that we receive the life of Christ by participation in His humanity.

Julie Canlis expresses this well when she says, 'Calvin resolutely held that creatureliness had its own appropriate forms for enjoying the divine life... Calvin believed that this did not need to happen at the expense of creatureliness. This is the supreme significance of the earthly life, or "flesh", of Christ: Christ's participation in our condition... allows us to participate in God in creaturely appropriate ways as well.'[71] Canlis is right to stress that this is where Calvin holds all God's blessings are stored. Christ's flesh is a synechdochal reference to His humanity.

---

68. Mark Garcia, *Life in Christ*, p. 132.

69. Mark Garcia, *Life in Christ*, p. 146.

70. John Calvin, *Calvin's Commentaries: The Gospel According to St. John 11–21 and the First Epistle of John*. Trans. T. H. L. Parker (Grand Rapids: Eerdmans 1959), p. 146; John Calvin, *In Evangelium Secundum Johannem Commentarius Pars Altera*, Ioannis Calvini Opera Exegetica (Genève: Librairie Droz 1998), p. 220.

71. Canlis, *Calvin's Ladder*, pp. 100–1.

She suggests that this language somehow marginalises the Spirit, citing Bruce McCormack who has the same concerns. The thought runs like this: if the flesh of Christ is indeed a fountain that pours into us the life of the Godhead that flows into itself, as Calvin says, then the Holy Spirit is bypassed and Christ is a mere channel.[72] However, this is not the case since Calvin held to the classic axiom of the inseparable operations of the Trinity grounded in its indivisible unity.[73] Calvin simply teaches that all God's blessings, given by the undivided Trinity, come in and through the incarnate Mediator. He does not sideline the Spirit; his primary statement in *Institutes* 3:1:1 alone is enough to render the proposal untenable. He makes this clear in his comments on John 17: 'From this, too, we infer that we are one with Christ; not because he transfuses his substance into us, but because by the power of his Spirit *(Spiritus sui virtute)* he communicates to us his life and all the blessings he has received from the Father.'[74]

For Calvin, union with Christ includes union in His ascension. Christ's bodily ascension is at the root of his opposition both to Roman and Lutheran doctrines of the Eucharist; for Christ, in His flesh, is now in heaven with the Father. This is His intercession, representing us in the presence of God.[75] In union with Him we have entrance to heaven, for 'we shall not doubt that we have an entrance in common with him who clothed himself with

---

72. Canlis, *Calvin's Ladder*, pp. 101–3, citing Bruce M. McCormack, 'What's at stake in current debates over Justification? The crisis of Protestantism in the West', in Mark Husbands and Daniel Treier (eds.) *Justification: What's at Stake in the Current Debates* (Downers Grove, Illinois: InterVarsity Press 2004), p. 105.

73. See Robert Letham, *The Holy Trinity: In Scripture, History, Theology, and Worship* (Phillipsburg: Presbyterian & Reformed 2004), pp. 252–68.

74. Calvin, *The Gospel According to St. John 11-21 and the First Epistle of John,* Trans. T. H. L. Parker (Grand Rapids: Eerdmans 1959), p. 148; Calvin, *In Evangelium Johannem Pars Altera*, p. 223.

75. Commenting on Hebrews 9:11, in John Calvin, *Calvin's Commentaries: The Epistle of Paul the Apostle to the Hebrews and the First and Second Epistles of St Peter.* Trans. William B. Johnston (Grand Rapids: Eerdmans 1963), pp. 119–20; John Calvin, *Commentarius in Epistolam ad Hebraeos Ioannis Calvini Opera Exegetica* (Genève: Librairie Droz 1996), pp. 138–40.

our flesh to make us participants in all blessings.'[76] Christ's goal
is to unite us to God, making us one with God the Father, to
make us sooner or later like God.[77] This is by no means contrary
to justification; for by imputation we are considered righteous
before God and 'from this also another benefit proceeds, viz:
that our works have the name of righteousness', this latter not
due to our own merit but from the Father. Both our person and
our works are justified, and 'the justification of works depends
on the justification of the person, as the effect from the cause.'[78]

4. Union with Christ and the Trinity

Jesus taught the disciples that no one can come to Him in faith
unless the Father draws him; it is a gift of God (John 6:44-45,
64-65). This, as Calvin put it, is the principal work of the Holy
Spirit.[79]

Again, 'we hold ourselves to be united with Christ by the secret
bond of his Spirit.'[80] The Spirit as the bond of union between the
Father and the Son was a theme in western trinitarianism going
back to Augustine.[81] There are problematic aspects to this line of
thought. It appears to imply that the Father and the Son need to

---

76. Commenting on John 3:13 in John Calvin, *Calvin's Commentaries: The Gospel
   According to St John 1–10*. Trans. T. H. L. Parker (Grand Rapids: Eerdmans 1961),
   pp. 71–72; John Calvin, *In Evangelium secundum Johannem Commentarius Pars Prior*,
   Ioannis Calvini Opera Exegetica (Genève: Librairie Droz 1997), p. 97.

77. See Calvin's comments on John 14:28, Calvin, Gospel of John and 1 John, pp.
   89–90; Calvin, *In Evangelium Johannem pars Altera*, pp. 155–7; and on 2 Peter 1:4,
   Calvin, *Commentaries on Hebrews and 1&2 Peter*, p. 330; John Calvin, *Commentarii
   in Epistolas Canonicas*, Ioannis Calvini Opera Exegetica (Genève: Librairie Droz
   2009), p. 328.

78. John Calvin, 'Antidote to the Council of Trent', in Beveridge and Bonnet (eds.),
   Selected Works of John Calvin: Tracts and Letters, 3:128.

79. Calvin, *Institutes*, 3:1:4.

80. Calvin, *Institutes*, 3:11:5.

81. Augustine, *De Trinitate*, 15:17:27, 15:27:50; PL, 42:1096–97, 1079–80; Lewis
   Ayres, *Augustine and the Trinity* (Cambridge: Cambridge University Press 2010),
   pp. 251–62.

be united and that it is the Spirit who does it.[82] Moreover, the Spirit seems subordinate in the sense of being merely a bond, the weight falling on the Father and the Son. This has given rise to suggestions that the Spirit has been seen as less than fully personal.[83]

The Spirit, in uniting us to Christ, overcomes the problem arising from the distance occasioned by the bodily ascension of Christ and so – as Calvin repeatedly says – joins things separated by distance. The transcendent Holy Spirit bridges heaven and earth; for Him it is no problem to engraft us into the ascended Christ. Consequently, Calvin says, 'we are one with Christ; not because he transfuses his substance into us, but because by the power of his Spirit he communicates to us his life and all the blessings he has received from the Father.'[84] Again, 'It is because he [Christ] consecrated himself to the Father that his holiness might come to us. For as the blessing is spread to the whole harvest from the first-fruits, so God's Spirit cleanses us by the holiness of Christ and makes us partakers of it. And not by imputation alone, for in that respect he is said to have been made to us righteousness... but he is also said to have been made to us sanctification, because he has, so to say, presented us to the Father in his own person (*in sua persona*) that we may be renewed to true holiness by his Spirit (*quia nos in sua persona quodammodo Patri obtulit*).'[85] As we will note, Calvin teaches that it is the Spirit who joins the faithful to Christ in the Lord's Supper, bridging the distance between them and the ascended Christ. Canlis writes that Calvin's trinitarian model preserves our humanity as we are not absorbed by the divine but have union with 'a *triune* God, whose own differentiation makes room for human particularity'.[86] I have argued along similar lines elsewhere.[87]

---

82. Augustine, *De Trinitate*, 8:10:14; PL, 42:960.

83. See Robert Letham, *The Holy Trinity*, pp. 189, 196.

84. Commenting on John 17:21 in Calvin, *Gospel of John and 1 John*, p. 148; Calvin, *In Evangelium Johannem Pars Altera*, p. 223.

85. Commenting on John 17:9, in Calvin, *The Gospel According to St. John 11-21 and the First Epistle of John*, p. 146; Calvin, *In Evangelium Johannem Pars Altera*, p. 220.

86. Canlis, *Calvin's Ladder*, p. 137.

87. Robert Letham, *The Holy Trinity*, pp. 458–78.

Some Christological issues are evident. In classic Christology, Christ perpetually has a human nature, body and soul. As a century later, the Westminster Assembly was to declare, His presence now at the right hand of the Father is His intercession on our behalf (*WLC* ,55). Indeed, He will never divest Himself of His assumed humanity or else we could not be saved. The incarnation is for eternity. Correlative with that is the statement in the Niceno-Constantinopolitan creed – directed against Marcellus of Ancyra – that Christ's kingdom will never end.

It is here that Calvin lapses. In his commentary on 1 Corinthians 15:28, he betrays an almost Nestorian division of the person of Christ and suggests that the assumed humanity will be discarded.

> But Christ will then hand back the Kingdom which he has received, so that we may cleave completely to God. This does not mean that he will abdicate from the Kingdom in this way, but will transfer it in some way or other (*quodammodo*) from his humanity to his glorious divinity, because then there will open up for us a way of approach, from which we are now kept back by our weakness. In this way, therefore, Christ will be subjected to the Father, because, when the veil has been removed, we will see God plainly, reigning in his majesty, and the humanity of Christ will no longer be in between us to hold us back from a nearer vision of God.[88]

In the overall context, Calvin stresses the unity of Christ's person and opposes the Nestorian heresy, so we can only conclude that his comments here are unfortunately clumsy. Instead of seeing Christ's mediatorial kingdom as under the rule of His *person*, it seems Calvin has placed it under His *human nature*. Since Christ's humanity has no independent existence, this statement has a worryingly Nestorian ring to it. Moreover, Calvin considers Christ's humanity to prevent us from having close union with God; the whole force of Scripture, not to say Calvin's own

---

88. John Calvin, *Calvin's Commentaries: The First Epistle of Paul the Apostle to the Corinthians*. Trans. John W. Fraser (Grand Rapids: Eerdmans, 1960) on 15:27, p. 327.

theology, suggests that it is the *means* by which we know God.
Thirdly, comes a comment that suggests that Christ's humanity
will at least fade from view so as to enable us to draw close to the
Father. Beyond this is the hint that Christ will be subordinated to
the Father, subjected in such a way that He will no longer hinder
us or 'hold us back from a nearer vision of God.'

This seems to be connected with what Calvin says in the
Institutes, 2:14:3

> Until he comes forth as judge of the world Christ will therefore
> reign, joining us to the Father as the measure of our weakness
> permits. But when as partakers in heavenly glory we shall see God
> as he is, Christ, having then discharged the office of mediator, will
> cease to be the ambassador of his Father, and will be satisfied with
> that glory which he enjoyed before the creation of the world.[89]

While not quite as alarming as the comment in the 1 Corinthians
commentary, there is more than a hint that Calvin sees the
mediatorial kingdom of Christ to end upon our glorification, at
His parousia. This runs counter to the declaration of the Niceno-
Constantinopolitan Creed that the kingdom of the crucified,
risen and ascended Christ will have no end, countering Marcellus
of Ancyra, who identified the kingdom of the Son to be from
the resurrection to the parousia.

Statements such as these gave rise to suspicions among
Roman Catholic theologians that Calvin was a closet Nestorian.
Weinandy dismisses these suggestions, although he acknowledges
that the accusations have been made and, with others, recognises
weaknesses in Calvin's grasp of the incarnation.[90] The focus on

---

89. Calvin, *Institutes*, 2:14:3.
90. Thomas G. Weinandy O.F.M. Cap., *Does God Suffer?* (Notre Dame, Indiana/
     Edinburgh: University of Notre Dame Press/T & T Clark2000), pp. 187–88.
     Weinandy recognises that 'once he [Calvin] entered into the ontology of the
     incarnation he became somewhat confused and ambiguous'. This, he concluded,
     was because Calvin understood the incarnation to be a union of two natures
     patterned on the union of soul and body in the human being. In this, we may
     suggest, Calvin was seeking to do justice to the humanity but in doing so, as
     David Willis acknowledged, he lost a grasp of the *communicatio idiomatum* based

the humanity of Christ, that His mediatorial work was according to both natures, may have given an impetus to such ideas but his comments both on 1 Corinthians 15:27 and in *Institutes* 2:14:3 were enough to raise eyebrows. In the *Institutes* he has just finished an attack on Nestorianism so it would be more than surprising if he intended to make remarks that could be interpreted that way. Perhaps he'd had a bad day at the office.

5. Union with Christ and the means of grace

Garcia sums up pithily, 'Christ, salvation, and sacrament… belong together in the sixteenth-century mind.'[91] For Calvin, Christ is the *raison d'être* of the sacraments. While they are never to be severed from the Word, yet they also offer us righteousness in Christ.[92] Since Calvin sees union with Christ fostered in the Lord's Supper we will note his treatment of the theme diachronically.[93]

In the first edition of his *Institutes*, published in 1536, Calvin writes of union with Christ in terms of engrafting in baptism. Paul does not exhort us to imitate Christ in His death and resurrection, Calvin insists, but says that through baptism we are made participants in His death so that we might be engrafted in him (*nempe quod per baptismum Christus nos mortis suae fecerit participes, ut in eam inseramur*). We receive the efficacy of His death and resurrection by the life-giving power of the Spirit (*simul etiam resurrectionis, in vivificatione spiritus*). He cites Titus 3:5, referring

---

on the unity of the *person* of Christ in the sense taught by Cyril, which was the standard Christological commitment of the church. See Edward David Willis, *Calvin's Catholic Christology. The Function of the So-Called Extra Calvinisticum in Calvin's Theology* (Leiden: E. J. Brill, 1966) pp. 3–5; Thomas G. Weinandy OFM Cap, 'Cyril and the Mystery of the Incarnation', in *The Theology of St. Cyril of Alexandria: A Critical Appreciation* Thomas G. Weinandy OFM; (London: T & T Clark2003), pp. 23–54. I discuss these questions in a forthcoming chapter on Christology in a symposium entitled *Reformation Theology*, to be published by Crossway.

91. Mark Garcia, *Life in Christ*, p. 149.

92. Mark Garcia, *Life in Christ*, p. 159.

93. The following discussion is closely based on a section in my book *Union with Christ* (Phillipsburg: Presbyterian & Reformed 2011), ISBN 978-1-59638-063-9, www.prpbooks.com, and is used with permission.

to baptism as the laver of regeneration and renewal. Baptism, Calvin says, is joined with repentance and regeneration in both John the Baptist and the apostles.[94]

In his *Romans Commentary* of 1539, in dealing with Paul's argument in chapter 6:5 he talks of Christ pouring His power into us, with the result that we share in His risen life, departing from our nature into His (*in eius naturam ex nostra demigramus*), the better nature of the Spirit renewing us.[95] According to Calvin, Paul means not only conformity to Christ's example but that secret union through which we are joined together with Him, so that He invigorates us by His Spirit, and pours His power into us (*sed arcanam coniunctionem, per quam cum ipso coaluimus, ita ut nos Spiritu suo vegetans, eius virtutem in nos transfundat*). As the graft has the same life as the tree into which it is ingrafted, so we are as much partakers of the life as of the death of Christ (*ita vitae Christi non minus quam et mortis participes nos esse consentaneum est*).[96] The word *insticii*, which translates the Greek *sumphutoi* - 'united' (ESV), 'be one with' (Louw & Nida), 'grow together' (Bauer, Arndt & Gingrich) – has great *energeia* or force, Calvin insists. Paul compares this union to a tree receiving sap from the root. There is however an evident disparity, Calvin comments, for the tree graft retains its natural quality in the fruit it produces. In spiritual engrafting, on the other hand, not only do we derive the strength and sap of the life which flows from Christ but we also pass from our nature into His. The efficacy of Christ's death and resurrection renews in us the better nature of the Spirit (*alteram quoque resurrectionis, ad renovandam in nobis meliorem spiritus naturam*).[97] Calvin here suggests that in union with Christ, Christ pours His life into us by the Spirit.

In his *Short Treatise on the Holy Supper of our Lord and only Saviour Jesus Christ* (1540) and his *Genevan Catechism* (1545), Calvin

---

94. OS, 1:129.

95. CO, 49:107; Calvin, *ad Romanos*, p. 121.

96. CO, 49:107; Calvin, *ad Romanos*, p. 120.

97. Calvin, *ad Romanos*, p. 121.

takes this idea further. In the *Short Treatise* he concludes that 'in receiving the sacrament in faith… we are truly made partakers of the real substance of the body and blood of Jesus Christ' and 'that the Spirit of God is the bond of participation'.[98] In the catechism he states that the Supper is not only a testimony or exhibition of Christ's benefits but in it we are made partakers of Christ's substance as we are united with Him (*je ne doubte par qu'il ne nous face participans de sa propre substance, pour nous unir avec soy en une vie*).[99]

The following year, in his *Commentary on 1 Corinthians*, Calvin reaffirms that in union with Christ we are given to share in His substance and life. In discussing 1 Corinthians 6:15, Calvin states that the spiritual union we have with Christ includes the body as well as the soul, so that we are flesh of His flesh, referencing Ephesians 5:30. The hope of the resurrection would be faint if our union with Him was not complete and total like that.[100]

It is in his comments on Paul's discussion of the Lord's Supper in 1 Corinthians 11:24 that Calvin is most expansive. The first thing in union with Christ is that we are united to Christ Himself; His benefits follow from the personal union (*Ego autem tunc nos demum participare Christi bonis agnosco, postquam Christum ipsum obtinemus*). We obtain Christ not so much when we believe He was sacrificed for us but when He dwells in us, when He is one with us, when we are members of His flesh and joined together with Him in one life and substance (*sed dum in nobis habitat, dum est unum nobiscum, dum eius sumus membra ex carne eius, dum in unam denique et vitam et substantiam [ut ita loquor] cum ipso coalescimus*). Christ does not offer only the benefit of His death and resurrection but the same body in which He died and rose (*sed corpus ipsum, is quo passus est ac resurrexit*). That body is really (*realiter*) and truly (*vere*) given to us in the Supper, as health-giving

98. Calvin, *Calvin: Theological Treatises*. Trans. & ed. J. K. S. Reid (Philadelphia: The Westminster Press 1954), p. 166.

99. CO, 6:127–8.

100. Calvin, *First Corinthians*, p. 130.

food for our souls. Calvin draws to his clinching conclusion: 'I mean that our souls are fed by the substance of his body, so that we are truly made one with him (*ut vere unum efficiamur cum eo*); or, what amounts to the same thing, that a life-giving power from the flesh of Christ is poured into us through the medium of the Spirit, even though it is at a great distance from us, and is not mixed with us' (*nec misceatur nobiscum*).[101]

Hence, for Calvin union with Christ comes to particular expression in the Eucharist. Here we are fed with the body and blood of Christ. This is not corporeal, as Rome and the Lutherans held in their different ways. Christ has ascended to the right hand of God; His body is far from us spatially. However, the Spirit unites things separated by distance, however great. In doing so, He enables us to feed on the glorified humanity of Christ.

Two years later, in 1548, Calvin wrote further on the theme in his Ephesians commentary. In dealing with the passage in chapter 5 where Paul compares the marriage relationship to that between Christ and the church, Calvin claims again that in union with Christ He communicates His substance to us so that we grow into one body (*ita nos, ut simus vera Christi membra, substantiae eius communicare et hac communicatione nos coalescere in unum corpus*). In saying this Paul testifies that we are of the members and bones of Christ (*Paulus nos ex membris et ossibus Christi esse testatur*). So, Calvin argues, in the Supper Christ offers His body to be enjoyed by us and to nourish us to eternal life (*corpus suum in Coena fruendum nobis exhibet, ut sit nobis vitae aeternae alimentum*).[102] On verse 31, Calvin states that such is the union between us and Christ, that in a sense He pours Himself into us (*se quodammodo in nos transfundit*). We are bone of His bones because, by the power of His Spirit, He ingrafts us into His body, so that from Him we derive life (*Spiritus virtute nos in corpus suum inserit, ut vitam ex eo hauriamus*).[103] We note the *quodammodo* – 'in a sense' Christ pours Himself into

---

101. Calvin, *First Corinthians*, 246; CO, 49:487.

102. Calvin, *Epistles of Paul*, pp. 208–9; Calvin, In Pauli Epistolas, XVI:272.

103. Calvin, *Epistles of Paul*, p. 209; Calvin, In Pauli Epistolas, XVI:273.

us. This alerts us to the point that Calvin is aware he is using language metaphorically, seeking to express in intelligible terms what transcends explanation. So much is evident when, on verse 32, he acknowledges that this 'is a great mystery... no language can do it justice... whatever is supernatural is clearly beyond the grasp of our minds.'[104]

These qualifications surface again in Calvin's celebrated comments on 2 Peter 1:4, written in 1551. We recall that Peter has said that God has given us His exceedingly great and precious promises, in order that – *inter alia* – 'we might become partakers of the divine nature'. Calvin recognises the superlative nature of this gift, especially seeing the depths to which we had sunk in sin: 'the excellence of the promises arises from the fact that they make us partakers of the divine nature, than which nothing more outstanding could be imagined' (*quo nihil praestantius cogitari potest*).[105] Indeed, 'it is the purpose of the gospel to make us sooner or later like God; indeed, it is, so to speak, a kind of deification.' (*Notemus ergo hunc esse Evangelii finem, ut aliquando conformes Deo reddamur; id vero est quasi deificari, ut ita loquamur.*) He goes on to say that 'nature' here does not mean essence but kind; we do not participate in the being of God but in His attributes, His qualities, for His nature refers to what He is like rather than who He is (*caeterum naturae nomen hic non substantiam sed qualitatem designat*).[106]

Garcia is wrong to rule out *theosis*, or deification, in Calvin – *quasi deificari* points in that direction. It stems from lack of familiarity on his part with the Eastern view of theosis.[107] Calvin's

---

104. Calvin, *Epistles of Paul*, pp. 209–10; Calvin, In Pauli Epistolas, XVI:273.

105. Calvin, *Commentaries on the Epistle to the Hebrews and 1 & 2 Peter*, p. 330; Calvin, *In Epistolas Canonicas*, XX:327.

106. Calvin, *Commentaries on Hebrews and 1 & 2 Peter*, p. 330; Calvin, *In Epistolas Canonicas*, XX:328.

107. This is evident in the entire lack in his bibliography of primary or secondary sources on the Greek patristic tradition. He assumes that the Eastern position necessarily entailed a merging of divine and human, a participation in the essence of God. In fact, his exposition of Calvin's views is very close to the Alexandrian tradition of theosis. See Mark Garcia, *Life in Christ*, pp. 209f, 257–8.

exposition here is quite compatible with what Athanasius or Cyril wrote.[108] On the other hand, the *quasi* indicates a certain ambivalence. His comments on this theme are usually surrounded by a phrase such as 'so to speak' (*ut ita loquor*), 'in a certain way' (*quodammodo*) or the like. It is possible, of course, that Calvin may not have been entirely aware of the doctrine of deification in the Greek patristic tradition himself. While he mined the works of the Fathers, he was dependent to a great extent on anthologies and used citations more as weapons in debate than as a dispassionate historical theologian.[109]

On the other hand, Garcia may be right in suggesting that Calvin's thought on union with Christ underwent a development in the 1550s. He does not think it changed substantially but rather it was enriched.[110] The qualification in his 2 Peter commentary is one matter. A new reticence seems to emerge in his commentary on the gospel of John, as well as in correspondence with Pietro Martire Vermigli, while he develops his teaching on the Holy Spirit as the bond of union with Christ in his 1559 edition of the *Institutes*.

In the *Commentary on John*, written in 1553, Calvin stresses that union with Christ is something that transcends our mental capacities and is known only in faith, as the Holy Spirit pours into us the life of Christ. He refers to 'the secret efficacy of the Spirit'. We cannot know by idle speculation what is the sacred and mystic union between us and Him and again between Him and the Father (*qualis sit sacra et mystica inter nos et ipsum unio, qualis rursum inter ipsum et Patrem*). The only way to know is when He

---

108. See Norman Russell, *The Doctrine of Deification in the Greek Patristic Tradition* (Oxford: Oxford University Press 2004), pp. 168–204; Robert Letham, *Through Western Eyes: Eastern Orthodoxy; A Reformed Perspective* (Fearn: Mentor 2007), pp. 243–65. In referring to Calvin's use of Cyrilline language on participation in Christ, Billings notes that 'overall he found him to be an ally in Trinitarian and Christological matters.' Billings, *Calvin*, pp. 49–50.

109. Anthony N. S. Lane, *John Calvin: Student of the Church Fathers* (Grand Rapids: Baker 1999), pp. 67–86, 170–5, 232–4.

110. Mark Garcia, *Life in Christ*, pp. 210–11.

pours His life into us by the secret efficacy of the Spirit (*quum vitam suam arcana Spiritus efficacia in nos diffundit*). This is the experience of faith.[111] Later, in commenting on John 17:21, he seems to contradict what he said in his Ephesians commentary and elsewhere. In this context, he denies that Christ transfuses His substance into us. Instead, we receive His life, communicated to us by the Holy Spirit (*Unde etiam colligimus nos unum cum Christo esse, non quia suam in nos substantiam transfundat, sed quia Spiritus sui virtute nobiscum vitam suam et quicquid accepit a Patre bonorum communicet.*)[112]

Two years later, in 1555, Calvin entered into the important exchange of letters with Pietro Martire Vermigli, to which we referred earlier.

In the following year, 1556, Calvin wrote his *Secunda defensio piae et orthodoxae de sacramentis fidei, adversus Joachimi Westphali calumnias*. Here he wrote that the soul has no less communion in the blood of Christ than we drink wine with the mouth (*nec minus sanguinis communionem anima percipiat, quam ore vinum bibimus*).[113]

Calvin's sermons on Ephesians were delivered close to the time he was editing the 1559 edition of the *Institutes*. In them he said that both sacraments direct us to Christ, to His sufferings and death. Since we are not angels we need these earthly means. In baptism, just as water washes away the filth of the body so the blood of Christ cleanses our souls.[114] The spiritual life we have with the Son of God is above nature.[115] So 'just as a graft that is set into a stock takes its sustenance from the same, so must we, by being grafted into our Lord Jesus Christ' and as a branch that 'receives sap and nourishment from the root if it is grafted into

---

111. Calvin, *Calvin's Commentaries: The Gospel According to St. John 11–21 and the First Epistle of John*. p. 84; J. Calvin, *In Evangelium Secundum Johannem Commentarius pars Altera*, Ioannis Calvini Opera Omnia (Genève: Librairie Droz 1998), XI/2:150.

112. Calvin, *The Gospel According to St. John 11-21 and the First Epistle of John*, p. 148; Calvin, *In Evangelium Johannem Pars Altera*, XI/2:223.

113. CO, 9:65.

114. Calvin, *Sermons on Ephesians*, pp. 579–81.

115. Calvin, *Sermons on Ephesians*, p. 614.

another… so it is with us'.[116] This is a high mystery – 'St. Paul was not able to express that grace, but rather showed us that it ought to ravish our minds in astonishment.'[117] If it puzzles us as to how Christ who is in heaven 'should nourish us with his own substance' we should repulse our folly in trying to measure what is infinite. 'Our Lord shows us that when he has joined us to his only Son, he has done so high and profound a work as overtops all our capacity to understand.'[118]

Lastly, in 1559 came the final Latin edition of the *Institutes*. Here Calvin made plain the connection between the work of Christ and that of the Holy Spirit. 'First, we must understand that as long as Christ remains outside of us, and we are separated from him, all that he has suffered and done for the salvation of the human race remains useless and of no value to us.' All that Christ possesses 'is nothing to us until we grow into one body with him'. It is through 'the secret energy of the Spirit, by which we come to enjoy Christ and all his benefits', for 'the Holy Spirit is the bond by which Christ effectively joins us to himself'.[119] For Calvin all Christ's work comes to benefit us only when we are united to Him. Union with Christ is the root of salvation, justification and sanctification included. This occurs through faith but faith itself is the fruit of the Holy Spirit's work. The Spirit unites us to Christ. First, the Father bestowed the whole fullness of the Spirit on Christ in a special way, so as to gather His people to the hope of the eternal inheritance.[120] Faith is the principal work of the Holy Spirit.[121] It occurs in our being united to Christ: 'for we await salvation from him not because he appears to us afar off, but because he makes us, engrafted into his body,

---

116. Calvin, *Sermons on Ephesians*, p. 615.

117. Calvin, *Sermons on Ephesians*, p. 615.

118. Calvin, *Sermons on Ephesians*, p. 616.

119. Calvin, *Institutes*, 3:1:1.

120. Calvin, *Institutes*, 3:1:2.

121. Calvin, *Institutes*, 3:1:4.

participants not only in all his benefits but also in himself.'[122] If we were to contemplate ourselves it would be sure damnation. 'But since Christ has been so imparted to you with all his benefits that all his things are made yours, that you are made a member of him, indeed one with him, his righteousness overwhelms your sins; his salvation wipes out your condemnation.' So 'we ought not to separate Christ from ourselves or ourselves from him.' As a result 'Christ is not outside us but dwells within us. Not only does he cleave to us by an indivisible bond of fellowship, but with a wonderful communion, day by day, he grows more and more into one body with us, until he becomes completely one with us.'[123]

In terms of justification this means that we are righteous only in Christ.[124] In this sense, union with Christ has priority to justification by faith. It is only as we are united with Christ that God accounts us righteous.

> Therefore, that putting together of Head and members, that indwelling of Christ in our hearts – in short, that mystical union – are accorded by us the highest degree of importance, so that Christ, having been made ours, makes us sharers with him in the gifts with which he has been endowed. We do not, therefore, contemplate him outside ourselves from afar in order that his righteousness may be imputed to us but because we put on Christ and are engrafted into his body – in short, because he deigns to make us one with him. For this reason, we glory that we have fellowship of righteousness with him.[125]

Precisely because righteousness is imputed to us because we are one with Christ – brought about by the Holy Spirit through faith – it is Christ's righteousness that is ours. 'You see that our righteousness is not in us but in Christ, that we possess it only

---

122. Calvin, *Institutes*, 3:2:24.

123. Calvin, *Institutes*, 3:2:24.

124. Calvin, *Institutes*, 3:11:8; OS, 4:190.

125. Calvin, *Institutes*, 3:11:10; OS, 4:191.

because we are partakers of Christ.'[126] Since 'all his things are ours and we have all things in him, in us there is nothing.'[127] As soon as we are engrafted into Christ through faith, we are made sons of God, heirs of heaven, possessors of life and all the merits of Christ.[128] Thus, we receive both justification and sanctification in union with Christ simultaneously, for Christ cannot be divided into pieces. We cannot possess Christ without at the same time being made partakers in His sanctification.[129] We have no hope of our future inheritance unless we have been united to Christ. The elect are so united to Christ that they have been called to participate in one God and Christ (*in unius Dei ac Christi participationem etiam vocati*).[130]

Therefore, according to Calvin, in the sacraments the benefits are conferred by Christ alone through the Holy Spirit, who makes us participators in Christ (*per Spiritum sanctum, qui nos facit Christi ipsius participes*).[131] Through baptism Christ makes us sharers in His death that we may be engrafted in it, the laver of regeneration.[132] So baptism is a token of our union with Christ.[133] Christ by sharing in our human mortality made us partakers in His divine immortality, raising our corruptible flesh to glory and incorruption (*quum humanae nostrae mortalitatis particeps factus nos divinae suae immortalitatis consortes fecit*).[134] This is applied to us through the gospel but more clearly through the sacred Supper, wherein the soul most truly and deeply becomes partaker of Christ as that it might be quickened to spiritual life by His power by true partaking of Him. So His life passes into us and is made

---

126. Calvin, *Institutes*, 3:11:23; OS, 4:206–7.

127. Calvin, *Institutes*, 3:15:5; OS, 4:245.

128. Calvin, *Institutes*, 3:15:6; OS, 4:245.

129. Calvin, *Institutes*, 3:16:1; OS, 4:248–9.

130. Calvin, *Institutes*, 4:1:2; OS, 5:4.

131. Calvin, *Institutes*, 4:14:16; OS, 5:274.

132. Calvin, *Institutes*, 4:15:5; OS, 5:288.

133. Calvin, *Institutes*, 4:15:6; OS, 5:289.

134. Calvin, *Institutes*, 4:17:4; OS, 5:345

ours (*ut vita sua in nos transeat*) just as when bread taken as food imparts vigour to the body.[135] Calvin explains how this happens.

> We can explain the nature of this by a familiar example. Water is sometimes drunk from a spring, sometimes drawn, sometimes led by channels to water the fields, yet it does not flow forth from itself for so many uses, but from the very source, which by unceasing flow supplies and serves it. In like manner, the flesh of Christ is like a rich and inexhaustible fountain that pours into us the life springing forth from the Godhead into itself. Now who does not see that communion of Christ's flesh and blood is necessary for all who aspire to heavenly life?[136]

This communion is achieved by the Holy Spirit. Even though it seems unbelievable since Christ's flesh is separated from us by such a great distance 'the secret power of the Holy Spirit towers above all our senses' and 'truly unites things separated by distance' in the Supper.[137] The bond of this connection is, then, the Spirit of Christ 'with whom we are joined in unity' and 'is like a channel through which all that Christ himself is and has is conveyed to us'. It is the Spirit who imparts to us the communion of His flesh and blood. 'On this account, Scripture, in speaking of our participation with Christ, relates its whole power to the Spirit.'[138]

Carl Mosser has argued that Calvin teaches a doctrine of deification.[139] He was strongly opposed by Jonathan Slater[140] but from assumptions that are akin to Nestorianism. Slater considers that Calvin treats the humanity of Christ as effectively

---

135. Calvin, *Institutes*, 4:17:5; OS, 5:346–7.

136. Calvin, *Institutes*, 4:17:9; OS, 5:350–1.

137. Calvin, *Institutes*, 4:17:10; OS, 5:351–2.

138. OS, 5:355–6; Calvin, *Institutes*, 4:17:12.

139. Carl Mosser, 'The Greatest Possible Blessing: Calvin and Deification', *SJT* 55 (2002), pp. 36–57.

140. Jonathan Slater, 'Salvation as Participation in the Humanity of the Mediator in Calvin's *Institutes* of the Christian Religion: A Reply to Carl Mosser', *SJT* 58 (2005), pp. 38–58.

autonomous; this precludes any idea of deification. Nestorius had no such doctrine of deification, of course, but at the price of jeopardising the unity of the person of Christ. In this, Slater's interpretation of Calvin is suspect. His citations of Calvin are limited to the *Institutes*. Moreover, the theological parameters on which he bases his claims are untenable. It indicates that objections to deification stem largely from a correct stress on the creator-creature distinction at the expense of their compatibility. This tendency yields a Nestorian Christology in which deity and humanity are kept separate, the unity of Christ's person – and the incarnation itself – undermined, and so His achievement of redemption jeopardised.[141] Billings is correct, to my mind, in affirming that 'Calvin's theology of participation emerges from a soteriology which affirms a differentiated *union* of God and humanity in creation and redemption.'[142] He adds that 'Calvin is willing to speak of the way in which believers are deified in redemption; yet this hyperbolic language does not imply, for Calvin, that distinctively divine attributes overwhelm human attributes in glorified believers.'[143] All this is so, while 'it is the intention of the gospel to make us sooner or later like God.'[144]

It seems to me that until around 1550 Calvin had some strong language about our participation in the substance of Christ's flesh, Christ pouring His life into us by the Holy Spirit, and wrote of our nature being changed. After that time, he seems to qualify those terms and to distance himself from the idea that somehow Christ's substance was in any way transmitted to us by the Holy Spirit in the Eucharist. However, this does not diminish his recognition that this is a mystery that transcends our capacities fully to grasp. Ultimately, Calvin's most frequent imagery is that the Holy Spirit unites us to Christ through faith and so the *life*

---

141. But see Calvin's comments on 1 Corinthians 15:27–28 and in *Institutes* 2:14:3, mentioned above, together with the discussion.

142. Billings, *Calvin*, p. 16.

143. Billings, *Calvin*, pp. 65–6.

144. Calvin, *Commentaries on Hebrews and 1&2 Peter*, p. 330; Calvin, *In Epistolas Canonicas*, p. 328.

of Christ – the risen and ascended Christ – is given to us to nourish us. At the root of this is that Christ has become one with us in the incarnation and consequently His flesh receives the life of the Godhead poured into it. From this we receive life in union with Him from the Holy Spirit through faith. Together with his concern for the integrity of the humanity of Christ this leads him to couch his language on themes like deification with *quasi* (a kind of), *ita ut loquor* (so to speak), or *quodammodo* (in a certain manner). In this he is opposing the Lutheran view of the *communicatio idiomatum* (communication of idioms) in which attributes of Christ's deity are transmitted to His humanity, thus blurring the distinction between the two and, in the eyes of the Reformed, undermining the humanity. He was not dealing with the Eastern teaching of *theosis*; the Lutherans were the innovators and Calvin was closer to the East than many have realised. Calvin repeatedly affirms a participation in Christ's substance by the power of the Spirit. It is a form of *perichoresis*, interpenetration, bringing us into union and participation in the life of the Trinity while remaining human, indeed ultimately receiving fulfilment as humans.[145] In Calvin's words, commenting on 1 John 4:15, 'we are united to God by Christ and… we can only be joined to Christ if God abides in us.'[146]

In summary, Calvin considers union with Christ to be a dominant soteriological theme. His agreement with Vermigli is clear but one wonders whether, by analysing union in a threefold way, they both were in danger of missing its integrated unity. With Calvin, within union with Christ, justification has a certain priority in relation to the start and foundation of the Christian life. However, in connection with the progress and goal of the Christian life, transformation through the means of grace assumes greatest prominence.

---

145. Billings, *Calvin*, pp. 61–5.

146. Calvin, *Calvin's Commentaries: The Gospel According to St. John 11–21 and the First Epistle of John*, p. 293.

Bibliography

Augustine. *De Trinitate*.

Ayres, Lewis. *Augustine and the Trinity*. Cambridge: Cambridge University Press 2010.

Billings, J. Todd. *Calvin, Participation, and the Gift: The Activity of Believers in Union with Christ*. Oxford: Oxford University Press 2007.

Calvin, John. 'Antidote to the Council of Trent', in Henry Beveridge and Jules Bonnet (eds.), *Selected Works of John Calvin: Tracts and Letters*. Grand Rapids: Baker 1983. Vol. 3:61-3.

―― *Calvin: Theological Treatises*. J. K. S. Reid. Philadelphia: The Westminster Press 1954.

―― *Calvin's New Testament Commentaries*. ed. D. W. Torrance and Thomas F. Torrance. Grand Rapids: Eerdmans 1959–1972.

―― *Calvin's Commentaries: The Gospel According to St. John 11-21 and the First Epistle of John*. T. H. L. Parker. Grand Rapids: Eerdmans 1959.

―― *Calvin's Commentaries: The First Epistle of Paul the Apostle to the Corinthians*. John W. Fraser. Grand Rapids: Eerdmans 1960.

―― *Calvin's Commentaries: The Gospel According to St John 1-10*. T. H. L. Parker. Grand Rapids: Eerdmans 1961.

―― *Calvin's Commentaries: The Epistle of Paul the Apostle to the Hebrews and the First and Second Epistles of St Peter*. William B. Johnston. Grand Rapids: Eerdmans 1963.

―― *Calvin's Commentaries: The Epistles of Paul to the Galatians, Ephesians, Philippians and Colossians*. T. H. L. Parker. Grand Rapids: Eerdmans 1965.

―― *Calvin's Commentaries: The Epistles of Paul the Apostle to the Romans and to the Thessalonians*. Ross MacKenzie. 1960; repr. Grand Rapids: Eerdmans 1973.

—— *Commentarii in Priorem Epistolam Pauli Ad Corinthios.* Strassburg: Per Wendelium Ribelium 1546.

—— *Commentarii in Pauli Epistolas.* Ioannis Calvini Opera Exegetica. Genève: Librairie Droz 1992.

—— *Commentarius in Epistolam Ad Hebraeos.* Ioannis Calvini Opera Exegetica. Genève: Librairie Droz 1996.

—— *Commentarius in Epistolam Pauli Ad Romanos.* Ioannis Calvini Opera Omnia. Genève: Librairie Droz 1999.

—— *Commentarii in Epistolas Canonicas.* Ioannis Calvini Opera Exegetica. Genève: Librairie Droz 2009.

—— *In Evangelium Secundum Johannem Commentarius Pars Prior.* Ioannis Calvini Opera Exegetica. Genève: Librairie Droz 1997.

—— *In Evangelium Secundum Johannem Commentarius Pars Altera.* Ioannis Calvini Opera Exegetica. Genève: Librairie Droz 1998.

—— *Institutes of the Christian Religion.* Trans. Ford Lewis Battles; ed. John T. McNeill. Philadelphia: Westminster Press 1960.

—— *Joannis Calvini Opera Selecta.* Ed. Petrus Barth and Guilielmus Niesel. 5 vols. Munich: Christoph Kaiser 1926-52.

—— 'Reply to Sadolet.' Vol. 1:37-38 in Henry Beveridge and Jules Bonnet (eds.), *Selected Works of John Calvin: Tracts and Letters.* Grand Rapids: Baker 1983.

—— *Sermons on the Epistle to the Ephesians.* 1577. Repr. Edinburgh: Banner of Truth 1973.

Canlis, Julie. *Calvin's Ladder: A Spiritual Theology of Ascent and Ascension.* Grand Rapids: Eerdmans 2010.

CO. *John Calvin: Opera quae supersunt Omnia,* Guilielmus Baum, Eduardus Cunitz and Eduardus Reiss (eds.) Brunswick: C. A. Schwetschke & Son 1863–1900.

Fesko, J. V. *Beyond Calvin: Union with Christ and Justification in Early Modern Reformed Theology (1517–1700)*. Göttingen: Vandenhoeck & Ruprecht 2012.

Gaffin, Jr., Richard B. 'Biblical Theology and the Westminster Standards', *WTJ* 65 (2003), pp. 165-79.

Garcia, Mark A. 'Imputation and the Christology of Union with Christ: Calvin, Osiander and the Contemporary Quest for a Reformed Model', *WTJ* 68 (2006), pp. 219-51.

Garcia, Mark. *Life in Christ: Union with Christ and Twofold Grace in Calvin's Theology*. Milton Keynes: Paternoster 2008.

Gatiss, Lee. 'The Inexhaustible Fountain of All Good Things: Union with Christ in Calvin on Ephesians', *Themelios* 34, no. 2 (2009).

Horton, Michael S. *Covenant and Salvation: Union with Christ*. Louisville: Westminster John Knox Press 2007.

Lane, Anthony N. S. *John Calvin: Student of the Church Fathers*. Grand Rapids: Baker 1999.

—— *Justification by Faith in Catholic-Protestant Dialogue: An Evangelical Assessment*. London: T & T Clark 2002.

Letham, Robert W. A. 'Faith and Assurance in Reformed Theology: Zwingli to the Synod of Dort', 2 vols. Ph.D. Unpublished thesis, University of Aberdeen 1979.

—— 'Faith and Assurance in Early Calvinism: A Model of Continuity and Diversity', in W. Fred Graham (ed.) *Later Calvinism: International Perspectives*. Kirksville: Sixteenth Century Journal Publishers 1994, pp. 355-84.

—— *The Holy Trinity: In Scripture, History, Theology, and Worship*. Phillipsburg: Presbyterian & Reformed 2004.

—— *Through Western Eyes: Eastern Orthodoxy; A Reformed Perspective*. Fearn: Christian Focus Publications 2007.

—— The Westminster Assembly: Reading Its Theology in Historical Context. Phillipsburg: Presbyterian & Reformed 2009.

Mosser, Carl. 'The Greatest Possible Blessing: Calvin and Deification', *SJT* 55 (2002), pp. 36-57.

Muller, Richard A. *The Unaccommodated Calvin: Studies in the Foundation of a Theological Tradition.* New York: Oxford University Press 2000.

Pettegree, Andrew. 'The Reception of Calvinism in Britain', in Wilhelm H. Neuser (ed.) *Calvinus Sincerioris Religionis Vindex: Calvin as the Protector of the Purer Religion.* Kirksville: Sixteenth Century Journal Publishers 1997, pp. 267-89.

PL. J. P. Migne et al., eds. *Patrologia cursus completus: Series Latina.* Paris 1878-90.

Russell, Norman. *The Doctrine of Deification in the Greek Patristic Tradition.* Oxford: Oxford University Press 2004.

Slater, Jonathan. 'Salvation as Participation in the Humanity of the Mediator in Calvin's *Institutes* of the Christian Religion: A Reply to Carl Mosser', *SJT* 58 (2005), pp. 38-58.

Torrance, James B. 'Covenant or Contract? A Study of the Background of Worship in Seventeenth-Century Scotland', *SJT* 23 (1970), pp. 51-76.

Weinandy, Thomas G., O.F.M. Cap. *Does God Suffer?* Notre Dame/Edinburgh: University of Notre Dame Press/T & T Clark 2000.

—— 'Cyril and the Mystery of the Incarnation' in Thomas G. Weinandy and Daniel A. Keating (eds.) *The Theology of St. Cyril of Alexandria: A Critical Appreciation.* London: T & T Clark 2003, pp. 23-54.

Wenger, Thomas L. 'The New Perspective on Calvin: Responding to Recent Calvin Interpretations', *JETS* 50 (2007), pp. 311-28.

Willis, Edward David. *Calvin's Catholic Christology. The Function of the So-Called Extra Calvinisticum in Calvin's Theology.* Leiden: E. J. Brill 1966.

QUESTIONS FOR DISCUSSION

This paper was first given at a theological conference and is focused upon Calvin. However, I have wanted to avoid unremitting discussion of the type one expects to find in a Calvin studies seminar. It is important to know what Calvin taught and to evaluate it from a range of angles. However, it is even more valuable – once that is done – to appropriate what is learned for our own time and place.

1. What are your thoughts on Calvin's teaching on union with Christ? Perhaps you could assess it from Biblical and theological angles. As one particular instance, is the frequent comment that this is incompatible with the imputation of the righteousness of Christ in justification sustainable?

2. How might the realisation that every aspect of our salvation is received in union with Christ affect the preaching and teaching of the church? How do you think union with Christ is best taught in a church context?

3. According to Calvin, in what distinct ways do the preaching of the Word and the sacraments present Christ to us and how, in particular, does this relate to union with Christ?

4. In a context where believers are taught that the Eucharist is a time simply to remember Christ's death, in an act of individual recollection of the past, or is merely symbolic, how might a theology of union with the ascended Christ change such a practice?

5. In virtue of the union Christ has established with His people, do you expect the ascended Christ to bless the preaching of His Word and the sacraments each and every time, and if so, why?

CHAPTER FOUR

The Communion Controversy: Owen and Sherlock on 'Union with Christ'

J. V. FESKO

Introduction

John Owen (1616–1683) is hailed as one of the Reformed tradition's greatest luminaries given the scholarly rigour and expansive nature of his writings.[1] Certainly the twenty-four published volumes of his writings attest to Owen's labours and confirm the high esteem placed upon them.[2] Despite the praise for his work and theology, not all appreciated Owen's contributions. During his own lifetime Owen came under withering criticism by William Sherlock (c. 1641–1707), who

---

1. Carl R. Trueman, *John Owen: Reformed Catholic, Renaissance Man* (Aldershot: Ashgate 2007), p. 1; Ryan M. McGraw, *A Heavenly Directory: Trinitarian Piety, Public Worship and a Reassessment of John Owen's Theology* (Göttingen: Vandenhoeck & Ruprecht 2014), p. 11; in general, also Peter Toon, *God's Statesman: The Life and Work of John Owen* (Exeter: Paternoster 1971).

2. John Owen, *The Works of John Owen*, 17 vols., ed. William H. Goold (Edinburgh: T & T Clark 1862); idem, *An Exposition of the Epistle to the Hebrews*, 7 vols., ed. William H. Goold (Edinburgh: Johnstone and Hunter 1854). Note, the original T & T Clark edition of Owen's works included *Theologumena Pantodapa* (1661), a work on theological prolegomena written in Latin. This work has been recently translated and published as John Owen, *Biblical Theology: The History of Theology from Adam to Christ* (Grand Rapids: Soli Deo Gloria Publications 2012).

published a work panning Owen's doctrine of union with Christ. Sherlock characterised Owen's view as unbridled mysticism and thus aligned him with Quaker theology. He also branded Owen's position as novel and therefore one to be rejected. Sherlock's heated rhetoric not only elicited a written response from Owen but a number of other theologians entered the fray. Owen and others met Sherlock's accusations of novelty and mysticism and countered that he was a Socinian.

This heated exchange between Owen and Sherlock was significant in its own day, but there is little secondary literature that explores the debate. In fact, the recently published *Research Companion to John Owen's Theology* does not list or mention Sherlock's critical treatise.[3] Paul Lim has a brief survey of the debate in his recently published book, *Mystery Unveiled*, as does Carl Trueman in his book on Owen.[4] The relative absence of secondary literature provides an excellent opportunity to shine new light upon Owen's theology of union with Christ. Rather than explore the doctrine abstracted from its historical context, the debate offers the opportunity to examine Owen's teaching under the fire of criticism. We can analyse Owen's doctrine, Sherlock's criticism, Owen's response, as well as the supporting literature from other debate participants. These different elements paint a full picture of Owen's doctrine of union with Christ. The debate also delivers a historical cross-section from a wide array of authors to measure the reception of the disputed doctrine in late seventeenth-century England. In other words, one of the regular claims that appears in secondary literature is that John Calvin (1509–1564) offered the paradigmatic formulation of union with Christ and that

---

3.   John W. Tweedale, 'A John Owen Bibliography', in Kelly M. Kapic and Mark Jones (eds.), *The Ashgate Research Companion to John Owen's Theology* (Aldershot: Ashgate 2012), pp. 12–16.

4.   Paul C. H. Lim, *Mystery Unveiled: The Crisis of the Trinity in Early Modern England* (Oxford: Oxford University Press 2012), pp. 204–14; Trueman, *John Owen*, pp. 123–4.

all subsequent Reformed theologians either reproduced or distorted his doctrine.[5] This debate presents the opportunity to see to what degree, if any, Calvin's formulations were invoked, whether by Owen or any other debate participant. Rather than determine Calvin's influence upon the tradition based upon contemporary esteem of his theology, this debate offers an answer to this question from seventeenth-century primary-source evidence.

The broader intent of this paper, then, is to survey the debate between Owen and Sherlock regarding their respective doctrines of union with Christ. The narrower focus is twofold. First, to show that the differences between Owen and Sherlock's doctrines of union with Christ lie in: (a) the nature of the union, (b) their respective doctrines of justification, and (c) the roles that they each give to the imputed righteousness of Christ. In a nutshell, Owen's doctrine of union encompasses the covenant of redemption, which acts as the forensic foundation for Owen's doctrine of union with Christ where believers lay hold of their redemption through mystical union with Christ. Second, this paper seeks to demonstrate a corollary thesis, namely, that Owen's doctrine of union with Christ was uniquely his own, one grown from a diverse body of sources, and not derivative of Calvin's formulation. In this respect, the debate reveals that Calvin played little to no role in any of the offered formulations. Such a conclusion challenges contemporary assumptions and

---

5.   For those who make this type of claim, see e.g., Richard B. Gaffin, Jr., 'Justification and Union with Christ', in David W. Hall and Peter A. Lillback (eds.), *A Theological Guide to Calvin's Institutes: Essays and Analysis* (Phillipsburg: P & R 2008), p. 248; William B. Evans, *Imputation and Impartation: Union with Christ in American Reformed Theology* (Eugene: Wipf & Stock/Paternoster 2008), pp. 261–7; Mark A. Garcia, *Life in Christ: Union with Christ and Twofold Grace in Calvin's Theology* (Milton Keynes: Paternoster 2008), pp. 267–8; Charles Partee, *Theology of John Calvin* (Louisville: Westminster John Knox 2008), pp. xii–xiii, 3–4; Lane G. Tipton, 'Union with Christ and Justification', in Scott K. Oliphint (ed.) *Justified in Christ: God's Plan for Us In Justification* (Fearn: Mentor 2008), p. 39; Marcus Peter Johnson, *One with Christ: An Evangelical Theology of Salvation* (Wheaton: Crossway 2013), pp. 91, 234.

claims about Calvin's influence upon the doctrine of union with Christ in the Reformed tradition.[6]

This paper proceeds in the following manner: (1) survey the genesis of the debate, rehearse the players, and set the stage for the key works under consideration; (2) explore Owen's views on union with Christ; (3) delve into Sherlock's criticisms of Owen and examine his doctrine of union with Christ; (4) survey Owen's response to Sherlock; and (5) offer analysis of the debate and make observations about Owen's doctrine in the light of the conflict, and prove the corollary thesis regarding the relatively minor influence of Calvin's doctrine of union with Christ in late seventeenth-century England.

1. Background to the Debate

Among the well-known works of the seventeenth-century, Owen's *Communion with God the Father, Son, and Holy Ghost* (1657) is certainly one of his more popular. In the present day, simplified versions of this work attest to its perceived importance.[7] But in the seventeenth-century not everyone was convinced of its significance or orthodoxy. William Sherlock was the dean of St Paul's Cathedral in London and his very first publication was *A Discourse Concerning the Knowledge of Jesus Christ, And Our Union*

---

6.   For Calvin's relative role within the tradition, see Philip Benedict, *Christ's Churches Purely Reformed: A Social History of Calvinism* (New Haven: Yale University Press 2002), pp. 76, 84, 104, 115, 118; Richard A. Muller, 'Reception and Response: Referencing and Understanding Calvin in Seventeenth-Century Calvinism', in I. Backus and P. Benedict (eds.), *Calvin and His Influence, 1509–2009* (Oxford: Oxford University Press 2011), pp. 182–201; idem, 'Demoting Calvin: The Issue of Calvin and the Reformed Tradition', in Amy Nelson Burnett (ed.) *John Calvin, Myth and Reality: Images and Impact of Geneva's Reformer* (Eugene: Cascade 2009), pp. 3–17; John Coffey, *Politics, Religion and the British Revolutions: The Mind of Samuel Rutherford* (Cambridge: Cambridge University Press 1997), p. 75.

7.   John Owen, *Communion with the Triune God*, ed. Kelly M. Kapic and Justin Taylor (Wheaton: Crossway 2007); idem, *Communion with God* (Puritan Paperbacks) *Treasures of John Owen for Today's Readers* (Edinburgh: Banner of Truth 1991). Note, I will cite *Of Communion with God the Father, Son, and Holy Ghost*, in *The Works of John Owen*, vol. 2, ed. William H. Goold (1965; Edinburgh: Banner of Truth 1997). Subsequent citations will refer to the page numbers of this edition.

and Communion with Him (1674).[8] Sherlock was in no way fond of what he perceived as mysticism in much of the popular theology of his day, which arose from among the Independents. Sherlock openly provoked conflict with the so-called mystics. On the heels of Sherlock's theological ridicule of Owen's work, a series of books and pamphlets were published in response. The first entry was from Owen himself, in his *A Vindication of Some Passages in a Discourse Concerning Communion With God* (1674).[9] Owen was exercised for two reasons: (1) because, in his estimation, Sherlock had misrepresented his views in a number of places, and (2) he was somewhat perplexed that Sherlock would publish a response and criticism to Owen's work seventeen years after its publication. Perhaps this latter reason was also an instance of Owen's reported impatience with personal criticism.[10]

In addition to Owen's response, there were a number of other theologians who joined the theological battle. Thomas Danson (bap. 1629–1694), a non-conformist theologian, published *A Friendly-Debate Between Satan and Sherlock* (1675), where he reported an imaginary dialogue between Satan and Sherlock in an effort to demonstrate the falsity of Sherlock's critique and his views on union.[11] Vincent Alsop (1630–1703) published *Anti-Sozzo sive Sherlocismus Enervatus* (1675), where he sought

8.   Biographical information has been drawn from, 'Sherlock, William, D. D. (1641? – 1707)', in Sidney Lee (ed.), *Dictionary of National Biography*, vol. 52, (New York: MacMillan Co. 1897), pp. 95–7. See also William Sherlock, *A Discourse Concerning the Knowledge of Jesus Christ, And Our Union and Communion with Him; to which is annexed a Defence and Continuation; with A Particular Respect to the Doctrine of the Church of England, and the Charge of Socinianism, and Pelagianism*, 3rd edn. (London: M. Clark for W. Kettilby 1678).

9.   John Owen, *A Vindication of Some Passages in a Discourse Concerning Communion with God*, in *The Works of John Owen*, vol. 2, ed. William H. Goold (1965; Edinburgh: Banner of Truth 1997). Subsequent citations will refer to the page numbers of this volume of Owen's works.

10.   Tim Cooper, 'Owen's Personality: The Man behind the Theology', in Kapic and Jones (eds.), *The Ashgate Research Companion to John Owen's Theology*, pp. 215–26.

11.   Thomas Danson, *A Friendly-Debate Between Satan and Sherlock: Containing A Discovery of the Unsoundness of Mr. William Sherlock's Principles* (London: 1675).

to align Sherlock's views with Socinianism.[12] Robert Ferguson (c. 1637–1714) contributed his *The Interest of Reason in Religion* (1675), which largely dealt with Sherlock's hermeneutical claims, namely, the role and nature of metaphor in the Scriptures.[13] Henry Hickman (bap. 1629–1692), a non-conformist pastor of an English congregation in Leiden, wrote *Speculum Sherlockianum* (1674).[14] Another non-conformist theologian, Samuel Rolls [or Rolles] (c. 1628–1680), wrote two briefer entries, *Prodromus, Or The Character of Mr. Sherlock's Book* (1674) and *Justification Justified* (1674).[15] The last of the anti-Sherlockian publications was Edward Polhill's (c. 1622–1694), *An Answer to the Discourse of Mr. William Sherlock* (1675).[16] Equally noteworthy is Polhill's later work, *Christus in Corde: or, The Mystical Union Between Christ and Believers* (1680), though this work lies beyond the purview of the 1674–75 debate.[17] Polhill nevertheless does engage Sherlock's views in this later treatise.

On the other side of the debate, Sherlock published a response to Owen, *A Defence and Continuation* (1675). Beyond this only one theologian, Thomas Hotchkiss, a bishop in the Church

---

12. Vincent Alsop, *Anti-Sozzo sive Sherlocismus Enervatus: In Vindication of Some Great Truths Opposed, and Opposition to Some Great Errors Maintained by William Sherlock* (London: Nathanael Ponder 1675).

13. Robert Ferguson, *The Interest of Reason in Religion; with the Import and Use of Scripture-Metaphors; and the Nature of the Union Between Christ and Believers* (London: Dorman Newman 1675).

14. Henry Hickman, *Speculum Sherlockianum: Or, A Looking-Glass In Which the Admirers of Mr. Sherlock May Behold the Man, as to His Accuracy, Judgment, Orthodoxy* (London: Thomas Parkhurst 1674).

15. Samuel Rolles, *Prodromus, or The Character of Mr. Sherlock's Book: Called A Discourse of the Knowledge of Jesus Christ. In Which the Evil Spirit, and Design, of that Book is Discovered, and Several Errours therein Confuted* (London: 1674); idem, *Justification Justified: Or the Great doctrine of Justification, Stated According to the Holy Scriptures* (London: 1674).

16. Edward Polhill, *An Answer to the Discourse of Mr. William Sherlock, Touching the Knowledge of Christ, and Our Union and Communion with Him* (London: B. Foster 1675).

17. Edward Polhill, *Christus in Corde: or, The Mystical Union Between Christ and Believers Considered, in its Resemblances, Bonds, Seals, Privileges and Marks* (London: Thomas Cockerill 1680).

of England, published a defence of Sherlock in two volumes, *A Discourse Concerning the Imputation of Christ's Righteousness* (1675, 1678).[18] These two works were written in response to Owen's *Communion* and Ferguson's *Interest in Reason in Religion*. Excluding Owen's initial work and Polhill's 1680 work on union, this 1674–75 debate produced a dozen works totalling over four thousand pages. If anything, these statistics indicate the ferocity of what the editor of Owen's works called 'the Communion Controversy'.[19]

The various titles also indicate the chief subjects of controversy: union with Christ, reason and revelation, hermeneutics (i.e., the proper understanding of scriptural metaphors), justification, and imputation. That debaters would identify each other as traffickers of novelty, heresy, Socinianism, and the like, also evinces the perceived dangers from each side. Also noteworthy is the fact that Sherlock and Hotchkiss were in the Church of England, whereas Owen and the others were exiled from it; they were non-conformists. More was at stake than merely theological jousting; rather, emotions undoubtedly ran high because of the perceived implicit vindication of greater ecclesiological commitments, whether for or against the Church of England.[20] Going forward, this modest paper cannot explore every claim in these dozen works. Nevertheless, as we explore Owen's doctrine and Sherlock's criticism, these other works can provide helpful contextual data to paint a fuller picture of the debate.

2. Owen on Union with Christ

While Owen deals with union with Christ in a number of his works, we will focus primarily upon the doctrine as it appears

---

18. Thomas Hotchkiss, *A Discourse Concerning the Imputation of Christ's Righteousness to Us, and Our Sins to Him* (London: Walter Kettilby 1675); idem, *The Second Part of a Discourse Concerning Imputed Righteousness in An Answer to Mr. Throughtons Late Book Intitled Lutherus Redivivus, and a Postscript Containing a Vindication of the Authors Doctrine in the Former Part, Against the Reflections of Dr. John Owen in His Late Book of Justification* (London: 1678).

19. Owen, *Vindication*, p. 276.

20. Trueman, *John Owen*, pp. 123–24; also Lim, *Mystery Unveiled*, pp. 203, 389–90.

in his *Communion* since this is ground zero of the controversy. Owen begins his work by explaining that our communion with God flows from our union with Christ.[21] In Owen's estimation, the Father holds out His love to the saints, and the saints return their love to the triune God.[22] But Owen stipulates that the Father's love is antecedent and our love is consequent; that is, God takes the initiative to love first.[23] The believer's communion with God begins once a person receives faith by the work of the Spirit, and this faith places us in fellowship with Christ, our Mediator.[24] For Owen, a Spirit-wrought faith places the believer in union with Christ, which he characterises as a 'conjugal relation'. Citing Song of Songs 2:16, 'My Beloved is mine, and I am his', Owen explains that everything Christ possesses belongs to His bride, and everything the bride possesses belongs to Christ.[25]

When Owen invokes the concept of a conjugal union he has several things in mind. Owen writes: 'Christ gives himself to the *soul*, with all his *excellences*, righteousness, preciousness, graces, and eminences, to be its Saviour, head, and husband, for ever to dwell with it in this holy relation.'[26] Among the texts to which Owen appeals, he quotes or cites Song of Songs 2:14; 4:8; 7:10, Matthew 11:28, Jeremiah 23:6, 1 Corinthians 1:30, and Isaiah 4:2.[27] Given this cluster of passages, especially those from Song of Songs, Owen's doctrine does not arise from an exclusively Pauline source, as it appears in some contemporary expositions, but from a broader canonical root, one that incorporates Pauline

---

21. Owen, *Communion*, p. 8.
22. Ibid., p. 22.
23. Ibid., p. 29.
24. Ibid., pp. 34, 40.
25. Ibid., p. 54.
26. Ibid., p. 56.
27. Ibid., p. 57.

branches.[28] In response to Christ's call, argues Owen, saints respond with their *'free, willing consent* to receive, embrace, and submit unto the Lord Jesus, as their husband, Lord, and Saviour, – to abide with him, subject their souls unto him, and to be ruled by him forever.'[29] Owen's broad and general terms give way to greater specificity in other works. In his *Exposition of Hebrews*, Owen argues that union with Christ 'is the cause of all other graces that we are made partakers of; they are all communicated to us by virtue of our union with Christ. Hence is our adoption, our justification, our sanctification, our fruitfulness, our perseverance, our resurrection, our glory.'[30]

But we would be remiss if we only focused upon the *applicatio salutis*, or the believer's mystical union with Christ (i.e., the believer entering into union with Christ by the Spirit-wrought faith and indwelling of the Holy Spirit). The believer's mystical union with Christ has roots that connect to the important doctrines of the incarnation and covenant of redemption. The believer's union has a resting place in the union of Christ's two natures, divine and human. Christ's suitability to save, and hence execute the office of mediator, arises from the grace of His union, the conjunction of the two natures of God and man (John 1:14; Isa. 4:6; Rom. 1:3; 9:5). The believer's communion with the

---

28.   cf. e.g., Richard B. Gaffin, Jr., *By Faith, Not by Sight: Paul and the Order of Salvation*, 2nd edn. (Phillipsburg: P & R 2013), pp. 40–8; Constantine R. Campbell, *Paul and Union with Christ: An Exegetical and Theological Study* (Grand Rapids: Zondervan 2012). Especially noteworthy is that Song of Songs was cited by some proponents of mystical union, which points in two potential directions: (1) it evinces the canonical footing of the doctrine, and (2) appeal to this book bears the influence of Bernard of Clairvaux and his sermons on Song of Songs where he expounded the doctrine of union with Christ. Polhill, for example, writes: 'The whole Book of the *Canticles* is a divine Ditty; which, under the parable of Marriage, streams all along, as a full torrent of Spiritual Love interchangeably passing between Christ and his Church.' (cf. Polhill, *An Answer*, pp. 403, 598; Bernard of Clairvaux, *Sermons on the Song of Songs*, 4 vols. [Collegeville: Cistercian Publications 1971–80]). For citations to Bernard, see Polhill, *An Answer*, pp. 132, 298, 310.

29.   Owen, *Communion*, p. 58. (Owen's italics)

30.   Owen, *An Exposition of the Epistle to the Hebrews*, 21:149–50. Note, Owen's work on Hebrews was published in 1668.

triune God is the effect of the union of Christ's two natures.[31] But beyond the incarnation, we must push behind the curtain of time and history and peer into eternity where the triune God established the plan of redemption. For Owen, such peering is not speculative, transgressing the boundaries of Scripture, but is part of the divinely-revealed economy of redemption.

Owen contends that by way of a covenant, or agreement, the Father constituted the Son as covenant surety, which is based upon his understanding and exegesis of Hebrews 7:22. As covenant surety Christ meets and supplies all of the necessary conditions to accomplish the redemption of the elect.[32] In *Communion*, however, Owen does not make explicit reference to the covenant of redemption; but the concept does appear substantively to undergird his argumentation at certain points.[33] Its architectonic significance appears, for example, in the Savoy Declaration (1658), in which Owen and Thomas Goodwin (1600–1680) explicitly inserted the doctrine into the Congregational version of the Westminster Confession of Faith.[34] In the wake of Sherlock's criticism and the Communion controversy, it does appear that the covenant of redemption would take on greater significance in Owen's theology.

As we return to Owen's *Communion*, we should note the ways in which he explores the various dimensions of the believer's union with Christ. Christ's union with the believer is mystical, a conjugal bond of love, but there are also legal dimensions to this bond. Why, for example, did Christ not contract the guilt of original sin? To answer this question Owen reflexes to the doctrine of imputation. Christ escapes the contagion of original

---

31. Owen, *Communion*, p. 51.

32. John Owen, 'Exercitation XXVIII: Federal Transactions Between the Father and the Son', in William H. Goold (ed.), *Exposition of the Epistle to the Hebrews*, vol. 2, pp. 77–97.

33. Owen, *Communion*, pp. 177–80.

34. Mark Jones, *Why Heaven Kissed Earth: The Christology of the Puritan Reformed Orthodox Theologian, Thomas Goodwin (1600–80)* (Göttingen: Vandenhoeck & Ruprecht 2010), pp. 126–7.

sin because He was never federally in Adam, and therefore was never legally liable to the imputation of Adam's sin.[35] Christ voluntarily assumed the legal liability for Adam's sin by virtue of the covenant of redemption, but not because of His descent from Adam. He was also preserved from original sin because of the miraculous nature of His incarnation (Luke 1:35).[36]

Legal concerns also appear in other areas of *Communion*, particularly with regard to Christ's satisfaction and the doctrine of justification. Owen believed that the 'complete obedience of Christ' was reckoned to believers.[37] In this respect Owen draws upon a number of texts including Genesis 2:17, Hebrews 2:14-15, Matthew 19:17, but especially noteworthy is Leviticus 18:5, 'Do this and live.'[38] Owen places the fulcrum of Christ's work upon His obedience, which he sets in contrast to the disobedience of Adam; he cites Romans 5:18-19 in support of this claim. Owen does not rest upon this lone Pauline text but reaches back to the Old Testament and Zechariah 3:3-5. Owen explains that the prophet presents a typical representation of our justification – the filthy robes represent the forgiveness of sins, secured by Christ's death, and the investiture with a clean robe represents the imputation of righteousness, which we receive by Christ's obedience.[39] This means that the believer receives the non-imputation of sin (forgiveness) as well as the imputation of Christ's righteousness by virtue of his union with Christ.[40]

Owen characterises the legal elements of our union with Christ as the 'grace of acceptation with God' which is fundamental to communion with Him. But Owen does not focus exclusively

---

35. Owen, *Communion*, p. 65.

36. Owen, *Communion*, p. 65.

37. This is likely a reference to both the active and passive obedience of Christ. cf. Savoy Declaration, XI.i; Carl Trueman, 'John Owen on Justification', in K. Scott Oliphint (ed.) *Justified in Christ: God's Plan for us in Christ* (Fearn: Mentor 2007), pp. 81–98.

38. Owen, *Communion*, pp. 162–3.

39. Owen, *Communion*, p. 164.

40. Owen, *Communion*, p. 170. Similar statements appear in Polhill, *An Answer*, p. 289.

upon justification and legal categories. As important as they are
to redemption and union with Christ, he also insists upon the
necessity of sanctification. The first grace of our acceptance with
Christ is justification and the second is sanctification. As Owen
writes: 'He doth not only justify his saints from the guilt of sin,
but also sanctify and wash them from the filth of sin.'[41] Owen's
emphasis upon justification and sanctification is important,
because as we will see below, Sherlock accused Owen of being
an antinomian. Owen was already sensitive to the accusation of
antinomianism because he responds to the possible objection
that, if Christ's obedience was imputed to the believer, then what
need is there for personal obedience?[42] For Owen, sanctification
was crucial in his understanding of communion with God
because believers had to understand how they were to maintain
their sense of acceptance with God, namely, daily renewing the
perception of comfort and life.[43]

Owen responded to the charge of antinomianism by first
referring to the covenant of redemption; he does this to ground
the believer's acceptance in Christ's work as covenant surety,
not in the believer's own obedience.[44] Owen was insistent that
our personal obedience rest in its proper place – it has no role
in our justification.[45] But Owen is quick to affirm that, though
our good works do not save us, God has nevertheless ordained
them, which is sufficient ground to affirm their importance and
necessity as part of our sanctification (Eph. 2:8-10). Not only
has God ordained them but they are the 'eminent immediate end
of the distinct dispensation of Father, Son, and Holy Ghost'.[46]
In support of the necessity of good works, Owen gives three
reasons: they are (1) a means unto an end, namely, that God has

41. Owen, *Communion*, pp. 169–70.
42. Ibid., pp. 176–7.
43. Ibid., p. 176.
44. Ibid., pp. 177–8.
45. Ibid., pp. 180–1.
46. Ibid., pp. 182–3.

ordained them, thus believers should perform them; (2) a pledge and testimony of our adoption; and (3) an expression of our thankfulness.[47]

To perform these good works, Owen maintains that the work of the Spirit is absolutely necessary. The Holy Spirit indwells a person and creates a habit of grace; Owen writes: 'This is that which I intend by this habit of grace – a new, gracious, spiritual life, or principle, created, and bestowed on the soul, whereby it is changed in all its faculties and affections, fitted and enabled to go forth in the way of obedience unto every divine object that is proposed unto it, according to the mind of God.'[48] Owen distinguishes *habitual grace* from *actual grace*, which he defines as the permeating 'divine influence and assistance, working in and by the soul any spiritual act or duty whatsoever, without any pre-existence unto that act or continuance after it.' Or, in simpler scriptural terms, God works in us both to will and to do. Habitual grace is the cause and principle of actual grace.[49] The indwelling power and presence of the Spirit, a correlate of our union with Christ, is part of the saints' communion with Christ.[50] Believers pursue holiness because of their union and communion with the triune God.

3. Sherlock on Union with Christ

A cursory reading of Sherlock's writings gives the impression that he holds to a common doctrine of union with Christ. He employs the same type of terminology that appears in numerous seventeenth-century works – Sherlock writes of union with Christ, justification, and sanctification. But beyond superficial resemblances, Sherlock was intent on demonstrating the novelty of the common view of mystical union. In his subsequent response to Owen's *Vindication*, Sherlock writes:

---

47. Owen, *Communion*, p. 186.
48. Ibid., p. 200.
49. Ibid., pp. 200–1.
50. Ibid., p. 206.

That in a late Discourse, according to my mean Abilities, I endeavoured to vindicate Christian Religion from those uncouth and absurd Representations, which some modern divines, who are the great Fomenters of our present Factions, have made of it: and herein I thought, I should do good service, not only to the common Cause of Christianity (which is exposed to the scorn of Atheistical Wits, for the sake of such Doctrins, as are so far from belonging to Christianity, that they seem to be invented on purpose to affront the general sense and understanding of Mankind,) but also to the best constituted Church in the World, which is rent and torn into a thousand Factions for the sake of these new Discoveries, which are admired for no other reason, but because they are not understood.[51]

Sherlock's contempt for these 'new discoveries' was likely fuelled by his perception that most of the proponents of mystical union were non-conformists, such as Owen. Sherlock's contempt is evident when he states that he wanted to vindicate the Christian religion from 'modern divines' who were 'great Fomenters of our present Factions'. In fact, some have noted that the immediate context of the debate was the ousting of Oliver Cromwell (1599–1658) and Owen with him.[52] In other words, Sherlock sought to kick Owen while he was down and further discredit him. In addition to Owen, Sherlock critically engages other non-conformist theologians, including Thomas Watson (1620–1686), Thomas Brooks (1608–1680), Thomas Jacombe (1623–1687), and Thomas Shephard (1605–1649).[53] Owen, thus, was not

---

51. Sherlock, *Defence and Continuation*, preface (fol. A2).

52. Lim, *Mystery Unveiled*, p. 203.

53. e.g., Sherlock, *Knowledge of Jesus Christ*, pp. 41–42, 171, 175, 210. cf. Thomas Watson, *Christ's Loveliness, or, A Discourse Setting Forth the Rare Beauties of the Lord Jesus, Which May Both Amaze the Eye, and Draw the Heart of a Sinner To Him* (London: Ralph Smith 1657); Thomas Brooks, *The Unsearchable Riches of Christ, or, Meat For Strong Men and Milke for Babes Held forth in Twenty-Two Sermons from Ephesians III, VIII* (London: John Hancock 1661); Thomas Jacombe, *Several Sermons Preach'd on the Whole Eighth Chapter of the Epistle to the Romans: Eighteen of which Preach'd on the First, Second, Third, Fourth Verses are Here Published*, vol. 1, pt. 1 (London: W. Godbid 1672); Thomas Shephard, *The Sound Beleever. A Treatise of Evangelicall Conversion* (London: Andrew Crooke 1653).

the only target, though he often bears the brunt of Sherlock's criticisms.

Sherlock's presuppositional difference with Owen lies in his approach to hermeneutics. Unlike Owen, Sherlock did not believe there was anything mysterious about the believer's union with Christ; hence, there was no mystical element to it.[54] Owen's error was that he wrested language of allusion and metaphor from its original context and misapplied it to his doctrine of union.[55] To posit an indwelling of the believer by the Holy Spirit, hence bringing him into union with Christ, entailed mixing of the essences of Christ with the believer.[56] Sherlock offers a counter-explanation of the language concerning union with Christ: 'That those Phrases and Metaphors which represent our Union to Christ, signifie our visible Society with the Church, and our sincere practice of the Christian Religion: When we joyn in Communion with the Church of Christ.'[57] When a person joins the church, then, he is in union with Christ, members and head, constitute one person – there is no mystery, riddle, or mystical aspect. Rather than *mystical* union with Christ, Sherlock denominates his own view as a *political* union with Him, an idea that appears in other theologians of the period such as Richard Baxter (1615–1691).[58]

Citing Colossians 2:10 in support, Sherlock claims that this text explains the true nature of Christ's relationship to His Church:

> He is the *Head and Husband*, because he is invested with Authority to govern; and the Church is *his Body and Spouse*, because it must be obedient to his Laws, and subject to his Government: As we know it is very familiar to call a Society of men, who live under the same Laws and Civil Government, a *body politick*, which

---

54. Sherlock, *Knowledge of Jesus Christ*, p. 87.

55. Ibid., p. 67.

56. Ibid., p. 182.

57. Ibid., pp. 119–20.

58. cf. Richard Baxter, *Of The Imputation of Christ's Righteousness to Believers* (London: Nevil Simmons 1675), p. 5.

signifies their subjection to the same Authority, as a body hath but one Head.[59]

Like Owen and other non-conformists, Sherlock refers to the same biblical language – head and body, husband and spouse – but he does not explain it in terms of mystical union but rather as a society. This does not mean that Sherlock rejects the idea that there is a spiritual dimension to his doctrine of union. Again, he uses similar nomenclature, but it has different theological content. Sherlock explains that the political union between Christ and the church can either be external and visible or true and real. External union is the manner by which 'hypocritical professors' are united to Christ. They merely profess to be united to Christ but their lives do not evidence their union with Him. Those in true and real union with Christ offer their sincere obedience and subjection to their Lord.[60]

For Sherlock, the visible profession of faith is the foundation for one's external political union to Christ, and the believer's new nature is the foundation of the real and spiritual union. Once again, there is familiar terminology (i.e., spiritual union) but Sherlock fills it with different theological content. First, spiritual union is the Christian's subjection of his mind and spirit to Christ as his spiritual king and placing one's soul and body under His government. According to Sherlock, this is the manner by which Christ is said to dwell in our hearts by faith (Eph. 3:17).[61] Second, spiritual union is participation in Christ's nature. By participation in His nature Sherlock means the following: Christ's gospel is the image of His mind, which He has transcribed in His laws. Therefore, sincere obedience to His laws is conformity to His nature (Phil. 2:15). To obey Christ's laws is to be conformed to His nature; hence, Paul describes this conformity of nature as having the Spirit of Christ (Rom 8:9).[62] Third, the pinnacle

---

59. Sherlock, *Knowledge of Jesus Christ*, p. 98.

60. Ibid., p. 103.

61. Ibid., p. 105.

62. Ibid., p. 106.

of the spiritual union is the mutual and reciprocal love shared between Christ and the believer. 'Love', writes Sherlock, 'is the great Cement of Union, which unites Interests, and thereby does more firmly unite Hearts.'[63] Sherlock's understanding of union does not involve the indwelling presence of the Spirit, and hence, contra Owen and other non-conformists, there is no mystical element to it.

Apparent in Sherlock's view is an impulse and emphasis upon the necessity of obedience. This is one of the hallmark aspects of Sherlock's doctrine of union, and one that stands in stark contrast to Owen's view. In Sherlock's estimation, one of the biggest problems with Owen's understanding of union was the emphasis the non-conformist divine placed upon the righteousness of Christ.[64] Sherlock flatly rejected the concept of the imputed righteousness of Christ.[65] He argued his case from a number of different premises: the concept is absent from the Old Testament, the gospels mention nothing of imputed righteousness, the gospels explicitly state the necessity of obedience for salvation, and the expression 'imputed righteousness of Christ' appears nowhere in Scripture.[66] When Paul precludes works from justification, he does not have in view obedience to the law but rather he seeks to exclude works of the ceremonial law, which is a mere external conformity to the moral precepts.[67] Thus when Paul opposes the righteousness of law to faith, he places external adherence in opposition to sincere obedience.[68] In addition to this, no Old Testament believer actually believed in Christ, which means that they could not lay hold of His righteousness. Rather, Abraham, for example,

---

63. Sherlock, *Knowledge of Jesus Christ*, p. 107.

64. Ibid., p. 144.

65. Ibid., pp. 145ff.

66. Sherlock, *Knowledge of Jesus Christ*, pp. 146–8, 150. (Polhill takes up the specific issue of the supposed lack of the doctrine of imputation in the gospels; Polhill, *An Answer*, p. 318).

67. Sherlock, *Knowledge of Jesus Christ*, pp. 151, 162–3.

68. Ibid., p. 168.

believed in the general promise of Christ, but Christ was not the formal object of his faith; Abraham believed in God.[69] For these reasons Sherlock concludes: 'Thus, you see, there is no foundation in Scripture for all this talk of a *Personal righteousness of Christ, inherent in him, and imputed to us.*'[70]

In his critique, Sherlock goes to the heart of what he perceives is the problem with Owen's view. Owen conceives of a union of persons, Christ and the believer, by which he partakes of Christ's personal graces. This union, argues Sherlock, commonly goes under the concepts of conjugal and legal unions.[71] Sherlock does not invoke the terms, but he likely has in view the distinction between the union formed between Christ and the elect in the covenant of redemption and the mystical union that occurs within the historical covenant of grace. The clue that points in this direction is that Sherlock specifically engages and rejects Owen's concept of Christ's role as *surety*. Recall, according to Owen, the Father appoints the Son as covenant surety in the covenant of redemption. Sherlock, however, distinguishes between *surety* and *covenant surety*. Sherlock readily grants that Scripture calls Christ surety (Heb. 7:22). According to Sherlock, a covenant surety simply ratifies a covenant, performs it, and guarantees that all of the promises of the covenant come to pass *if* the terms and conditions are met. A surety, by contrast, vicariously carries out all of the requirements of the covenant – he fulfils all of the covenant conditions. This is the view that Sherlock attributes to Owen, and the view he categorically rejects.[72]

Understandably, Sherlock's doctrine of justification was considerably different than Owen's. Sherlock's view has great similarities to the doctrine of Baxter. In particular, like Baxter, Sherlock believed that Christ did not come to fulfil the law on behalf of believers. Instead,

---

69.   Sherlock, *Knowledge of Jesus Christ*, pp. 152, 156.

70.   Ibid., p. 170.

71.   Ibid., p. 174.

72.   Ibid., p. 179.

Christ came to fulfil and recalibrate the law's demands.[73] In contrast to Owen, who cites Leviticus 18:5 as the core principle of the law, namely, 'Do this and live', Sherlock argues that Christ fulfilled the law so that the new requirement is sincere obedience.[74] Sherlock writes: 'Now this is the thing in question, whether we must be made righteous with the perfect Righteousness of Christ imputed to us, or whether God will for the sake of Christ dispence with the rigour of the Law, and accept of a sincere and Evangelical obedience, instead of a perfect and unsinning Righteousness.'[75] For Sherlock, there is no imputation of the active and passive obedience of Christ.[76] Christ suffers the curse of the law and His righteousness is the foundation of the covenant, the means by which we are accepted, and the platform from which believers offer their own sincere obedience in fulfilment of the law.[77]

Sherlock's understanding of Christ's work and justification stands in contrast to Owen's view because of the latter's emphasis upon mystical union and imputed righteousness. He believed that such a construction was inherently antinomian. Again, like Baxter, Sherlock believed that, if one placed union with Christ prior to accomplished holiness, it was fertile ground for antinomianism.[78] It fosters antinomianism because placing union before holiness, and hence the imputation of Christ's righteousness, crowds out any place for the believer's sincere obedience.[79] Beyond this, Sherlock objects to union before holiness on two grounds. First, he objects to the idea that everything the sinner does prior to union is characterised as sin. Second, Sherlock observes:

---

73. cf. e.g., Richard Baxter, *Confession of His Faith: Especially Concerning the Interest of Repentance and Sincere Obedience to Christ, in our Justification and Salvation* (London: Tho. Underhil 1654), p. 296; idem, *A Treatise of Justifying Righteousness in Two Books* (London: Nevil Simmons 1676), p. 7.

74. Sherlock, *Knowledge of Jesus Christ*, p. 187.

75. Ibid., p. 196.

76. Ibid., p. 207.

77. Ibid., p. 209.

78. cf. e.g., Baxter, *Confession*, pp. 158–9.

79. In addition to Owen, others advocated the priority of union to obedience (see Polhill, *An Answer*, pp. 118, 194, 203).

These men constantly place *our Justification before our Sanctification*, that we are first accounted holy by God, before we are made holy; now our Justification follows our Union to Christ, and our Sanctification follows our Justification, and therefore we must first be united to Christ, so as to have a title to all the Promises of the Gospel, to Justification and Eternal Life, before we are sanctified, that is, before we are made holy.[80]

He does not invoke the term, neither does Owen for that matter, but Sherlock objects to the concept of the golden chain (or order of salvation), where Reformed theologians typically placed justification before sanctification.[81]

Sherlock recognised that Owen and others spoke of the importance and necessity of sanctification, but in his judgment their doctrines of sanctification were deficient. It was not enough to talk of proving your justification by your sanctification, that is, that good works evidence a justifying faith.[82] Moreover, non-conformists like Owen often characterised sanctification as being imperfect, which means that a saint could not actually contribute good works to justification because they are stained by sin.[83] Given the imperfection of sanctification, the believer had to rest upon the imputed righteousness of Christ. Sherlock believed that such notions were pure antinomianism, and he therefore aligned Owen with Tobias Crisp (1600–1643) and John Saltmarsh (d. 1647), two of the seventeenth-century's most notorious antinomians.[84] Sherlock believed that Owen's doctrine of sanctification left no room for the believer's obedience and ran counter to a number of scriptural passages (e.g., John 14:23; 15:10).[85]

---

80. Sherlock, *Knowledge of Jesus Christ*, p. 211.

81. On the historic early modern Reformed understanding of the order of salvation, see J. V. Fesko, 'Romans 8.29–30 and the Question of the *Ordo Salutis*', *Journal of Reformed Theology* 8 (2014), pp. 35–60, esp. 41–50.

82. Sherlock, *Knowledge of Jesus Christ*, p. 228.

83. Ibid., p. 230.

84. Sherlock, *Knowledge of Jesus Christ*, p. 252; cf. Tobias Crisp, *Christ Alone Exalted* (London: William Parkhurst 1690); John Saltmarsh, *Sparkles of Glory, or, Some Beams of the Morning-Star* (London: Giles Calvert 1647).

85. Sherlock, *Knowledge of Jesus Christ*, p. 253.

In summary, Sherlock taught a doctrine of political union with Christ, one by which believers professed their faith, joined the church, placed themselves in subjection to Christ's rule, and sought conformity to Christ's image through sincere obedience to the law. The one in union with Christ was not indwelled by the Spirit because such a notion would require the mixing of Christ's essence with the believer. Moreover, the believer did not receive the unscriptural notion of His imputed righteousness. Rather, Christ modified the requirements of the law so that sincere obedience was the new standard. With a foundation of Christ's suffering and obedience, the believer had a platform to offer his own sincere obedience to the new form of the law.

4. Owen's Response

As one can well imagine, Owen was quick to respond, at least as one measures time in the seventeenth-century. He responded with his *Vindication* and refused to renounce his views. Rather than retreat from the quarrel, Owen asserted the truthfulness, antiquity, and catholicity of his doctrine of union with Christ.[86] Throughout Owen's response he appeals to a number of theologians from the ancient church but he also draws upon the names of many of his contemporaries. He quotes Richard Hooker's (1554–1600) definition of union with Christ, for example, to demonstrate that his own doctrine aligned with this venerable Church of England luminary.[87] Notable in this extensive quote, nearly five pages in volume 2 of Owen's works, is Hooker's appeal to Cyril of Alexandria (c. 376–444) and Augustine (354–430). Owen's citation of Hooker accomplished several things: (1) it demonstrated that, even though he was a non-conformist, he was nevertheless aligned with one of the Church of England's best-known theologians; (2) his doctrine was associated with ancient views expressed by Cyril and Augustine; (3) Hooker argues that believers participate

---

86. Owen, *Vindication*, p. 279.

87. Owen, *Vindication*, p. 280; cf. Richard Hooker, *Of the Lawes of Ecclesiastical Politie* (London: William Stansbye, 1622), V.56 (pp. 304–9).

in Christ by virtue of the indwelling presence of Christ; and (4) that this union involves both the imputation and infusion of righteousness. Beyond Hooker, Owen invokes the names of John Jewell (1522–1571), John Whitgift (c. 1530–1604), James Ussher (1581–1656), Joseph Hall (1574–1656), John Davenant (1572–1641), John Prideaux (1578–1650), Edward Reynolds (1599–1676), William Whitaker (1548–95), Matthew Sutcliffe (1550–1629), the English delegation to the Synod of Dort (1618–19), John Downame (1571–1652), Martin Luther (1483–1546), and even Roman Catholic theologian Robert Bellarmine (1542–1621).[88] The effect of citing these many names was to prove that Owen was not introducing anything new or heterodox, but that he adhered to a common doctrinal view.

Beyond proving the antiquity and catholicity of his doctrine, Owen sought to clarify and restate a few important points, which broadly cover the nature of union, justification, the necessity of good works, and the Socinian nature of Sherlock's view.[89] Concerning union, Owen was unfazed by Sherlock's criticisms. Far from run from the mystical nature of union, Owen fully embraced it:

> But it is the union of believers unto the person of Christ which is spiritual and mystical, whereby they are in him and he in them, and so are one with him, their head, as members of his mystical body, which is pleaded for herein, with the free communications of grace, righteousness, and salvation, in the several and distinct ways whereby we are capable to receive them from him, or be made partakers of them.[90]

Regarding justification and sanctification, Owen seems to spend more space defending the necessity of sanctification and good works. Perhaps Sherlock's accusation of antinomianism stung more sharply than his rejection of imputation? Nevertheless,

---

88. Owen, *Vindication*, pp. 304, 320.
89. Ibid., p. 310.
90. Ibid., p. 313.

Owen enlists a number of points to emphasise the necessity of good works, such as the fact that they are required given that they are ordained by God, the final cause of salvation, eminently useful to others, because of the justified state of believers, required in the new covenant, and are expressions of the believer's thankfulness.[91] In glaring contrast to Sherlock, Owen identifies the key issue of contention that divides his doctrine of union from Sherlock's: 'I confess this whole discourse proceedeth on the supposition of the imputation of the righteousness of Christ unto us for our justification.'[92] Owen predicated the necessity of good works, and hence the believer's sanctification, upon the foundation of the imputed righteousness of Christ.

Owen does not greatly elaborate on what he means by this statement about imputation, but two clues provide likely answers. First, later in his *Vindication* Owen makes general reference to the covenant of redemption and points readers to his exercitation on the subject, presumably Exercitation XXVIII: 'On Federal Transactions Between the Father and the Son'.[93] This raises a second point. Owen does not elaborate the concept of imputation here in his *Vindication*, but he does offer a number of clear statements in a subsequent work published shortly thereafter. Just three years after Sherlock's work was published, Owen wrote *The Doctrine of Justification by Faith* (1677). To be sure, Sherlock's name never appears in the book; Owen was content to focus upon the doctrine of Richard Baxter.[94] In fact, Owen writes: 'I lay more weight on the steady direction of one soul in this inquiry, than on disappointing the objections of twenty wrangling or fiery disputers.'[95] Owen notes that there are 'at present various contests about the doctrine of justification,

---

91. Owen, *Vindication*, pp. 315–20.

92. Ibid., p. 320.

93. Ibid., p. 355.

94. Carl R. Trueman, *The Claims of Truth: John Owen's Trinitarian Theology* (Carlisle: Paternoster 1998), p. 25; idem, 'John Owen on Justification', p. 83.

95. Owen, *Justification*, in *Works*, 5:4.

and many books published in the way of controversy about it, yet this discourse was written with no design to contend with or contradict any, of what sort or opinion soever.'[96] So, for all intents and purposes, Owen supposedly does not have Sherlock in view.

Nevertheless, several statements point us to Sherlock's looming shadow. First, Owen notes that the doctrine he presents in his work has been accused of having 'an unfriendly aspect towards the necessity of personal holiness, good works, and all gospel obedience in general, yea, utterly to take it away.'[97] This was one of Sherlock's principal criticisms against Owen – antinomianism. Second, Owen invokes the 'Papists' as opponents of the doctrine during the Reformation, and then introduces the fact that the same charge 'was afterward renewed by the Socinians, and continueth still to be managed by them.'[98] Owen accused Sherlock of being a Socinian because he turned the grace of God into an epistemological category. That is, grace is equal to truth, and if people simply reform their lives according to God's grace (read truth), then they too can be saved. This in Owen's mind was unreconstructed Pelagianism.[99] Given these two facts, to quote a different Sherlock, Sherlock Holmes and *The Hound of the Baskervilles* to be precise, 'The world is full of obvious things which nobody by any chance ever observes.' In other words, though Owen does not mention his name, given the chronological proximity to the Communion controversy, the concern about accusations of antinomianism, and invoking the threat of Socinianism, despite Owen's silence about Sherlock, he undoubtedly is part of Owen's interrogative and theological context.

What in Owen's work on justification illuminates Owen's broader point about imputation in his *Vindication*? In what way

---

96. Owen, *Justification*, in *Works*, 5:4–5.

97. Ibid., 5:5.

98. Ibid., 5:5.

99. Owen, *Vindication*, p. 350; cf. Polhill, *An Answer*, p. 209.

is imputation foundational to the believer's holiness and good works? Owen explains the foundational nature of imputation under two different concepts: the covenant of redemption and the order of salvation. In his work on justification, as in his *Communion* and *Vindication*, Owen affirms the necessity and importance of union with Christ:

> That there is such a union between Christ and believers is the faith of the catholic church, and has been so in all ages. Those who seem in our days to deny it, or question it, either know not what they say, or their minds are influenced by their doctrine who deny the divine persons of the Son and of the Spirit. Upon supposition of this union, reason will grant the imputation pleaded for to be reasonable; at least, that there is such a peculiar ground for it as is not to be exemplified in any things natural or political among men.[100]

Again, though he never mentions his name, Sherlock seems to be a target, as Owen mentions the doctrine's antiquity and the subject of political union, two issues raised by Sherlock.[101] Nonetheless, from within this context Owen identifies that mystical union is the 'immediate foundation of the imputation of the satisfaction and righteousness of Christ unto us.' We lay hold of Christ's imputed righteousness, argues Owen, because of our 'actual coalescenscy into one mystical person with him by faith.'[102]

But Owen pushes further back, beyond the mystical union that believers have with Christ. Owen explains that the 'imputation of sin unto Christ was antecedent to any real union between Christ and sinners' even though 'the imputation of his righteousness unto believers is consequential in order of nature unto their union

---

100. Owen, *Justification*, in *Works*, 5:209.

101. Sherlock's doctrine of political union came under significant criticism. Danson, for example, suggested that because Christ was lord over all, which includes Satan, it should follow that Satan is in political union with Christ (Danson, *Friendly-Debate*, p. 38). In his later treatise, Polhill engages the doctrine without mentioning Sherlock (Polhill, *Christus in Corde*, p. 116).

102. Owen, *Justification*, in *Works*, 5:218; cf. Danson, *Friendly-Debate*, p. 37.

with him, whereby it becomes theirs in a peculiar manner.'[103]
Christ receives the imputed sin of the elect before they enter into
real, or mystical, union with Him, while, according to the order
of nature, believers receive Christ's righteousness after they are in
mystical union with Him. What accounts for the logical order of
these two imputations? Owen explains: 'The first spring or cause
of this *union*, and of all the other causes of it, lie in that *eternal*
compact that was between the Father and the Son concerning the
recovery and salvation of fallen mankind.'[104]

In Owen's mind, the Father imputed the sins of the elect
to Christ in the covenant of redemption.[105] Christ receives the
imputed sins of the elect because He is surety, and He is therefore
legally responsible for all covenant requirements on behalf of His
confederated bride.[106] On this point Owen's influence and input
into the Savoy Declaration sheds some light on the relationship
between imputation and the covenant of redemption. Owen
and the Congregationalists modified the original statement from
Westminster Confession XI.iv: 'God did from all eternity decree
to justify all the elect, and Christ did in the fullness of time die
for their sins, and rise again for their justification: nevertheless,
they are not justified *personally*, until the Holy Spirit doth in due
time actually apply Christ unto them' (emphasis).[107] For Owen,
there is a sense in which the elect are justified in Christ prior to
their profession of faith, but they are nevertheless not *personally*
justified until the Holy Spirit applies redemption.[108]

Owen rests imputation upon two points: the covenant of
redemption and the order of salvation. Recall that Sherlock

---

103. Owen, *Justification*, in *Works*, 5:354.

104. Ibid., 5:179.

105. Ibid., 5:179–80.

106. Ibid., 5:182. For similar views, see Jacombe, *Several Sermons*, p. 50.

107. Jones, *Why Heaven Kissed Earth*, pp. 230–8.

108. Owen does not employ the category, though Rolles does mention the distinction
     between *active* justification (the imputation of Christ's righteousness in the covenant
     of redemption) and *passive* justification (the temporal reception of righteousness by
     faith in the covenant of grace) (Rolles, *Justification Justified*, pp. 1–2).

accused Owen and others of erroneously placing justification prior to sanctification. According to Sherlock, prioritising justification before sanctification was an error that led to antinomianism. Nevertheless, Owen was not cowed by Sherlock's criticism and doubled-down on the priority of justification. Owen explains: 'The plain truth is, the apostle speaks not one word of the *necessity* of our *sanctification*, or *regeneration*, or *renovation* by the Holy Ghost, *antecedently* unto our justification.' Furthermore, 'Nor is there intimated by him any order of *precedency* or connection between the things that he mentions, but only between justification and adoption, justification having the priority in order of nature: "That being justified by his grace, we should be heirs according to the hope of eternal life."' Owen repeats his point again in slightly different language: 'But that it is necessary that we should be sanctified, that we may be justified before God, who justifieth the ungodly, the apostle says not in this place, nor any thing to that purpose.' [109] Owen insists upon placing justification before sanctification in the order of salvation, or to use his terms, the order of nature.

5. Analysis

Primary thesis: imputed vs. personal righteousness
What accounts for Owen and Sherlock's widely divergent doctrines of union with Christ? Owen, for one, constructed his doctrine from a broadly catholic basis. As noted above, Owen cited numerous sources to support his view including patristic theologians such as Augustine, Cyril of Alexandria, and contemporaries like Richard Hooker. Sherlock's doctrine, however, has little historical mooring. For whatever accusations of novelty that Sherlock might cast upon Owen, Sherlock's doctrine is actually the newer of the two. In this respect Sherlock's doctrine bears the rationalising tendencies of Socinianism,

---

109. Owen, *Justification*, in *Works*, 5:133. Others similarly prioritise justification to obedience (see Polhill, *An Answer*, pp. 146, 158, 485, 587).

the young bastard child of the Reformation. At many points Sherlock eliminates the category of mystery, a concept that theologians had employed for ages, and in its place articulated a rational account of how Christ enters into union with believers. Sherlock's view can be characterised as a meeting of the minds, one where believers assent to the goodness of Christ's law and then offer their loving obedience in response. Given, moreover, that Sherlock defines grace, not as God's favour by which He regenerates and effectually calls people by the work of the Spirit, it seems difficult to avoid the Socinian label that Owen and others attached to his doctrine. Sherlock's doctrine of union, therefore, ultimately rests upon the believer's sincere obedience. Owen's, by contrast, rests upon the imputed righteousness of Christ, which finds its origins in the covenant of redemption, and its historical application in the mystical union between Christ and the believer. The instrument of this union is not reason, as with Sherlock, but a God-given, Christ secured, Spirit-wrought gift of faith.

Given these radically different versions of union with Christ, it is no wonder that they produce very dissimilar doctrines of communion. While Sherlock does emphasise that his understanding of communion encompasses the loving obedience of the believer to and for Christ, when he discusses the final judgment an entirely different element surfaces – fear. In a work written later in his life, Sherlock repeatedly invokes the importance of fear of judgment and condemnation as a motivation for good works.[110] Sherlock, for example, writes: 'Fear of a Future Judgment makes us truly and sincerely good.'[111] In this extended treatise, Sherlock only invokes the name of Christ to remind his reader that they will appear before Him for judgment. For Sherlock, justification awaits the final judgment, and not a moment sooner. Even with Abraham works precede his justification. Sherlock contends that God 'called *Abraham* out of *Ur* of the *Chaldees*,

---

110. See, e.g., William Sherlock, *A Practical Discourse Concerning a Future Judgment*, 2nd edn. (London: W. Rogers 1692), pp. 100, 142, 144, 350.

111. Sherlock, *Future Judgment*, p. 144.

and having tried his Faith and Obedience, entered into Covenant with him.'[112] Sherlock believed that 'Holiness is essential to a justifying Faith'.[113] Anything less than this was, in Sherlock's mind, false vain confidence, a presumptuous reliance upon Christ, and antinomian at its core.[114] Since believers are judged by their sincere obedience, Sherlock also offers the hope that unbelievers will find similar acceptance:

> I cannot but hope, that Christ in judgment of their [heathens'] Works will make the same favourable allowances to them, which the Gospel makes to those, who do believe in Christ: that is to say, that he will allow of the Repentance of a Heathen, if it were sincere and hearty, and did reform his Life, as well as of the Repentance of a Christian; that he will overlook the same Defects and Imperfections in the good Actions of Heathens, who lived vertuous Lives, who worshipped the One true God, and observed the natural Rules of Sobriety, Justice, and Righteousness, that he will in the Actions of Christians.[115]

Such a statement certainly confirms the anthropocentric and thus Socinian character of Sherlock's doctrine of union with Christ. Those unbelievers who nevertheless live virtuous lives may escape damnation, which seems to relativise the difference between being in and out of union with Christ.

Owen, by contrast, never lost sight of the need for Christ, whether in the present or at the divine bar for the final judgment. Owen believed that inherent righteousness was always imperfect, which means that the stain of sin always tainted the believer's good works, no matter how virtuous they might be. Hence, the believer's works were always insufficient to stand scrutiny for one's justification. Justification always, therefore, had to rest upon the

---

112. Sherlock, *Future Judgment*, p. 197.

113. Ibid., p. 343.

114. Ibid., pp. 339, 343, 356.

115. Ibid., pp. 359–60. This was one of the bigger sticking points in the debate, namely, justification by sincere obedience (Rolles, *Justification Justified*, p. 90; idem, *Prodromus*, p. 33; Polhill, *An Answer*, p. 136).

perfect imputed righteousness of Christ.[116] Owen was insistent upon this even in the face of Roman Catholic claims regarding an initial justification by baptism and a final justification at the consummation: 'Some affirm that the apostle excludes all works from *our first justification*, but not from the second; or, as some speak, the continuation of our justification.'[117] Owen rejected this twofold understanding of justification because, in his mind, justification rests entirely upon the pardon of sin and imputation of Christ's righteousness.[118] To highlight this point and relate it to the events at the final judgment, Owen distinguishes between the essence and manifestation of justification – the essence is Christ's righteousness and its manifestation or declaration will occur at the final judgment. 'Yet is it not a *second justification*', writes Owen, 'for it depends wholly on the *visible effects* of that faith whereby we are justified, as the apostle James instructs us; yet is it only one single justification before God, evidenced and declared, unto his glory, the benefit of others, and increase of our own reward.'[119] For Owen, Christ never recedes into the background but rather forms the very ground by which the believer stands on the last day before the divine bar.

Secondary thesis: Calvin's relative absence

A secondary outcome of this investigation lies in the bibliographic data that the Communion Controversy provides. It may come as a surprise to some, but Calvin's relative absence from the debate is conspicuous. Despite the flurry of cited authorities Calvin's name appears only four times in over four thousand published pages. He is but one brilliant light in

---

116. Owen, *Justification*, in *Works*, 5:172–3.

117. Ibid., 5:284–5.

118. Ibid., 5:138.

119. Ibid., 5:139. For similar analysis, see Rolles, *Justification Justified*, pp. 104–5. Noteworthy is that Rolles rejects the idea that at the final judgment works were a synecdoche for the believer's faith (*Justification Justified*, p. 79). Others, such as Jacombe, argued that the elect were completely exempt from condemnation at the final judgment because of their justification (Jacombe, *Several Sermons*, pp. 1–39, esp. 19, 22).

a larger universe brimming with stars. Owen's response and other works of the 1674–75 debate reveal the catholicity of the Reformed doctrine of union with Christ. The following table illustrates this point:[120]

Name	Affiliation	Times cited
Augustine	Patristic	25
Robert Bellarmine	Roman Catholic	13
John Davenant	Anglican	13
James Ussher	Anglican	13
Chrysostom (c. 349–407)	Patristic	9
Richard Hooker	Anglican	6
Martin Chemnitz (1522–1586)	Lutheran	5
Thomas Gataker (1574–1654)	Reformed	5
William Perkins (1558–1602)	Reformed	5
Girolamo Zanchi (1516–1590)	Reformed	5
Lancelot Andrews (1555–1626)	Anglican	4
Theodore Beza (1519–1605)	Reformed	4
John Calvin	Reformed	4
David Pareus (1548–1622)	Reformed	4
John Prideaux	Reformed	4
Seth Ward (1617–1689)	Anglican	4
Matthew Wren (1585–1667)	Anglican	4
Ambrose (c. 337–397)	Patristic	3
Bernard of Clairvaux (1090–1153)	Medieval	3
Cyril of Alexandria	Patristic	3
James Durham (1622–1658)	Reformed	3
William Ames (1576–1633)	Reformed	2
Robert Abbot (1560–1617)	Anglican	2
Edward Reynolds	Anglican	2
William Whitaker	Anglican	2

120. This list of names is drawn from Owen, *Vindication*; Danson, *Friendly-Debate*; Hickman, *Speculum Sherlockianum*; Rolles, *Prodromus*; and idem, *Justification Justified*. Debate participant's names have been excluded given that they naturally appear numerous times.

Among the fifty other names that appear only once, there are numerous Reformed, Lutheran, Roman Catholic, patristic, and medieval theologians. Some might counter that such citation patterns are only natural given Sherlock's claims of novelty. Debate participants sought to prove the catholicity, antiquity, and orthodoxy of their claims.

Yet, when one compares citation patterns to Thomas Jacombe's work, one that Sherlock included with his initial criticism of Owen, and one that predates the controversy, the same picture emerges. There are thirty-four names cited in one thirty-five page sermon specifically on union with Christ:[121]

Name	Affiliation	Times cited
Thomas Aquinas (1225–1274)	Medieval	3
Martin Luther (1483–1546)	Lutheran	3
Gulielmus Bucanus (d. 1603)	Reformed	2
John of Damascus (676–749)	Medieval	2
Peter Lombard (1100–1160)	Medieval	2
Peter Martyr Vermigli (1499–1562)	Reformed	2
Amandus Polanus (1561–1610)	Reformed	2
Girolamo Zanchi	Reformed	2
Heinrich Alting (1583–1644)	Reformed	1
William Ames	Reformed	1
Aristotle (384–322 B.C.)	Philosopher	1
Bernard of Clairvaux	Medieval	1
Theodore Beza	Reformed	1
Anthony Burgess (d. 1664)	Reformed	1
Francis Cheynell (1608–1665)	Reformed	1
Ralph Cudworth (1617–1688)	Anglican	1
Cyprian	Patristic	1
Cyril of Alexandria	Patristic	1
John Davenant	Anglican	1
Guilielmus Estius (1542–1613)	Roman Catholic	1

---

121. These names appear in Jacombe, *Several Sermons*, pp. 41–86. Note, there are several names that I was unable to identify: Bodium, Nemes, Newson, and Cornelius Mussus.

Franciscus Gomarus (1563–1641)	Reformed	1
Hugo Grotius (1583–1645)	Remonstrant	1
Justinian I (c. 482–565)	Patristic	1
David Pareus	Reformed	1
William Perkins	Reformed	1
Johannes Piscator (1546–1625)	Reformed	1
Obadiah Sedgwick (c. 1600–1658)	Reformed	1
Tertullian (c. 160–220)	Patristic	1
François Vatable (d. 1547)	Humanist	1
Richard Vines (1599–1656)	Reformed	1

Keep in mind, this is one sermon, and while Jacombe likely did not cite all of these names from the pulpit, his desire was to include them in the published version so that readers could see the pluriform sources from which he constructed his doctrine.

These citation patterns support the corollary thesis, namely, that the reception of Calvin's doctrine of union with Christ has been greatly exaggerated in our own day. The Reformed tradition was pluriform, eclectic, and sought insights from contemporary, medieval, and patristic sources. This corollary thesis returns the investigation to the nature of the Communion Controversy insofar as it further evidences the specious nature of Sherlock's claims of novelty. Sherlock, not Owen and the other non-conformists, promoted a novel doctrine of union. Owen's doctrine of union with Christ was rooted in the catholic tradition. Indeed, Owen was a Reformed Catholic, and his doctrine of union reveals the catholicity of his views.

Conclusion

The Communion Controversy of 1674–75 deserves greater attention, more so than this modest paper has been able to offer. Chances are that several doctoral dissertations lie buried within the small pond of four thousand pages of fiery barbs exchanged between Sherlock, Owen, and the other participants. Nevertheless, this debate affords the opportunity to read Owen's doctrine of union with Christ in its historical context rather than abstracted from it. Such a contextual reading enables investigators to see how imputation, indwelling, faith, union, and communion all function in Owen's theology. The controversy also reveals how Owen and others responded to significant criticism at numerous points and reveals the catholic rather than Calvinistic nature of their doctrine of union with Christ.

QUESTIONS FOR DISCUSSION

1. What are the key differences between Owen and Sherlock's doctrines of union with Christ?

2. Is Sherlock's doctrine truly Socinian in nature?

3. Should the catholicity of Owen's doctrine of union impact our own methodology and formulations of the doctrine?

4. To what extent was Owen's doctrine impacted by Bernard of Clairvaux and Song of Songs?

5. Is Owen's use of the term habit in relation to sanctification problematic, i.e., habitual vs. actual grace?

CHAPTER FIVE

'Union with Christ' and Justification

David McKay

The doctrines of union with Christ and of justification have been
the subject of extensive discussion in recent years and both have
generated numerous scholarly studies. Some radical rewriting
of both doctrines have been proposed as a result, for example,
of developments in Pauline studies (as in the New Perspective
on Paul) and in historical theology (such as the New Finnish
interpretation of Luther).[1] Within the Evangelical and Reformed
family considerable work has also been done, producing, for
example, the 'Christological realism' proposed by Marcus Peter
Johnson.[2] Debates about forensic versus participationist, *ordo
salutis* versus *historia salutis*, and other related issues occupy many
pages and sometimes raise temperatures.

Is there anything more to be said? A theme which was once
central to treatments of these topics, but which has received much
less attention recently, is that of covenant. Some writers, such as

---

1. A useful survey is the essay 'Where We Are: Justification under Fire in the
    Contemporary Scene' by David Van Drunen in R. Scott Clark (ed.) *Covenant,
    Justification, and Pastoral Ministry*, (Phillipsburg: P & R Publishing 2007).

2. Marcus Peter Johnson, *One with Christ. An Evangelical Theology of Salvation*
    (Wheaton: Crossway 2013).

Johnson, reject a covenantal approach to union with Christ and
related subjects. Others make some use of the covenant theme, but
give it a fairly limited role in their formulation of doctrine. Among
contemporary theologians Michael Horton[3] and the contributors to
the symposium cited above (see note 1) do make extensive use of
covenant theology, but they would appear to be in a small minority.

Nevertheless it seems to me that the covenant motif offers
a fruitful framework for understanding both union with Christ
and justification. The approach in this study will be first to
examine the basics of covenant theology and then to consider
how it might shape our thinking about union with Christ and
justification. The aim is not to engage in a purely historical
exercise but rather to offer a fresh consideration of a valuable
and, I believe, biblical tradition that takes into account modern
discussions and debates. There is not space to engage in detailed
critiques of the major contemporary reconstructions of these
doctrines, but these will be taken into account where possible.

1. A covenantal framework

What is a covenant? Definitions have often been given which
lean heavily on customary practices in the Near East in Old
Testament times. These have some value, but ultimately biblical
usage is to be our guide. Many definitions lay heavy emphasis on
legal and contractual categories. These elements must be taken
into account, but such definitions do not seem to get to the heart
of what a covenant is.

One helpful, concise definition of covenant in relation to the
covenants of Scripture is provided by the Scottish theologian
Robert Rollock in his 1597 work *A Treatise of God's Effectual
Calling*: 'The covenant of God is a promise under some certain
condition.'[4] Four centuries later Jonty Rhodes offers, 'A covenant

---

3.   Michael S. Horton, *Covenant and Salvation: Union with Christ*, (Louisville and
      London: Westminster John Knox Press 2007).

4.   Robert Rollock, *A Treatise of God's Effectual Calling*, 1603 edition, translated by H. Holland
      in *Select Works of Robert Rollock* (Edinburgh: Woodrow Society 1844–1849), p. 34.

is a conditional promise.'[5] This is a helpful approach, bringing together the gracious element of promise and the aspect of obligation which the conditions impose.

These elements come together in the institution of marriage which is portrayed in Scripture as a covenant relationship and which is often, especially in the Prophets, such as Hosea, employed as an illustration of God's covenant with His people. Since that is the case, a covenant might be defined as *a bond of love*.[6] There is a bond because commitments and promises are made and consequent obligations imposed, yet it is rooted and grounded in love. Thus God says to His people in Ezekiel 16:8: 'I made my vow to you and entered into a covenant with you . . . and you became mine.'[7]

A bond of love is thus forged, and it is important to stress this, lest the covenant should be viewed solely in terms of a cold, legalistic transaction. It is nevertheless a bond: it binds the parties to fulfil certain obligations concerning which they have made solemn promises. Thus in a marriage the cry, 'We don't love each other any more' does not remove the obligations or end the marriage. On the other hand, when love is missing, the marriage covenant becomes a bondage. This approach to the covenants holds together love and law, both of which are crucial to a biblical understanding of union with Christ and justification.

The very first chapters of the Bible need to be viewed covenantally. Although the word 'covenant' does not appear in these chapters, the basic elements of a covenant are present. Certain God-given provisions govern the life of Adam (and Eve) in Eden. There are commands regarding procreation and dominion in Genesis 1:28-30. More specific direction is provided in Genesis 2:16-17 regarding the prohibition on eating from the

---

5.   Jonty Rhodes, *Raiding the Lost Ark. Recovering the Gospel of the Covenant King* (Nottingham: InterVarsity Press 2013), p. 20.

6.   This is covered in more detail in David McKay, *The Bond of Love. God's Covenantal Relationship with His Church* (Fearn: Mentor 2001).

7.   All biblical quotations are from the ESV unless otherwise indicated.

tree of the knowledge of good and evil. Although there is only one prohibition, the whole future of Adam (and his descendants) hangs upon it.

Adam is left in no doubt regarding the covenant requirements that God has laid down for him, and the divine sanctions against the covenant breaker are made equally clear. In Genesis 2:17 the warning is given that 'in the day that you eat of it, you shall surely die'. That threat of judgment on the covenant breaker implies a corresponding gracious promise on God's part to the covenant keeper. If death is to be the consequence of disobedience, then obedience will entail the continuance of 'life', not merely as biological existence but as life in the fullest sense, life in fellowship with God. Through Adam's continued covenant obedience his relationship of love and trust with God will continue; God will be glorified and man will find the fulfilment for which he was created.

A bond of love was established in Eden. A very significant text in this regard is Hosea 6:7, which deals with Israel's sin of covenant breaking. According to the most satisfactory rendering, the verse reads: 'But like Adam they transgressed the covenant.'[8] The implication of the verse is that Adam was a party to a covenant in Eden, with the Lord obviously being the other party.

Although some have opted for names such as Covenant of Creation or Covenant of Nature, most have designated the covenant in Eden the *Covenant of Works*. This term may be used as long as we recognise that, of himself, man is unable to accumulate merit and so put God under some obligation to bless. The principle stated by Jesus in Luke 17:10 is always true: 'When you have done all that you were commanded, say, "We

---

8.   The proposed alternatives are unconvincing. 'Like man/men, they have broken the covenant': how else could men break the covenant but 'like men'? On this translation the verse is stating the obvious. 'As at Adam, they have broken the covenant': no-one can suggest what (presumably well-known) episode is in view if this is the correct translation, not to mention how forced a translation of the Hebrew it is.

are unworthy servants; we have only done what was our duty".'
God may nevertheless choose to bestow blessing on the basis of
His servants' obedience or lack of it. It is for this reason that the
obedience of Adam in Eden is of such importance. To fail to
render the obedience required by the covenant would entail ruin
for himself and, as we shall see, for all his descendants.

It is clear in Scripture that Adam in Eden acted not only as
an individual but also as a representative of the whole human
race that would derive its existence from him. In the language
of 1 Corinthians 15:22 we are 'in Adam': there is a covenantal
union between Adam and his descendants. This fact emerges
in the way in which the relationship between fallen Adam and
his descendants is described in several New Testament passages.
Death, in its fullest sense, is the lot of every human being, not
through personal repetition of the pattern of temptation and
fall in Eden but as a result of spiritual – covenantal – solidarity
with Adam. As 1 Corinthians 15:22 indicates, 'in Adam all die'.
In that text a vitally important parallel between Adam and Christ
is stated: 'as in Adam all die, so in Christ all will be made alive.'
Just as those who are united to Christ receive the benefits of His
redemptive work, so those who are united to Adam receive the
poisoned fruit of his disobedience.

The parallels between Adam and Christ are explored more
fully in Romans 5:12-19. The heart of Paul's argument is found
in verse 19: 'For as by the one man's disobedience the many
were made sinners, so by the one man's obedience the many
will be made righteous.' Union with Adam is set in contrast to
union with Christ: the covenantal headship of Adam with the
covenantal headship of Christ. In union with Adam the human
race is declared guilty before God and condemned to death, and
human nature is corrupted at its very roots. These are the results
of Adam's disobedience and loss of righteousness for those
who are 'in' him. The guilt and condemnation will be addressed
by justification and the corruption by sanctification, which will
be made possible by the obedience and righteousness of Christ
provided for all who are in covenant union with Him.

If the plight of man is to be understood covenantally, is there warrant for understanding God's provision of a solution covenantally? Is there, as many Reformed theologians have believed, a *Covenant of Redemption*, a covenant established within the Trinity that provides the basis for salvation? The concept has often been dismissed as absurd or entirely speculative, and as Geerhardus Vos, a supporter of the concept, states: 'It has not always been defended too happily exegetically.'[9] That said, however, it is exegetically defensible and contributes significantly to our understanding of union with Christ and all that results from that union. As Brian Vickers says:

> As Adam lived in a covenantal relationship with God, so too Jesus, in his role as second Adam and Son of God, relates to God his Father in what resembles a covenantal relationship . . . The purposes of God unfold in Scripture through a series of Covenants (with Adam, Noah, Abraham, Moses, David, and the New Covenant), but the redemptive relationship between the Father and the Son is not merely a linear step in the series but the basis for the covenantally enacted plan of salvation.[10]

We must proceed with great care and reverence to avoid reading into Scripture things that are not there or forcing it to fit a preconceived scheme. It does appear, however, that behind our experience of salvation lies a covenantal arrangement made within the Trinity before time began.

It is noteworthy that during His earthly ministry Jesus had a deep awareness of fulfilling a mission with which He had been charged: 'I have come down from heaven, not to do my own will but the will of him who sent me' (John 6:38). He goes on to specify that this involves not losing any of 'all that he has given me' (v. 39). He has been sent to provide salvation for a people *given*

---

9.   Geerhardus Vos, 'The Doctrine of the Covenant in Reformed Theology' in Richard B. Gaffin, Jr. (ed.), *Redemptive History and Biblical Interpretation. The Shorter Writings of Geerhardus Vos* (Phillipsburg: P & R Publishing 1980), p. 252.

10. Brian Vickers, *Justification by Grace through Faith* (Phillipsburg: P & R Publishing 2013), p. 41.

to Him (see also John 17:2, 6, 9, 24) and the giving is expressed in Ephesians 1:4 as pre-temporal: 'He chose us in him before the foundation of the world.'

Covenantal language is used specifically in a passage such as Psalm 89:3: 'I have made a covenant with my chosen one; I have sworn to David my servant.' The immediate context is the renewal of God's covenant with David in 2 Samuel 7:12-14, but the quotation from this passage in Hebrews 1:5 shows that the ultimate reference is to David's descendant, the Lord Jesus Christ. This Christological perspective is also evident in Isaiah 42:6: 'I will give you as a covenant for the people, a light for the nations.' The Servant of the Lord who is in view here is often regarded as Israel, but the fulfilment in Christ is made clear when Simeon speaks of Him as 'a light for revelation to the Gentiles' (Luke 2:32).

Mention has already been made of the parallels between Adam and Christ in 1 Corinthians 15:22 and Romans 5:12-19. These texts will require further consideration but at this point we may say that the language of 'in Adam' and 'in Christ' is the language of covenantal representation. Adam was constituted the covenant head of the human race by the Covenant of Works: Christ was constituted the covenant head of His elect people by the Covenant of Redemption.

As far as the content of the Covenant of Redemption is concerned, it may be summarised succinctly in Horton's words: 'The Father elects a people in the Son as their mediator to be brought to saving faith by the Spirit.'[11] We may briefly flesh this out as follows:[12]

- *the Father,* for His part, gives to the Son a people whom He will redeem (John 17:2, 6), sends Him to be their representative (John 3:16; Rom. 5:18-19), in a human body and soul

---

11. Michael Horton, *God of Promise: Introducing Covenant Theology* (Grand Rapids: Baker Books 2006), p. 6.

12. Wayne Grudem, *Systematic Theology. An Introduction to Biblical Doctrine* (Nottingham: InterVarsity Press 1994), pp. 518–19.

(Col. 2:9; Heb. 10:5), accepts Him as the representative of the redeemed (Heb. 9:24), promises Him universal dominion (Matt. 28:18) and the outpouring of the Holy Spirit to apply redemption (Acts 1:4; 2:33).

- *the Son,* for His part, undertakes to become incarnate and live under the law (Gal. 4:4; Heb. 2:14-18), rendering perfect obedience to the Father (Heb. 10:7-9), including death on the cross (Phil. 2:8), ensuring that none of those given to Him would be lost (John 17:12).

- *the Holy Spirit* must not be overlooked in a properly Trinitarian formulation of the covenant. His role is to equip the incarnate Son with everything necessary for the fulfilment of His mission (Matt. 3:16; Luke 4:1, 14, 18; John 3:34) and to apply to the elect the benefits of redemption by which they are united to Christ (John 14:16-17, 26; Acts 1:8; 2:17-18, 33).

As Horton notes:

> The covenant of redemption underscores not only God's sovereignty and freedom in electing grace, but the Trinitarian and, specifically, Christ-centred character of that divine purpose. It all takes place 'in Christ'; hence the emphasis in covenant theology on the theme of 'Christ the mediator'.[13]

The way in which those 'chosen in Christ' benefit from the work of Christ on their behalf is also to be thought of covenantally. The eternal redemptive purpose of God unfolds historically in terms of what has been called the *Covenant of Grace*, the bond of love between God and His people.

At the heart of this covenant, which God sovereignly and graciously establishes, is the promise found, for example, in the words of Leviticus 26:12: 'I will walk among you and will be your God, and you shall be my people.' As Brian Vickers notes: 'This refrain, or something similar to it, is found in every covenantal

---

13. Michael Horton, *God of Promise*, p. 80.

era.'[14] Covenant, indeed, is one of the unifying themes in the unfolding of God's redemptive purpose. Thus when God establishes His covenant with Abraham in Genesis 17, He promises: 'I will establish my covenant between me and you and your offspring after you throughout their generations for an everlasting covenant, to be God to you and to your offspring after you' (v. 7). This covenant thread can be traced all the way through the Scriptures. Thus when the prophets look forward to the New Covenant, the promise that it will embody is again 'I will be their God, and they shall be my people' (Jer. 31:33). Further examples are to be found in Jeremiah 32:38 and Ezekiel 36:28; 37:27. When the new heaven and the new earth, the goal of God's redemptive plan, are described in Revelation 21, the 'loud voice from the throne' declares: 'Behold, the dwelling place of God is with man. He will dwell with them, and they will be his people, and God himself will be with them as their God' (Rev. 21:3).

The central covenant promise is of a new relationship to God that results from the atoning work of Christ. He fulfils the role of Mediator, dealing with the sin that destroyed the covenant in Eden and providing every blessing that the people of God require, ending with the full enjoyment of eternal life in the new creation. The fruit of eternal love to the utterly undeserving, this is indeed a Covenant of Grace. In covenantal union with Christ His people receive all the blessings of salvation which He has secured, including justification, adoption and sanctification, leading to resurrection and glorification which will mark the entrance of risen believers into the fullness of eternal life in fellowship with God. Passages such as 1 Corinthians 15:12ff. and Philippians 3:20-1 reveal a little of the wonders that God still has in store for His covenant people. As an expression of the infinite love of God, the Covenant of Grace cannot fail to reach its ordained goal. Nothing can separate us from God's love 'in Christ Jesus our Lord' (Rom. 8:38-9). Even the faith that is man's

---

14. Brian Vickers, *Justification by Grace through Faith*, p. 21, n.8.

response to God's initiative of grace is a divine gift (Eph. 2:8-9) and so all glory accrues to Him.

With this covenantal framework in mind we may now go on to see, in relation particularly to justification, the truth of John Murray's view that, 'Union with Christ is really the central truth of the whole doctrine of salvation not only in its application but also in its once-for-all accomplishment in the finished work of Christ.'[15]

2. Christ our Representative

With reference to the redemptive, propitiatory work of Christ, Paul in Romans 3:26 states that God's provision in Christ 'was to show his righteousness at this present time, so that he might be just and the justifier of the one who has faith in Jesus.' In addressing the sin of covenant-breaking rebels, guilty in Adam, God must be just, otherwise He would deny Himself in admitting them into fellowship with Himself. Thomas Boston states the problem and the solution in this way:

> The elect of God, lying under the breach of the first covenant, were dead in law, as being under the curse. They could not be restored to life in the eye of the law, but upon the fulfilling of the righteousness of the law; the which they not being able to do for themselves, Christ in the covenant undertook to do it for them; and thereupon was made the promise of their justification.[16]

If, as we have argued, the covenant is a bond of love, it involves more than legal considerations and relationships; it does nevertheless include the legal dimension. God cannot be in loving fellowship with those who are under the curse of the broken law

---

15. John Murray, *Redemption Accomplished and Applied* (Grand Rapids: Eerdmans 1955), p. 161.

16. Thomas Boston, *A View of the Covenant of Grace,* 1734 edition (Lewes: Focus Christian Ministries Trust 1990), p. 109. Although Boston did not accept the terminology Covenant of Redemption/Covenant of Grace, but held to a single covenant, his statement is still valid.

in Adam. Hence the need for the atoning work of the Christ who is, in Sinclair Ferguson's striking phrase, 'Adam in reverse'.[17]

Talk of justification takes us into the realm of law courts and legal proceedings, and consequently justification is rightly described as *'forensic'*. Although this is often disputed in recent writing on the subject, the traditional approach appears to be correct. In an exhaustive study of 'justification' language in both Old and New Testaments,[18] John Murray has demonstrated that in the overwhelming majority of cases the action in view is a *declaration* of a person's righteous standing. Thus when God 'justifies' someone, He is not making him righteous but declaring him to be righteous. According to Deuteronomy 25:1 judges settling a dispute 'justify the righteous and condemn the wicked' (NASB). The judges do not make either party righteous or wicked, but declare what their legal standing actually is. Justification stands in opposition to condemnation (as also in Prov. 17:15).

Not only is this the case in the Hebrew of the Old Testament, the same is true in the Greek of the New Testament. We read in Matthew 12:37: 'for by your words you will be justified, and by your words you will be condemned.' As Murray's analysis shows, when Paul in Romans 8:33 states, 'It is God who justifies', he has in his view God's declaration that His people are righteous in His sight. Robert Reymond sums up thus: 'This biblical evidence makes it clear that justification is a juridical or forensic determination made by a judge.'[19] Justification relates to the legal standing of a person before God, not to his spiritual condition. The law is, of course, God's own law, the expression of His holiness, not some external legal requirement. The sinner's condition of spiritual deadness is addressed in regeneration; his status of guilt and defilement by justification.

---

17. Sinclair B. Ferguson, *The Christian Life. A Doctrinal Introduction* (London: Hodder and Stoughton 1981), p. 95.

18. John Murray, *The Epistle to the Romans*, 1968 edition (Grand Rapids/Cambridge: Eerdmans 1997), volume 1, appendix A, pp. 336–62.

19. Robert L. Reymond, *A New Systematic Theology of the Christian Faith* (Nashville: Thomas Nelson 1998), p. 745.

A common objection to a forensic, declarative view of justification is that it involves a legal fiction whereby God pretends that those who are actually sinful are in fact righteous. We will engage with questions about the basis of justification below, but some response to the objection may be made at this point. If God were to pretend that those who are sinful are righteous He would be contradicting His own nature and behaving unrighteously. Part of the answer to this apparent problem relates to the availability of a righteousness that God takes into account in His declaration, namely the righteousness of Christ. Another consideration is noted by John Murray: 'The peculiarity of God's action consists in this that he causes to be the righteous state or relation which is declared to be.'[20] God grants to the sinner who has been regenerated and united to Christ a new judicial standing. God constitutes him righteous and can thus in perfect justice declare him to be righteous. God's act of justification is *constitutive* as well as *declarative*. That is the significance of Romans 5:19: 'For as by the one man's disobedience the many were made sinners, so by the one man's obedience the many will be made righteous.' This must be linked with verse 17 which speaks of 'the free gift of righteousness'. God constitutes His people righteous and then passes the appropriate judicial verdict upon them, not only that they are 'not guilty' but also that they are positively righteous.

To discover the righteousness which God takes into account in justification, and so to see how He is just as well as the justifier of those who have faith in Jesus, we need to consider the role of the Son as our representative.

The parallels and contrasts between Adam and Christ set out by Paul in Romans 5 take us to the heart of the matter. Both act in a representative, covenantal capacity. Union with Adam brings death and separation from God. If men are to be restored to covenant fellowship with God their sin and covenant-breaking must be addressed. As Donald Macleod puts it: 'The covenant-*breaking* of the First Man (and of all mankind) is covered by

---

20. John Murray, *Redemption Accomplished and Applied*, p. 123.

the covenant-*keeping* of the Last Man, the Lord Jesus Christ.'[21] In undertaking in the Covenant of Redemption to save those whom the Father had given Him, the Son committed Himself to the path of obedience which required the keeping perfectly of the law of God, specifically the requirements of the Covenant of Works, and the bearing of the sins of His people who have broken that covenant. In other words, the righteousness that is necessary for justification is provided by Christ for all who are 'in him'.

Christ is perfectly qualified to be our representative in His covenantal, redemptive work. As the eternal Son, the second Person of the Trinity, His work has infinite value, so that the innumerable multitude given to Him by the Father will be saved, and there is no doubt that this is the gracious initiative of God throughout. We must also stress equally strongly, however, that it is the *incarnate* Son who represents us. We must not lose sight of the truth of Hebrews 2:17: 'Therefore he had to be made like his brothers in every respect, so that he might become a merciful and faithful high priest in the service of God, to make propitiation for the sins of his people.' Robert Letham sums up the necessity of the Son's taking human nature thus:

> Christ, in his incarnate life and ministry, was the second Adam. Man had sinned; man must put things right, not only by avoiding sin but by actually rendering to God the obedience that Adam failed to supply.[22]

By virtue of the virgin birth (better, the virgin conception) by the power of the Holy Spirit, the corrupting link with Adam was broken. Alone of the human race, Jesus of Nazareth was not 'in Adam'.

Incarnation of itself, however, is not sufficient to explain the redemptive nature of Christ's work. It is when we see the role

---

21. Donald Macleod, *A Faith to Live By* (Fearn: Christian Focus 1998), p. 98.

22. Robert Letham, *Union with Christ in Scripture, History and Theology* (Phillipsburg: P & R Publishing 2011), p. 58.

assigned to and accepted by Him in the Covenant of Redemption that we have the necessary explanation. We may note the description of Christ in Hebrews 7:22 as the 'guarantor' (ESV), 'guarantee' (NIV, NASB) or 'surety' (AV) of 'a better covenant'. The surety is one who undertakes to be responsible for the meeting of another party's legal obligations. On this basis Christ has undertaken the obligations of His elect people. As Scottish theologian Hugh Martin demonstrates at length, the covenantal framework offers the best explanation of Christ's role. As Martin says of 'the everlasting covenant oneness' that exists between Christ and His people:

> That is the great underlying relation. That is the grand primary conjunction between the Redeemer and the redeemed, which alone bears up, and justifies, and accounts for all else in respect of relation which can be predicated as true concerning them.[23]

The righteousness required for justification is that provided by the obedience of Christ on behalf of His people. It has become traditional in theology to distinguish between the 'active' and 'passive' obedience of Christ, although Brian Vickers comments that 'it is practically impossible to separate obedience neatly into two parts'.[24] Broadly speaking, the 'passive' obedience of Christ is His enduring death on the cross (although at no point is He a helpless 'passive' victim), whilst His 'active' obedience is His perfect keeping of God's law throughout His life. The two elements are interwoven and inseparable, and as we will see, both are necessary for justification. This is well summarised in covenantal terms by Scott Clark:

> I contend that, as the voluntary surety entailed by the covenant of redemption between the Father and the Son (*pactum salutis*) and as the Second Adam required by the Covenant of Works,

---

23. Hugh Martin, *The Atonement: In its Relations to the Covenant, the Priesthood, the Intercession of Our Lord,* 1870 edition. (Edinburgh: Banner of Truth 2013), pp. 23–8.

24. Brian Vickers, *Justification by Grace through Faith*, p. 39.

God the Son became incarnate to fulfil the legal obligations of these covenants. By his active suffering obedience to God's law as expressed in these covenants, he not only propitiated the divine wrath and expiated sin but also merited justification and eternal life for his people.[25]

The damage done by the sin of Adam for all those 'in Adam' is undone by the obedience of Christ for all those 'in Christ'. As John Fesko states the situation:

> There is a parallel between the two federal heads, the first and last Adams: just as Adam's disobedience and guilt are imputed to those whom he represents, so too Christ's obedience, or righteousness, is imputed to those whom he represents.[26]

3. Redemption accomplished

As John Murray says: 'Union with Christ is really the central truth of the whole doctrine of salvation not only in its application but also in its once-for-all accomplishment in the finished work of Christ.'[27] It is to that finished work that we now turn our attention, bearing in mind the comment of Herman Bavinck that, 'There is no sharing in the benefits of Christ unless we share in His person, because the benefits are not to be separated from the person.'[28] This truth flows from Paul's statement in Ephesians 1:3 that God 'has blessed us in Christ with every spiritual blessing in the heavenly places.'

It is particularly important to bear in mind that justification entails more than the forgiveness of sins, however wonderful that in itself might be. In justification God declares those who are in

---

25. R. Scott Clark, 'Do This and Live' in *Covenant, Justification and Pastoral Ministry*, pp. 243–4.

26. J. V. Fesko, *Justification. Understanding the Classic Reformed Doctrine* (Phillipsburg: P & R Publishing 2008), p. 135.

27. John Murray, *Redemption Accomplished and Applied*, p. 161.

28. Herman Bavinck, *Our Reasonable Faith: A Survey of Christian Doctrine*, 1867 edition (Grand Rapids: Baker Book House 1977), p. 399.

Christ positively righteous. As far as forgiveness is concerned, Paul in Romans 4:7-8 can quote David's words in Psalm 32:1-2: 'Blessed are those whose lawless deeds are forgiven, and whose sins are covered; blessed is the man against whom the Lord will not count his sin.' Paul also speaks, however, of a further dimension of justification when he refers in Romans 5:17 to 'the abundance of grace and the free gift of righteousness' which come 'through the one man Jesus Christ'. He repeats the thought in verse 19 when he says that 'by the one man's obedience the many will be made righteous'. Justification confers not only a status of 'not guilty' but also a status of 'righteous', such that God's people receive 'the righteousness of God through faith in Christ Jesus for all who believe' (Rom. 3:22).

The source of the righteousness required so that God can justify the ungodly whilst Himself remaining just (Rom. 3:26) is the obedience of Christ, our covenant head, in both His life and His death. The obedience of Christ is thus set against the disobedience of Adam in a passage such as Romans 5:12ff.

In what is traditionally termed His 'passive obedience', Christ bore the full penal consequences of the sins of all of those 'chosen in him' from eternity. This is indicated in His own statement that 'the Son of Man came not to be served but to serve, and to give his life as a ransom for many' (Mark 10:45). The same perspective informs Old Testament passages such as the portrayal in Isaiah 53 of the Suffering Servant who was 'wounded for our transgressions . . . crushed for our iniquities' (v. 5) and New Testament passages such as 1 Peter 1:18-19: 'you were ransomed . . . with the precious blood of Christ, like that of a lamb without blemish or spot.' The language of the atoning sacrifice of a lamb is found in John the Baptist's reference to 'the Lamb of God, who takes away the sin of the world' (John 1:29). Paul describes the redemptive action of God thus: 'For our sake he made him to be sin who knew no sin, so that in him we might become the righteousness of God' (2 Cor. 5:21); and again: 'Christ redeemed us from the curse of the law by becoming a curse for us – for it is written, "Cursed is everyone who is hanged on a tree".' (Gal. 3:13). Thus by 'becoming obedient to the point of death, even death on a cross' (Phil. 2:8), Christ has taken the punishment due to the covenant-breaking of His people, dying 'the righteous for the unrighteous' (1 Pet. 3:18).

More must be said regarding Christ's obedience, however, and this brings into account His 'active obedience'. As James Buchanan rightly observes:

> The precept, not less than the penalty, of the Law must be fulfilled; and His fulfilment of both is the complete satisfaction which he rendered to the Law and Justice of God.[29]

Since this is the case, there is great merit in Robert Reymond's description of this aspect of Christ's work as His 'preceptive obedience',[30] thus avoiding any suggestion that He was 'passive' in offering Himself on the cross.

In Eden God required perfect fulfilment of His law on the part of Adam as covenant head of the human race in the Covenant of Works. The fact of the fall, with its terrible consequences for all mankind, does not abolish the divine requirement for perfect obedience to His Law. The demand throughout human history remains: 'You shall therefore love the LORD your God and keep his charge, his statutes, his rules, and his commandments always' (Deut. 11:1). Sin indeed is defined in 1 John 3:4 as 'lawlessness', and this includes not only the breaking of particular commands but also the failure to keep the Law's requirements. If sinners are to be declared righteous in God's sight, that perfect obedience is necessary, yet the sinner is unable to supply it.[31]

This underlines the crucial importance of the active, preceptive obedience of Christ. At His baptism, in response

---

29. James Buchanan, *The Doctrine of Justification*, 1867 edition (Grand Rapids: Baker Book House 1977), p. 308.

30. Robert L. Reymond, *A New Systematic Theology of the Christian Faith* (Nashville: Thomas Nelson 1998), p. 631.

31. John Murray, 'The Obedience of Christ' in *Collected Writings of John Murray, vol. 2* (Edinburgh: Banner of Truth 1977), p. 151.

to John's reluctance, Jesus stated the necessity for this act, and for His life of obedience: 'Let it be so now, for thus it is fitting for us to fulfil all righteousness' (Matt. 3:15). As John Murray comments: 'This shows that the fulfilment of righteousness in all its detail and extent was the demand of Jesus' commission.' Throughout His public ministry Jesus testified to His delight in obeying His Father's commands. As the covenant head of His people He rendered full and willing obedience to God's Law throughout His life. He was 'born under the Law, to redeem those who were under the Law' (Gal. 4:4) and nothing less than perfect obedience was required. Thus He could testify: 'For I have come down from heaven, not to do my own will but the will of him who sent me' (John 6:38). What the law requires must be done on behalf of and in the place of His covenant people.[32]

It is in this context that Romans 5:12-21 is to be understood.[33] The two covenant heads are set in contrast, one disobedient, bringing death for all who are 'in' him, the other obedient, bringing life for all who are 'in' Him (as indicated also in 1 Cor. 15:22). The disobedience of 'the first man' is matched by the obedience of 'the last Adam', to use Paul's terminology in 1 Corinthians 15:45. As Paul expresses it in Romans 5:19: 'For as by the one man's disobedience the many were made sinners, so by the one man's obedience the many will be made righteous.' Sinners will, in Christ, be declared righteous because Christ's obedience satisfies divine justice and provides the required righteousness which the 'works of the law' (Rom. 3:20) could never provide. In view are condemnation and justification, the contrast underlining the forensic, declarative nature of justification. In Christ there is 'the grace of God and the free gift by the grace of that one man Jesus Christ' (Rom. 5:15), and the legal basis for this blessing is His obedience. In verse 16 Paul is even more specific: 'the free

---

32. On Christ as Substitute and as Representative, see Robert Letham, *Union with Christ*, pp. 60–2.

33. This passage is expounded helpfully by Scott Clark in 'Do This and Live', pp. 246–9.

gift following many trespasses brought justification', and in verse 17 he states that the free gift is 'righteousness'. Paul does not separate out different aspects of Christ's obedience (active and passive) but treats it as a seamless whole, such that he can say, 'one act of righteousness leads to justification and life for all men' (v. 18) and 'by the one man's obedience the many will be made righteous' (v. 19).

The obedience of Christ throughout His life and on the cross is therefore the source of the righteousness required by His people, dealing both with the penalty incurred by the broken law and with the need for perfect law-keeping. For those 'in Christ' all of this is provided.

4. Christ the Justified One

Every spiritual blessing that believers receive is 'in Christ', as Ephesians 1:3 indicates. As noted above in a quotation from Herman Bavinck, in relation to Christ 'the benefits are not to be separated from the person'.[34] Believers are united in covenant bonds with Christ crucified and risen. This leads Lane Tipton to comment:

> Union with Christ is a soteric replication in the structure of the believer's life-experience of what happened antecedently in the life-experience of Christ, namely death and resurrection.[35]

Combining Ephesians 2:5-6, regarding believers, with Ephesians 1:19-20, regarding Christ, we see that such an assertion is warranted. Not only are the life-experiences parallel; that of Christ is the ground for that of believers 'in him'.

As Tipton argues, Christ's bodily resurrection, as an eschatological event in salvation history, includes within it His own justification, adoption and sanctification. This is demonstrated

---

34. See note 28 above.

35. Lane G. Tipton, 'Union with Christ and Justification' in K. Scott Oliphint (ed.), *Justified in Christ. God's plan for us in Justification*, (Fearn: Mentor 2007), p. 25. The following paragraphs are indebted to Tipton's article.

with respect to justification by a text such as 1 Timothy 3:16 'vindicated (or justified) by the Spirit'; with respect to adoption by Romans 1:4 'declared to be the Son of God in power according to the Spirit of holiness by his resurrection from the dead'; and with respect to sanctification by Romans 6:9-11 which among other things states that 'the death he died he died to sin, once for all, but the life he lives he lives to God' (v. 10). The pattern is humiliation followed by exaltation. To speak of Christ justified in, or by, the Spirit points to His relationship to the Spirit-wrought act of re-creation that dawns in His resurrection. By the mighty working of the Spirit He becomes the first participant in the new order of glory and imperishability which Paul describes in 1 Corinthians 15:42-9. Christ's resurrection, understood as His justification, places Him as second Adam and as Messiah in full possession of eschatological righteousness. 'Jesus' justification in the Spirit is an irreversible and declarative act that demonstrates his eschatological righteousness', says Tipton.[36]

How is this so? The resurrection of Jesus as His justification follows from the fact that He died as a substitutionary sacrifice for His people, thereby bearing the just wrath and condemnation of God upon the sins of His people. This is evident from texts such as Romans 3:24-5; 4:5; 2 Corinthians 5:21 and Hebrews 9:26-8. When He was 'made sin' the judicial verdict of guilt and condemnation was pronounced upon Him, a verdict which can be reversed only by a judicial declaration of justification, stating His righteousness in God's sight. When the covenantal character of Jesus' obedience is recognised, namely the way in which His active and passive obedience satisfies the just demands of the Covenant of Works, then it is clear that His resurrection must involve a judicial declaration of His righteousness.

The resurrection therefore includes as one of its aspects the declaration by God the Father that the incarnate Son has met in full all the demands of divine justice arising from the breaking of

---

36. Tipton, 'Union with Christ and Justification' in K. Scott Oliphint (ed.), *Justified in Christ. God's plan for us in Justification*, p. 30.

the Covenant of Works by Adam and, consequently, all who are 'in him', both in regard to the positive precept and also in regard to the penal sanction. Christ has thus provided the obedience necessary for the salvation of those given to Him in eternity. Since He truly bore their guilt and condemnation in His life and His death, it follows that his resurrection includes a justifying dimension whereby He is declared righteous in God's sight.

Christ, crucified and risen, therefore contains within Himself every soteriological benefit conferred on His people in the Covenant of Grace. In this regard we may note 1 Corinthians 1:30: 'He is the source of your life in Christ Jesus, whom God made our wisdom and our righteousness and sanctification and redemption.' This ESV translation obscures somewhat the fact that Paul defines the 'wisdom' that Christ has been made for us as righteousness, sanctification and redemption (the NIV brings this out well). 'In Christ' is to be found the full, multifaceted reality of salvation. In Him there is righteousness, sanctification and redemption: He has become the crucified and resurrected embodiment of them for His covenant people.

Christ's obedience unto death and His consequent resurrection thus have absolutely decisive significance for the justification of believers. He was 'delivered up for our trespasses and raised for our justification' (Rom. 4:25). Christ was not justified until His resurrection: that is the moment of divine declaration. By virtue of their covenantal union with Him, Christ's people are comprehended within that event. As Paul puts it in Romans 6:4: 'Just as Christ was raised from the dead by the glory of the Father, we too might walk in newness of life.' The comprehensive 'newness of life' entailed by union with the risen Christ includes believers' justification. Christ's resurrection has unique relevance to the justification of believers since His acquittal, the declaration of His righteousness, is effected in His resurrection. Christ rises for His own justification and also for the justification of believers. As Tipton puts it:

> By virtue of faith union with the resurrected Christ, all of his meritorious active and passive obedience, all that he is as crucified and raised unto justification, is reckoned to believers.[37]

---

37. ibid., p. 32.

5. Justified in Christ

> It is essential to the heart of the gospel to insist that God declares
> us to be just or righteous not on the basis of our actual condition
> of righteousness or holiness, but rather on the basis of Christ's
> perfect righteousness, which he thinks of as belonging to us.[38]

In these words Wayne Grudem accurately sums up one of the
issues at the heart of Reformation debates between Protestantism
and Roman Catholicism, an issue which recent discussions of
justification show to be of abiding significance. The fundamental
question is whether justification is based on something God does
for us or something He does *in* us. The current official position
of Rome, as stated in the *Catechism of the Catholic Church*, is clearly
the latter:

> Justification is conferred in Baptism, the sacrament of faith.
> It conforms us to the righteousness of God, who makes us
> inwardly just by the power of his mercy.[39]

The Reformation, and biblical, perspective is that justification
is something that God does for us, a constitutive declaration of
righteousness that He makes on the basis of a righteousness
external to the sinner. For Rome, infused righteousness is the
key; for the heirs of the Reformation it is imputed righteousness
that is crucial.

When God by the powerful regenerating work of the
Holy Spirit brings a sinner into the bond of love which is the
Covenant of Grace, that sinner is united to Christ in His death
and resurrection and becomes the beneficiary of all the blessings
purchased by the Saviour. In the language of 1 Corinthians 1:30,
noted above, He is 'our righteousness and sanctification and
redemption'. When dealing with this issue Calvin divided the
benefits of union with Christ into two:

---

38.   Wayne Grudem, *Systematic Theology. An Introduction to Biblical Doctrine*, p. 727.

39.   *Catechism of the Catholic Church* (Dublin: Veritas 1994), §1992, p. 433.

By partaking of him, we principally receive a double grace [*duplicem gratiam*]: namely, that being reconciled to God through Christ's blamelessness, we may have in heaven instead of a Judge, a gracious Father; and secondly, that sanctified by Christ's spirit we may cultivate blamelessness and purity of life.[40]

The basis on which a sinner is justified before God is not anything in himself but solely the righteousness of Christ, which is counted by God as belonging to those who are 'in him'. This is the language of 'imputation' which draws on texts such as Romans 4:6: 'David also speaks of the blessing of the one to whom God *counts* righteousness apart from works.' The verb Paul uses, *logizesthai,* has the sense of 'count, reckon, impute'. Thomas Schreiner defines it in this way:

The conception is that something is reckoned to a person that is not inherent to him or her . . . God's righteousness is not native to human beings; it is an alien righteousness granted to us by God's grace.[41]

In the same vein John Piper notes: 'Paul speaks immediately in terms of something *external* (a wage) being credited to our account, rather than something *internal* (faith) being treated as righteousness.'[42] This is the third strand of imputation in the New Testament, with the sin of Adam imputed to all 'in him', the sin of the elect imputed to Christ and finally the righteousness of Christ imputed to those 'in him'. Justification therefore involves 'the righteousness from God that depends on faith' (Phil. 3:9), 'the righteousness of God through faith in Jesus Christ for all who believe' (Rom. 3:22).

---

40. John Calvin, *Institutes of the Christian Religion*, 1559 edition. Trans. Ford Lewis Battles (Philadelphia: The Westminster Press 1960), III.xi.i. Note Richard B. Gaffin's correction to 'by his Spirit' in 'Justification and Union with Christ' in David W. Hall and Peter A. Lillback (eds.) *A Theological Guide to Calvin's Institutes. Essays and Analysis* (Phillipsburg: P & R Publishing 2008), p. 252, n.8.

41. Thomas R. Schreiner, *Romans*. Baker Exegetical Commentary on the New Testament (Grand Rapids: Baker Books 1998), p. 215.

42   John Piper, *Counted Righteous in Christ. Should We Abandon the Imputation of Christ's Righteousness?* (Wheaton: Crossway Books 2002), p. 56.

Another crucial text in relation to the reception of justification is 2 Corinthians 5:21: 'For our sake he made him to be sin who knew no sin, so that in him we might become the righteousness of God.' We do not have space to enter into the complex debates that have raged around terms such as 'the righteousness of God'. We agree, however, with the conclusion of Brian Vickers who, after painstaking exegesis of the verse in context, states:

> The meaning of 'become the righteousness of God' is qualified by the short but powerful phrase 'in him'. This is not an abstract notion of righteousness conceived as a mere transaction, but a declaration that whoever is 'in Christ' has a right standing before God owing to the fact that he is in union with Christ.[43]

Paul brings together becoming a new creation, being united to Christ in His death and resurrection and becoming the righteousness of God in Christ. Of God's people, Vickers says: 'They "become" God's righteousness, and are declared to be righteous, just as they are united with Christ who is the embodiment and revelation of God's righteousness.'[44] By virtue of union with the crucified and risen Christ, their covenant head, who is now the Justified One, they too are justified by virtue of His perfect righteousness being imputed to them.

It is important to see that it is the righteousness of Christ in its fullest sense, His righteousness constituted by both His active and His passive obedience, that is counted as belonging to His people. The plight in which sinners find themselves as covenant-breakers underlines the fact that this must be the case if they are to be justified. In Eden Adam was not only free of sin, he was positively righteous in God's sight. As 'very good' according to Genesis 1:31, he was not merely in a state of moral neutrality, he was positively righteous. That position was forfeited by the fall for Adam and for those 'in him', and so sinners require both the forgiveness of sin

---

43. Brian Vickers, *Jesus' Blood and Righteousness. Paul's Theology of Imputation* (Wheaton: Crossway Books 2006), p. 183.
44. ibid., p. 187.

and the gift of positive righteousness if they are to be righteous in God's sight. Thus justification entails the forgiveness of sin on the basis of Christ's redemptive suffering (His passive obedience) and also positive righteousness on the basis of Christ's life of perfect holiness (His active obedience). Although some who accept the imputation of Christ's passive obedience have rejected the idea of the imputation of His active obedience, it seems clear that both elements are necessary for justification.

The active/passive distinction with respect to Christ's obedience and consequent righteousness has value as a tool for theological analysis of His saving work, but it is significant that Paul, for example, writes in a passage such as Romans 5:12-21 of Christ's righteousness without distinguishing elements within it. Paul here contrasts the disobedience of the first Adam with the obedience of the last Adam, the former bringing condemnation, the latter justification and eternal life. On the one hand 'one trespass led to condemnation for all men' (Rom. 5:18). It is straightforward to see this as Adam's single act of eating the forbidden fruit, thus breaking the covenant with God. Paul then goes on to say, 'so one act of righteousness leads to justification and life for all men.' What is the 'one act'? It does not seem warranted to confine the reference to a single moment in Christ's experience, such as the crucifixion. Fesko is right to comment,: 'It is impossible to isolate the crucifixion from the life and resurrection of Christ in connection with justification.'[45] John Murray expresses this perspective helpfully:

> The righteousness of Christ is regarded in its compact unity in parallelism with the one trespass, and there is good reason for speaking of it as the one righteous act because, as the one trespass is the trespass of the one, so the one righteousness is the righteousness of the one and the unity of the person and of his accomplishment must always be assumed.[46]

---

45. J. V. Fesko, *Justification. Understanding the Classic Reformed Doctrine*, p. 155.

46. John Murray, *The Epistle to the Romans,* (Grand Rapids/Cambridge: Eerdmans 1968), ad loc. (I.201–202). Some writers, such as John Piper, disagree with this exegesis of Romans 5:18 whilst still arguing for the imputation of Christ's active obedience.

The ground of justification is the righteousness of Christ as He paid the penalty due to His people's law-breaking and as He Himself rendered perfect obedience to the divine Law. That righteousness is imputed to all who are 'in him'. God regards them as having provided that righteousness although it was provided by their Substitute who at every point acted for them. Although many objections have been raised against the concept of imputation of Christ's righteousness or, in a more limited way, against the imputation of the active obedience of Christ (Scott Clark answers seven in his study of the subject),[47] this is the heart of the biblical doctrine of justification, without which the gospel is lost. Those brought into the Covenant of Grace received the gift of an 'alien' righteousness, the righteousness of Christ in His life, death and resurrection. Far from being based on a legal fiction, justification is grounded in the comprehensive obedience of the incarnate Son of God, the covenant head of those chosen 'in him' in eternity.

6. Grace, faith and works

In conversion the Spirit of God brings sinners into the Covenant of Grace, the bond of love between the Triune God and His people, the Mediator of the covenant being the Lord Jesus Christ who shed 'the blood of the eternal covenant' (Heb. 13:20). God's people are brought into union with the three Persons of the Trinity, each of whom is said to indwell them. Thus Jesus says in John 14:23: 'If anyone loves me, he will keep my word, and my Father will love him, and we will come to him and make our home with him.' In the same chapter Jesus speaks of the outpouring of the Holy Spirit and tells His disciples: 'You know him, for he dwells with you and will be in you' (v. 17). It is, however, the believer's union with Christ that is the focus of attention in the New Testament.

---

47. Clark answers objections that the doctrine leads to Antinomianism, diminishes the cross, relies on Roman categories of merit, relies on a legal fiction, makes the filial superior to the legal, should be replaced by union with Christ, and is not confessional. See R. Scott Clark, 'Do This and Live', pp. 252–65.

At the heart of the gospel we have 'the riches of the glory of this mystery, which is Christ in you, the hope of glory' (Col. 1:27). Christ is in His people and they are in Him. Christ continues to make known the Father's name to His disciples 'that the love with which you have loved me may be in them, and I in them' (John 17:26). Crucified and risen with Christ, believers experience the Covenant of Grace as a living, loving relationship rooted in His work for them as their covenant representative. The legal and the experiential come together in the Covenant of Grace as the Lord's people experience all the blessings secured for them by His obedience on their behalf, including justification, adoption and sanctification.

With regard to the sinner's reception of justification, several issues require some consideration since error in any of these areas rips the heart out of the gospel.

Grace

As Paul states in Romans 3:24, we are 'justified by his grace as a gift through the redemption that is in Christ Jesus'. Paul regularly refers to righteousness as a 'free gift' (e.g., Rom. 5:15, 17) and in one of the best-known texts setting out the heart of the gospel, Ephesians 2:8-9, we are told: 'For by grace you have been saved through faith. And this is not your own doing; it is the gift of God, not a result of works, so that no-one may boast.'

Grace is at the heart of all God's covenantal dealings with man: even the Covenant of Works in Eden was a gracious provision of God for the blessing of Adam and his posterity. God is under no necessity of nature to deal with man in these loving ways. When God rewards works, it is not because of some obligation that He must meet, but rather because He has graciously placed Himself by covenant in such a position.

In the New Testament presentation of justification there is therefore a clear antithesis between the principle of grace and the principle of works. The two cannot be combined in any way without destroying the principle of grace. Paul makes this clear, for example, in Romans 11:5-6, when he refers to the remnant chosen by grace and states: 'So too there is a remnant, chosen by grace. But if it is by grace, it is no longer on the basis of works; otherwise grace would no longer be grace.' The principle of grace excludes the principle of works.

The greatest care must be exercised to maintain this antithesis since compromise is fatal to a biblical understanding of justification. An outright denial of grace in favour of works is not necessary; a mixing of the principles is all that is required. Thus Roman Catholic theology speaks much of grace in relation to salvation, in particular to justification. In the *Catechism of the Catholic Church* we read: 'Our justification comes from the grace of God.'[48] Leaving aside the fact that Rome's definition of justification includes sanctification and renewal, we note that grace is 'infused by the Holy Spirit into our soul to heal it of sin and to sanctify it.'[49] Grace enables man to co-operate with God on the basis of the freedom of his own will (which has not been lost in the fall). Much is made of 'the free response of man': 'Grace responds to the deepest yearnings of human freedom, calls freedom to co-operate with it and perfects freedom.'[50] The fatal compromise is thus made, allowing something in man to be taken into account in justification. The Pauline antithesis no longer holds.

Faith

Union with Christ is a faith-union and justification is by faith alone. Although Luther was attacked by opponents when he translated Romans 3:28 as 'by faith *alone*', adding a word absent from the Greek, Luther was theologically correct. In the previous verses Paul indicates that Christ and His propitiation are 'to be received by faith' (v. 25) and that God is 'the justifier of the one who has faith in Jesus' (v. 26). In Romans 4 Paul develops at length the antithesis between justification on the basis of works

---

48.   *Catechism of the Catholic Church*, §1996, p. 434.

49.   ibid., §1999, p. 434.

50.   ibid., §2022, p. 439.

and justification on the basis of faith, as exemplified in the experience of Abraham. In addition, a text such as Ephesians 2:8-9, quoted above with reference to grace, demonstrates that faith, itself a divine gift, stands in absolute contrast to works in the realm of salvation.

Leaving aside debates as to whether God's covenant with His people is 'conditional' or 'unconditional', it is clear that faith is required of those who would enjoy the blessings of the covenant, including justification. Neither the sovereignty nor the grace of God is compromised by this requirement since God graciously supplies what He requires by the powerful working of the Holy Spirit who produces faith in the elect, as He opened the heart of Lydia (Acts 16:14).

The biblical understanding of saving faith is well summed up in Chapter XIV of the Westminster Confession of Faith: 'the principal acts of saving faith are accepting, receiving and resting upon Christ alone for justification, sanctification and eternal life, by virtue of the covenant of grace.' This may be combined with the statement in Chapter XI: 'Faith, thus receiving and resting on Christ and His righteousness, is the alone instrument of justification.' This contrasts sharply with the Roman Catholic view which, whilst speaking of the necessity of faith for justification, views that faith in a very different way. Drawing on Aquinas, Rome begins with the necessity of *fides informis* – an intellectual assent to church dogma. To this must be added *fides formata caritate*. As Robert Godfrey helpfully explains, 'Saving faith must be more than unformed faith. To unformed faith must be added love, which gives form, life and saving effect to faith.'[51] The way in which this perspective destroys justification by faith alone is evident from Canon 11 of the sixth session of the Council of Trent:

> If any one saith, that men are justified, either by the sole imputation of the justice of Christ, or by the sole remission of sins, to the exclusion of the grace and the charity which is

---

51. W. Robert Godfrey, 'Faith Formed by Love or Faith Alone? The Instrument of Justification' in *Covenant, Justification and Pastoral Ministry*', p. 269.

poured forth in their hearts by the Holy Ghost, or is inherent in them; or even that the grace, whereby we are justified, is only the favour of God: let him be anathema.[52]

Fatally, justification is tied to something God does *in* the sinner.

The sole instrumentality of faith for justification must be maintained. Paul speaks of justification 'by' (*dia*) or 'through' (*ek*) faith – both in Romans 3:30 for example, but never 'on the basis of faith'. The meritorious ground of justification is the righteousness of Christ, never the faith of the believer. This is not contradicted in any way by Genesis 15:6, quoted by Paul in Romans 4:3, 'Abraham believed God, and it was counted to him as righteousness.' At first sight it might appear that this text is teaching that although Abraham had no works as a basis for justification, he did have faith, which God accepted in the place of works and on that basis declared him righteous in His sight. If that were indeed the case, faith would have become a basis for the declaration of righteousness, rather than the imputed righteousness of Christ, and indeed faith would have become a kind of 'work' produced by Abraham, and, it may be supposed, other justified sinners.

What are we to make of this possibility? The context of Paul's quotation should immediately make us wary of such a position: he argues vigorously and at length that 'by works of the law no human being will be justified in his sight' (Rom. 3:20), he sets the principles of faith and works in antithesis (4:4-5) and concludes 'to the one who does not work but trusts him who justifies the ungodly, his faith is counted as righteousness' (4:5). How therefore is this latter expression, together with the example of Abraham, to be understood? Having recognised that 'The passage is notoriously complex',[53] Don Carson exegetes the verses

---

52. The Canons and Decrees of the Council of Trent, Session 6, Canon 11 in Philip Schaff (ed.) *The Creeds of Christendom: With a History and Critical Notes*, 6th edition, revised by David S. Schaff (Grand Rapids: Baker Book House 1983), 2.112–113.

53. D. A. Carson, 'The Vindication of Imputation. On Fields of Discourse and Semantic Fields' in Mark Husbands and Daniel J. Treier (eds.) *Justification. What's at Stake in the Current Debate*, (Downers Grove and Leicester: InterVarsity Press and Apollos 2004), p. 56.

painstakingly against the background of contemporary Jewish thought and concludes, in agreement with Herman Ridderbos, that 'this crediting of faith as righteousness [is] an instrumental usage'.[54] This faith is imputed as righteousness because it is faith in the God who will fulfil the promise of the 'seed', the word concerning Christ's redemptive work. As Carson expresses it:

> The righteousness that God imputes to the ungodly is bound up with his promises concerning the seed, and thus ultimately with his word concerning Christ's death and resurrection. Faith in such a God is faith that is imputed as righteousness, not because the faith is itself meritorious but because it focuses absolutely on the God who justifies the ungodly by the means he has promised.[55]

Nothing in Genesis 15:6 undermines the principle of 'faith alone' or of the righteousness of Christ as the sole basis for justification.

Works

We have noted above that the principles of grace and faith stand in an antithetical relationship to works in relation to justification. It needs to be recognised, however, that justifying faith 'is not alone in the person justified, but is ever accompanied with all other saving graces, and is no dead faith, but worketh by love' (Westminster Confession of Faith, XI.2). True faith is invariably accompanied by good works. Thus in Ephesians 2:10 Paul, having just stated that salvation is by grace through faith, goes on to say that we are 'created in Christ Jesus for good works, which God prepared beforehand, that we should walk in them.' Such joyful good works are done in willing obedience to God's Law, the believer's guide for life in the Covenant of Grace. It is for this reason that God's people can sing, 'Oh how I love your law!' (Ps. 119:97) and John can

---

54. Carson, 'The Vindication of Imputation. On Fields of Discourse and Semantic Fields' in Mark Husbands and Daniel J. Treier (eds.) *Justification. What's at Stake in the Current Debate*, p. 66.

55. ibid., p. 67.

write: 'This is the love of God, that we keep his commandments. And his commandments are not burdensome' (1 John 5:3). It is clear throughout Scripture that God's love demonstrated in His covenant requires a response of love which expresses itself in willing obedience to His Law. Thus Paul, who opposed any notion of justification by works of the law can ask, 'Do we then overthrow the law by this faith?' and respond 'By no means! On the contrary, we uphold the law.' (Rom. 3:31)

This explains how we are to understand James' assertion that 'a person is justified by works and not by faith alone' (James 2:24). At first sight this appears to be a flat contradiction of Paul's doctrine of justification by faith, but careful attention to the context of such statements in the whole letter shows that the 'justification' of which James speaks is the believer's demonstrating his genuine, saving faith to the surrounding world by his works. Paul deals with how a sinner may be justified before God: James deals with how he demonstrates that standing to others. The two apostles do not conflict in any respect.[56] Such evidential works will be the basis of rewards at the Last Day (2 Cor. 5:10), but never of justification.

Conclusion

By virtue of union with Christ in the Covenant of Grace, the 'righteous' verdict of the Judge before whom they will stand at the Last Day has already been pronounced on those who are 'in him'. By virtue of His perfect righteousness, imputed to them, the burden of their sin and guilt has been lifted, they are counted righteous in God's sight and are set free to serve God in joyful obedience to the law which could never justify them. From first to last it is the fruit of the infinite, eternal love of the Triune God who justifies the ungodly on the basis of the life, death and resurrection of the incarnate Son. All the glory and praise thus belong to God alone.

---

56. See e.g., Wayne Grudem, *Systematic Theology. An Introduction to Christian Doctrine*, pp. 730–2.

QUESTIONS FOR DISCUSSION

1. What misunderstandings of the doctrine of justification have you encountered?

2. How does a covenantal approach enhance our understanding of union with Christ and justification?

3. Some theologians consider union with Christ to be a consequence of justification, rather than justification to be a consequence of union. How significant are such differences in relating these two truths?

4. What is lost when the active obedience of Christ is not taken into account in formulating the doctrine of justification?

5. How may the linked truths of union with Christ and justification be applied pastorally?

6. How may we present the doctrine of justification in a culture that has little or no conception of divine law or of personal sin?

CHAPTER SIX

◆

'Union with Christ' and Sanctification

Paul Wells

Relating union with Christ to sanctification presents a dual challenge. Firstly, the scope of both subjects is very broad. It embraces both the person and work of Christ and new life in Him from its inception to its heavenly conclusion. Secondly, the absence of a biblical-theological emphasis on either or both subjects creates false expectations regarding Christian living.

A distorted view or neglect of the biblical doctrine of union with Christ will lead to a drift away from New Testament fundamentals. Individualism that forgets the corporate and covenantal perspectives of union with Christ is the blight of western evangelicalism. Furthermore, when the centrality of union with Christ is absent from the understanding of believers, the link between the history of salvation and the order of salvation is eclipsed. The resulting subjectivism tends to look for the assurance of salvation in experiences.

Shifting the focus to sanctification, another set of issues arises. For over two centuries evangelicalism has spawned holiness movements that range from forms of legalism to downmarket mysticism. 'Mistakes about holiness however sincere', as J. I. Packer reminded us, 'will lock one into unreality and strain in a way that destroys either the joy or honesty of one's inner life, or perhaps both together.'[1] The consequences are far reaching. Such mistakes lead to attitudes of judgmentalism, self-satisfaction and spiritual pride, as well as 'love-only' antinomianism or the legalism that are the eczema of evangelical churches. Some of the most draining conflicts in the church arise because of false spirituality.

It is just as important to strike a biblical balance with regard to union with Christ and sanctification as with Christ and justification. Sanctification has to have its proper place as a *sine qua non* for every believer as the work of God, no less than justification. We forget all too easily that even the regenerate, and we ourselves, are devious and rebellious at heart and, as such, are never free from the lure of sin, particularly in a day when sin is trivialised.

1. Biblical Sanctification or Performance Holiness?

The formal structural issues raised by these subjects generate questions of their own in different ways, but should not cause us to overlook the central material problem regarding holiness itself. Is there not a distance between modern understandings of *holiness* and biblical *sanctification*?

Packer also wrote, in 1984, that 'holiness is a neglected priority throughout the modern church generally' and 'a fading glory in today's evangelical world'.[2] He seemed to suggest that holiness is a known quality and that its demise is regrettable. However, is it not legitimate to ask whether the ideas of holiness current in the context of the modern post-romantic world marked by the optimistic progress of humanism, individual self-fulfilment, rampant liberalism and western cultural superiority do not themselves produce unhealthy attitudes? Until the rise of the

---

1.   J. I. Packer, *Keep in Step with the Spirit* (Leicester: InterVarsity Press 1984), p. 122.
2.   ibid., p. 99.

charismatic movement, which has replaced one version of holiness with another, holiness-talk took over the field formerly occupied in Protestantism by the biblical sanctification of reformed and puritan theology, which was of another ilk, simply because holiness was discussed in the context of the *ordo salutis*, against a backdrop of covenant theology and the centrality of Christ's office as mediator. Isolated from this matrix, holiness assumes another meaning, more often than not either Arminian or sacramental.

The following argument will propose that it is beneficial to be more circumspect in our way of speaking about holiness. Even if holiness and sanctification translate the same Greek word (*hagiazo*), they do not have the same meaning or a conflated meaning, nor are they inter-changeable. The difference between holiness and sanctification is brought out when the mediating concept of righteousness (and the role of God's law) is introduced between the two. This will allow us to situate theologically not only the difference between holiness and sanctification but also between justification and sanctification as works of a holy God.

To put it more concretely: when we sing 'only Thou are holy, merciful and mighty', we confess that there is no holiness outside the holy Trinity. In Christ one person of the Trinity became incarnate and suffered for us,[3] so manifesting the unique holiness of God in the flesh and establishing righteousness for the ungodly. It is only through restoration to righteousness in Christ that we can be associated in any way with divine holiness and consequently be sanctified in union with Him. Without the intermediating step of 'Christ our righteousness', we have no part in holiness, but through Christ's righteousness we are sanctified and called to live consecrated to Him. In other words, our sanctification is only and ever a derivative and dependent God-graced holiness, never complete in this life, resting on union with Christ.

---

3.   cf. R. Letham, *Union with Christ, In Scripture, History and Theology* (Phillipsburg: P & R Publishing 2011), p. 32.

Commenting on the *Heidelberg Catechism* (q.60), 'God, without any merit of mine, but only of mere grace, grants and imputes to me the perfect satisfaction, righteousness and *holiness* of Christ', A. Kuyper stated: '*Sanctification* and *holiness* are two different things. Holiness, in the 60th question, has reference, not to personal dispositions and desires but *to the sum total of all the holy works required by the law.* Sanctification, on the contrary, refers not to any work of the law, but exclusively to the work of *creating holy dispositions in the heart*.'[4] Note, sanctification is God 'creating' holy dispositions, not us obtaining them by spiritual gymnastics. If, when we enter glory, we do so with Christ's imputed righteousness and holiness, during our earthly pilgrimage we enjoy sanctification, the divine renewal of holy dispositions of heart that foster obedience and service.

We will explore briefly, in what follows, this distinction between holiness and sanctification in the context of union with Christ. The main interest of this approach is that when sanctification is considered as the gracing of holy dispositions in union with Christ's righteousness and holiness, God is honoured as the author of salvation in sanctification as much as in justification. Any separation between justification and sanctification that 'divides Christ' and leaves us to 'satnav' our sanctification through seeking and getting holiness, is revealed for what it is – an incipient synergism that will inevitably lead to uncertainties and frustrations or to hypocritical dissimulation. Yet a common misunderstanding of holiness based on a performance mentality seems to prevail: God justifies us but we have to 'work out our own salvation' by becoming more holy. However, if it is down to us to 'let go and let God', we will soon be taking over and not letting God, because He is not a smooth enough operator for our liking. We will be in danger of hiding the reality in the pious language of divine guidance.

As B. B. Warfield commented in his discussion of the 'Higher Life' movement: 'The correlate to a free salvation is trust; the correlate to a conditional salvation is performance. Trust and

---

4.   A. Kuyper, *The Work of the Holy Spirit* (Grand Rapids: Eerdmans 1969), pp. 453–4, (italics are Kuyper's).

performance are contradictions. A 'Do' religion and a 'Trust' religion
are irreconcilable. . . We cannot look to ourselves for the decisive
act in our salvation and at the same time be looking to God for
all.'[5] G. C. Berkouwer as well indicated the tendency in pietism to
abstract sanctification from faith and justification:

> The renewal is not a mere supplement, an appendage, to the
> salvation given in justification. The heart of sanctification is
> the life which feeds on this justification. There is no contrast
> between justification as an act of God and sanctification as
> an act of man. The fact that Christ is our sanctification is not
> exclusive of, but inclusive of, a faith which clings to him alone in
> all of life. Faith is the pivot on which everything revolves. Faith,
> though not itself creative, preserves us from autonomous self-
> sanctification and moralism.[6]

These comments point to the fact that by seeing the order of
salvation in holiness-righteousness-sanctification, we may also
avoid both the legalism and antinomianism that rear their heads
so frequently in this context. Union with Christ in sanctification
will always lead back to Christ as mediator, over against all
naturalistic religion and philosophical idealism.[7] There are *no*
'holy men' and there is no moral *summum bonum* outside of Christ.
Is not this what Jesus Himself meant when He said, 'Outside of
me you can do nothing' (John 15:5)?[8]

In addition, and perhaps most important, the *person* of Christ
as mediator will be recognised as central in the whole soteric
process, not only in His life and passion as the author, but also in
His ascended ministry as the One who sanctifies and completes
salvation (*teleioten*, Heb. 12:2). So it will remain in glory.

After briefly (ii) defining the terms, we will consider: (iii)
righteousness and holiness in Adam and Christ as the context

---

5.   B. B. Warfield, *Works,* VIII (Grand Rapids: Baker Book House 1982 [1932]),
      p. 555.

6.   G. C. Berkouwer, *Faith and Sanctification* (Grand Rapids: Eerdmans 1952), p. 93.

7.   E. Brunner, *The Mediator* (London: Lutterworth Press 1934), chs I–II.

8.   Unless otherwise shown biblical quotations are from the ESV.

of sanctification in the covenant of grace; (iv) definitive sanctification in Christ as the status of believers; (v) transformative sanctification as lifestyle and (vi) the tension in the struggle for sanctification that precedes final glorification with Christ.

2. Mediation, Union with Christ and Sanctification

It is a reflection on our modern mindset that holiness is generally thought of in terms of individual progress, and I fear that this presentation will hardly be sufficient to break that mould. However, sanctification in Christ is a cosmic reality and the classic reformed *ordo salutis* presents an all-englobing movement of which the death and resurrection of Christ are the wellspring. The destination is the new creation into which no defilement will enter (Rev. 21:27). In this movement 'precisely by electing, calling, justifying, sanctifying and glorifying particular people, the triune God is drawing mere individuals in their subjectivity into a historical drama of cosmic proportion. As individuals . . . they become part of the new creation. . . a redeemed humanity.'[9] If the message of the New Testament does concern the salvation of individuals, this is because they are caught up in a cosmic movement in which the creation itself, the church and believers, all await the consummation of Christ's kingdom. As a body, the church grows into Christ as the 'fullness of him who fills all in all' and all reality, natural and historical, is placed under Christ to that end (Eph. 1:23). The order is cosmic, corporate-ecclesial and personal, and in talking about the individual we should not forget that the context is the corporate renewal of creation.[10]

---

9.   M. S. Horton, *Covenant and Salvation. Union with Christ* (Louisville: Westminster John Knox Press 2007), p. 36. Horton ably criticises the 'new perspective on Paul' for playing down the centrality of the universal aspects of sin and redemption in Romans.

10.   As J. Webster indicates in the structure of his book, *Holiness* (London: SCM Press 2003), which talks about the holiness of God, of the Church and of Christians in that order.

2.1 Key concepts

This movement is rooted in the mediatorial function of the second person of the Trinity, the one Lord Jesus who is mediator of angels[11] and of all creation. He is the true image represented in the Adamic creation,[12] the head of the covenant of grace and the Lord of the new creation. H. Bavinck repeats what had already been said by Calvin on this subject: 'While the creation is a work of the whole Trinity, it cannot be denied that in Scripture it also stands in a peculiar relation to the Son . . . Christ is not only the mediator of re-creation but also of creation.'[13] As the active presence in creation, the Word and wisdom of God sets the scene for subsequent action as the Word revealed in the unfolding of divine revelation in covenantal history.[14]

Union with Christ is the concrete effect of the unique mediation of the Word and the substance of that reality. If the expression 'does not occur in the Bible, it fairly describes the central reality of revealed salvation, from its eternal design to its eschatological consummation.'[15] Union is not a single condition, constant throughout history, but rather a series of conditions anchored in God's eternal purpose. It is the most basic thing that can be said about salvation, as Jesus saves by uniting us to Himself, through the work of His Spirit, according to the plan of the Father. Even if believers are in Christ by election before the foundation of the world and before their baptism, they are only savingly so in Christ subsequent to effectual calling, justification

11. On Calvin's debates with Francesco Stancaro, see J. Tylanda, 'Christ the Mediator: Calvin versus Stancaro', *Calvin Theological Journal* 7 (1972), pp. 5–16. See also S. Edmondson, *Calvin's Christology* (Cambridge University Press 2004), ch. 1.

12. P. E. Hughes, *The True Image* (Grand Rapids: Eerdmans 1989), III.

13. H. Bavinck, *Reformed Dogmatics,* II (Grand Rapids: Baker Academic 2004), p. 423. On Calvin and Bavinck, see J. T. Billings, *Union with Christ. Reframing Theology and Ministry for the Church* (Grand Rapids: Baker Academic 2011), pp. 70–86.

14. P. Wells, 'Calvin and Union with Christ: the Heart of Christian Doctrine' in J. R. Beeke and G. J. Williams, (eds.) *Calvin. Theologian and Reformer,*. (Grand Rapids: Reformation Heritage Books 2010), ch. 4.

15. R. B. Gaffin, 'Union with Christ : Some Biblical and Theological Reflections', in A. T. B. McGowan (ed.) *Always Reforming* (Leicester: Apollos 2006), ch. 8.

and the exercise of faith.[16] Concerning the time of union, Kuyper distinguishes five stages: the decree of God, the incarnation, regeneration, the first exercise of faith, the conscious enjoyment of it and finally union in glory after death. S. Ferguson simplifies this schema to three moments: the eternal, the incarnational and the existential.[17]

Sanctification begins in us with the existential laying hold on Christ by faith. Believers are, as rebellious creatures, outside Christ until drawn into Him by faith, called *insitio in Christum* by classic reformed theology and described as a 'real, wholesale, spiritual and indissoluble union of the persons of the elect with the divine-human person of the Redeemer, so that for the former the latter is exactly the same as soul is for body.'[18] They are so intimately united to Christ that they become one body and one spirit with Him (1 Cor. 6:17; 12:13), a reality described by a series of New Testament metaphors and by Calvin as engrafting, indwelling and participation.[19] The mutual communion in a single unity echoes trinitarian unity in which the divine persons are together a single entity. It is often described by five attributes with legal, objective and existential aspects as a union that is real, inclusive, indissoluble, spiritual and mystical.[20] The whole is often termed 'mystical' as a corporal unity that is *secret*, not natural but spiritual. Since the expressions spiritual and mystical are subject to misunderstanding, R. Gaffin has suggested that *mystical* should be taken in the sense of the New Testament *mysterion*. It indicates that 'what has been hidden with God in his eternal purposes now, finally, has been revealed in Christ, particularly in his death and

---

16. J. Frame, *Systematic Theology* (Phillipsburg: P & R Publishing 2013), pp. 913f.

17. Kuyper, op. cit., pp. 335–7; S. B. Ferguson, *The Holy Spirit,* (Leicester: InterVarsity 1996), pp. 106–111.

18. H. Heppe, *Reformed Dogmatics* (Grand Rapids: Baker 1978), p. 511.

19. Wells, op. cit., pp. 73–82.

20. Heppe, op. cit., p. 512, quoting P. Van Mastricht, *Theoretico-practica Theologia*, 1725, VI, v, pp. 10–13. cf. L. Berkhof, *Systematic Theology* (Grand Rapids: Eerdmans 1953), p. 450, who uses the attributes organic, vital, spiritual, reciprocal, personal and transformational.

resurrection, and is appropriated by faith (Rom. 16:25; Col. 1:26-7; 2:2).'[21] This proviso provides a necessary historico-redemptive mooring of union in the *ordo salutis* and the accomplishment of the plan of salvation.

Because of the very nature of union with Christ, sanctification could hardly be considered an evanescent reality, but must be an expression of God's faithfulness to His promises. It is as real in the application of salvation to believers as it is in the promises made to the mediator Himself concerning its accomplishment. Christ's mediation binds together in one movement redemption accomplished and applied in the *ordo salutis*.

2.2 The language of sanctification

When the New Testament usage of the words sanctification/holiness is considered, we find rather unexpected angles in the light of what 'holiness' has come to mean, particularly in contexts where progress toward perfection is taken as the norm for Christian experience. The verb *to sanctify*, the noun *sanctification* and the adjective *holy* rarely have the sense of progressive ethical renewal.[22] The dominant meaning indicates the status of consecration to God which results from being set apart for His service. *Hagiasmos*, used ten times in the New Testament,[23] is translated either by sanctification or holiness in different versions. If in some cases the context does suggest dynamic renewal and progressive sanctification, it is best understood, as D. Peterson states, 'as a state of holiness arising from God's consecrating work in Christ. The motivation and power to express that

---

21. Gaffin, op. cit., p. 272. The mystery of the kingdom and the hidden glory of the suffering and all-powerful Messiah it unfolds, G. K. Beale and B. L. Gladd, *Hidden But Now Revealed. A Biblical Theology of Mystery* (Nottingham: Apollos 2014), pp. 320–39.

22. *Hagiazein, hagiasmos* and *hagios,* used 28x, 10x and 233x respectively; see D. Peterson, *Possessed by God. The New Testament Theology of Sanctification and Holiness* (Leicester: Apollos 1995), pp. 139–42. *Hosiotes* and *hosios,* used 3x, refer to devotion to God.

23. See Peterson's chart, ibid., p. 140: The ten references (translated sanctification and holiness five times each in the KJV) are Rom. 6:19, 22; 1 Cor. 1:30; 1 Thess. 4:3, 4, 7; 2 Thess. 2:13; 1 Tim. 2:15; Heb. 12:14; 1 Pet.1:2.

holiness is given to believers by the indwelling Holy Spirit.'[24] Packer comments that 'the positional holiness of consecration and acceptance underlies the personal transformation that is normally what we have in mind when we speak of sanctification.'[25] However, contrary to common parlance, the biblical use pleads that sanctification be understood as relational holiness based on God's act of consecration, followed by the consequent dedication to the Lord in practical living.

In the context of union with Christ, sanctification is primarily a question of *status*, based upon the imputation of Christ's righteousness, accompanied by the holiness resulting from union with Christ, who has defeated sin and death. The *dynamic* aspect of sanctification, referred to in terms of growing in grace, conformity to Christ's image and the struggle against sin, refers to the active faith of the person who is indwelt by the Spirit, sharing in Christ's holiness and ruled by it. Being 'perfected' (*teteleiotai*) in the love of God, abiding in Christ, means walking in the same way that He walked (1 John 2:5-6). Progressive sanctification is subsidiary to the definitive relation with Christ, which is the matrix for Christian growth.

This is a different slant from the one we are most accustomed to. Peterson goes so far as to state that 'sanctification means being appropriated by God and dedicated to him by the saving work of his Son . . . Sanctification has to do with the identity and status of those who are "in Christ".'[26] It is the making holy of a life given by the Lord, describing the definitive situation of the believer in Christ, no less granted than justification itself. As J. Webster says:

> The sanctifying Spirit is *Lord*; that is, sanctification is not in any straightforward sense a process of cooperation or coordination between God and the creature, a drawing out or building upon some inherent holiness of the creature's own. Sanctification is

---

24.   ibid., p. 142.

25.   cf. Packer, op. cit., p. 104.

26.   Peterson, op. cit., p. 40.

making holy. Holiness is properly an incommunicable divine attribute; if creaturely realities become holy, it is by virtue of election, that is, by a sovereign act of segregation or separation by the Spirit of the Lord.[27]

Sanctification or holiness is therefore primarily a geographical concept as R. Letham says, because God has removed the believer from one place to a new spiritual situation. In a definitive sense this removal 'has already taken place in Christ by the power of the Holy Spirit.'[28] The difference between justification and sanctification lies perhaps in the sense that the first does not have an eschatological reference, whereas the second includes the idea of process, although justification is also an anticipation of the final eschatological verdict to be pronounced in and by Christ.

How does this perspective fit in with the history of salvation and the reformed interpretation of it in terms of creation-fall-redemption?

3. Righteousness and Holiness in Adam and in Christ

God's nature is to be holy; His holiness is eternal; He can no more not be holy than He cannot be God.[29] Although holiness ultimately belongs only to God, in so far as creation is a divine work, it mirrors the creator. Holiness is God's gift to creation in three senses, ontological, epistemological and ethical, and man is created with a holy nature. As the image of God, he can truly know and serve Him in righteousness. Man's holiness is derived and reflective, just as his living is derived life and his immortality is not a natural possession. The primal garden was a holy sanctuary consecrated by the presence of God for communion, and man was called in that context to glorify the enthroned Creator. The

---

27. J. Webster, *Holy Scripture: A Dogmatic Sketch* (Cambridge: Cambridge University Press 2003), p. 27.

28. Letham, op. cit., p. 87.

29. Webster, *Holiness*, p. 42.

creation was a royal protectorate to be consummated in the cosmic sabbath.[30] Man's holiness was therefore conditional, derived and dependent, awaiting consummation through enacted righteousness in accordance with God's command. When Adam fell, what he lost was righteousness, holiness and truth, which are only restored in Christ (Eph. 4:24, Col. 3:10).

3.1 Holiness and righteousness

Kuyper correctly drew a foundational distinction between holiness and righteousness, the first concerning the realm of being, the second involving status.[31] If God's holiness is eternal, belonging to His nature and having trinitarian expression, divine righteousness belongs not to His nature as such, but is the expression of the sum of His divine attributes and His holy kingship over creation. Holiness is inherent in the divine nature, whereas divine righteousness does not manifest itself until it is displayed in creation, through the existence of a jural relationship binding God and man. In the Adamic administration man was called to conform to the divine law and display righteousness in obedience to divine sovereignty, and in this way to demonstrate his inner constitutional holiness externally.

The fall was a rebellion against God's kingly status, a denial of His righteous sovereignty and law, and it demonstrated an inner corruption of holiness that led to the rejection of God. By overturning God's rule, Adam lost righteousness under the law and entered into condemnation and death, because the relation with God was severed. The divine curse is a result of unrighteousness and the corresponding loss of holiness. Man becomes a child of wrath; that is his *nature*, because holiness has given way to the pollution and stain of sin. He is unrighteous in terms of the divine law, that is his *status*, because of his refusal of divine kingship and disobedience. When Adam lost his holiness, he created a universal problem for humanity, and consequently

---

30. M. G. Kline, *Kingdom Prologue. Genesis Foundations for a Covenantal Worldview* (Overland Park: Two Age Press 2000), ch. 3.

31. Kuyper, op. cit., p. 444.

there are, after Adam, no holy human beings outside of Jesus, the second Adam.

This contrast between holiness and righteousness has multiple and far-reaching consequences. Existentially, what do sinners do? As covenant breakers, they seek to avoid God's righteousness by denying His sovereignty, hiding like Adam and Jonah did, pretending they can do enough to be acceptable to God; alternatively they deny the existence of a binding divine law, natural or revealed. God's righteousness antagonises sinners who curse God by blaming Him for their own faults. Guilt-transference is the sinful reaction to the righteous demands of the Lord. The holiness of God, on the other hand, arouses in sinners a feeling of lack and shame because of the stain of sin and hopelessness. Not guilt and condemnation, but emptiness and meaninglessness lead to the search for ersatz forms of holiness, idols, and counterfeit spiritualities. False religion always proposes fake holiness without righteousness and sinners hide from the demands of divine sovereignty in its practices.

3.2 Justification and sanctification

This contrast is also the foundation of the theological distinction between sanctification and justification. The latter is related to the demands of God's law and their fulfilment. Since the fall the way of holiness is shut tight to unrighteous sinners. Works cannot justify because they can never help us to progress an iota toward the holiness required for communion with God. Justification logically precedes sanctification as a divine act, complete in itself, in the place of the absence of human merits. It is the righteousness of God, grace apart from the law. Its status exists because of 'alien' righteousness. Holiness is not the result of anything we can do to attain it. It is freely gifted to us as God unites us to His holy One, the Lord Jesus. We rest in Christ's holiness, we receive a new nature in Christ and, as children of God, grow in grace as the dynamic of trust increases, in deepened dependence on Him.[32] Holiness is not acquired through performance, nor can performance justify; it can only create deceptive self-righteousness and an illusion of holiness. This is why union with Christ is the essence of sanctification. It indicates that sanctification does not mean getting more holy through acts of righteousness, nor is it testable by the fact that 'every day in every way I'm getting better and better'. If we grow in grace in union with Christ, we never get beyond 'miserable sinner Christianity', Luther's *simul justus et peccator*.[33]

3.3 The covenant of grace and incarnation

All this has a bearing on Christ's work in the covenant of grace, programmed in the eternal covenant of redemption, which is the basis of all the historical covenants.[34] According to God's eternal plan, Christ fulfils the covenant of works broken in Adam and is the mediator of a new covenant of grace.[35] Two aspects of Christ's work bear on the righteousness and holiness we receive from Him as mediator; He fulfilled both these conditions to make saving union with Himself possible. Union with Christ is firstly a consequence of His holy incarnational union with humanity and secondly, in our humanity He fulfilled 'all righteousness' (Matt. 3:15).

The eternal Word took human nature into personal union with His divinity and joined Himself to humanity forever. Consequently 'the basis of our union with Christ is Christ's union with us in the incarnation.'[36] In the Lord Jesus human nature was sanctified in communion with the divine nature, in the womb of the virgin, in His growth (Luke 2:52), His baptism,

---

32.   Kuyper, op. cit, pp. 440–3 on justification and sanctification.

33.   cf. Warfield's admirable remarks on 'miserable sinner Christianity' in op. cit., VII, 179ff.

34.   Horton, op. cit., p. 130.

35.   G. Vos, 'The Doctrine of the Covenant in Reformed Theology', in R. B. Gaffin, Jr., (ed.), *Redemptive History and Biblical Interpretation* (Phillipsburg: P & R Publishing 1980), pp. 234–67.

36.   Letham, op. cit., p. 21 and all ch. 2; cf. Peterson, op. cit., ch. 2.

His transfiguration, His suffering and finally His death and resurrection. The life-sanctification of His humanity was an ongoing dynamic drama enacted in the time between the miracles of the virgin birth and the resurrection. Human nature itself is saved and made holy in the person of Jesus. There was no divine-human life in His person since the creator-creature distinction 'is inviolate, *and also* the compatibility of God and man'.[37] The Word entered the conditions of creation in order to renew creation, and did so as His flesh was suffused with the holy qualities of divinity, renewing humanity. In John 10:36 Jesus described Himself as 'the one whom the Father has sanctified (*hegiasen*) and sent into the world'. He reconsecrated defiled humanity in His body, to become a temple for holy service to God. However, the incarnation is for atonement; Jesus consecrates Himself by laying down His life for the sheep (10:11-30), and fulfils the will of the Father (4:34). He dedicates Himself to become a sacrifice for sins. In John 17:19 he prays, 'for their sakes (the disciples) I sanctify myself so that they may also be sanctified in truth.'

In Hebrews 2:10-11 we again find the word *sanctify*: 'he who sanctifies and they who are sanctified all have one origin' – that is God the Father, who 'in bringing many sons to glory makes the founder of their salvation perfect through suffering.' This text is often interpreted as referring to Christ's accomplishment of the covenant of redemption, in particular in the light of verse 13. The Father as the origin of salvation consecrates the Son to His service, and those being brought to glory are sanctified together with him. They are united in the Son, who Himself becomes perfect though suffering, to accomplish the Father's purpose of consecration for salvation. This note is again sounded in Hebrews 10:9-10. The Son comes to accomplish the will of the Father and 'by that will we have been sanctified through the offering of the body of Jesus Christ once and for all', repeated in 10:29 in 'sanctified by the blood of the covenant'. In these cases 'the verb *to sanctify* is primarily employed in a covenantal sense.

---

37. ibid., p. 36.

Christ's sacrifice binds men and women to God in a new relation of heart-obedience.'[38] The perfecting (*teleo*) of Christ referred to in Hebrews 2:10, 5:9 and 7:28 is not a moral action, even if the holiness required for drawing near to God is not absent from the thought. It refers primarily to the high-priestly ministry of Christ who has fulfilled God's promises in establishing the final covenant with a 'better hope' than the old covenant, introducing believers into the eternal security of the kingdom.[39]

Sanctification in these instances is not inner holiness. It is receiving renewed dispositions from Christ, who alone is holy, and being reformatted in His holiness. This consecration is for covenant service in following Him. 'By a single offering he has perfected (*teteleioken*) for all time those who are being sanctified (*tous hagiazomenous*)' indicates that what we receive in Christ in the dynamic of sanctification is nothing other than what is already complete in His finished work (10:14).

3.4 Righteousness and holiness in Christ

Christ is our holiness as He sanctifies our human nature. He is our righteousness as He obeys God's law. Union with Christ rests on His work of righteousness on our behalf. If His holiness does not directly constitute the basis for our sanctification in union with Him, Christ's justice does, as He fulfils God's legal requirements. Adam not only did not achieve righteousness through obedience, but he also inherited death because of rebellion and disobedience. As the second Adam Christ assumes both the outcomes of the original sin. Not only does He carry out complete obedience to God's law, but He suffers the consequences of our disobedience in our place. His active and passive obedience, which are often distinguished as two forms of obedience, in fact make up the one obedience of the one mediator. The covenant of grace is constructed on both the debris of Adam's failure and the success of Christ's obedience in fulfilling the conditions of the covenant

38. Peterson, op. cit., p. 35.

39. ibid., pp. 36f.

of works. In His role as mediator Christ not only took Adam's place, but also our place to do the works we could not do and pay the price we could not pay.

The outcome of the obedience of Christ, active and passive, is that in Christ we are justified, as if we had never sinned and had rendered complete obedience to God's covenant ourselves.[40] As our surety, Christ is the author of reconciliation in making payment for sin, resulting in the remission of sin (2 Cor. 5:19). He is our righteousness and our peace, apart from any work, on the basis of His work alone (Rom. 4:5-6). What belongs to Christ is ours because of union with Him; it is received by imputation, because what is properly Christ's is legally imputed to us.[41] Imputation is a double act of God, simply because the theological distinction between active and passive obedience is made to elucidate the function of the one justice of the one Christ, which is counted as a whole to sinners.[42] Nor is it feasible to say that we are justified by incorporation into Christ not by imputation, as we cannot be united to Christ if we are unholy and have not received imputed righteousness from Christ. For this reason, as Gaffin says, 'while there is no imputation without union or antecedent to union, neither is there union without imputation.'[43]

Although reformed theology has occasionally used the word 'imputed' in the context of sanctification, Scripture does not speak this way in a conceptual sense. The holiness of Christ is imparted to us in union with Christ because we are united to Him as our covenant head and as a result of the righteousness of

---

40. *Heidelberg Catechism*, q.60.

41. H. Bavinck, *Reformed Dogmatics,* IV (Grand Rapids: Baker Academic 2008), pp. 212–14, calls this extrinsic imputation, as the person justified in a legal sense is ungodly in the ethical.

42. It is difficult to see how one obedience could be separated from the other in the act of imputation. See C. R. Venema, *The Gospel of Free Acceptance in Christ* (Edinburgh, Banner of Truth 2006), pp. 246–9; J. Buchanan, *The Doctrine of Justification* (Edinburgh: Banner of Truth 1961 [1867]), pp. 332–3.

43. Gaffin, art. cit., p. 286.

Christ received for remission of sin in justification. So the order is – first the *righteousness* of Christ imputed, then the *holiness* of Christ imparted in sanctification through (*dia*) faith by which we believe into (*pisteuein eis*) Christ. Sometimes the word 'infusion' has been used by Turretin, Bavinck and others, in the context of sanctification, in contrast with justification. While the legal merit of Christ's righteousness cannot become ours by infusion but only by imputation,[44] the personal holiness of Christ has a sanctifying effect because we are one with Him. So F. Turretin says, 'we put on Christ as righteousness and sanctification (Gal. 3:27); righteousness, which takes away the guilt of sin and covers; sanctification which every day removes and washes away pollution.'[45] Whereas justification is an immediate act of God, sanctification is mediate through the work of the Holy Spirit and the infusion of Christ's graces in us, as we live personally in a new relation with Him.

To sum up, distinguishing between righteousness and holiness on the one hand, and justification and sanctification on the other, is capital. The first were lost simultaneously in Adam's sin and are restored simultaneously to humanity in Christ who alone is righteous and holy. Believers receive the righteousness of Christ in justification, being freed from guilt and the demands of the law, and His holiness in sanctification. Both graces are restored in the triangular union with Christ dear to Calvin. Although ontologically holiness precedes righteousness, as the law flows from a holy God, and Christ fulfils all righteousness as the holy One, in soteriology righteousness through justification must precede sanctification. The work of sanctification cannot begin until we are counted righteous for the sake of Christ. Both graces proceed from union with Christ, even though justification is first as 'the main hinge on which religion turns'.[46] This is why any

---

44. J. Buchanan, op. cit., p. 321.

45. F. Turretin, *Institutes of Elenctic Theology*, II (Phillipsburg: P & R Publishing 1994), p. 691; Bavinck, op. cit., IV, pp. 249–50.

46. J. Calvin, *Institutes of the Christian Religion*, III.xi.1.

reversal of order leads to works religion and self-sanctification for salvation, and was vigorously rejected by the reformers as contrary to the sovereignty of grace.

4. Definitive Sanctification in Christ, the Status of Believers

The *ordo salutis* is based on the accomplishment of salvation by Christ and presents a sequence in which its benefits are unfolded in the lives of believers. [47] More generally, it is the ongoing application of the once-for-all salvation accomplished in the history of salvation.[48] Union with Christ itself has broader scope than the *ordo*, beginning in eternity past and ending in eternity future, via the segment of time in which believers receive and live in the hope of salvation. 'Union with Christ is in itself a very broad and embracive subject', says J. Murray, ' . . . the whole process of salvation has its origin in one phase of union with Christ and salvation has in view the realization of other phases of union with Christ.'[49] If justification has priority, being declarative and forensically determinative for the entire order,[50]

---

47. Discussions about the *ordo salutis* are numerous and complex. See R. A. Muller, *Calvin and the Reformed Tradition. On the Work of Christ and the Order of Salvation* (Grand Rapids: Baker Academic 2012), chs. 6, 7. Muller is against the idea that union with Christ in Calvin's thought was replaced by the *ordo* as a logical structure in later reformed theology. He indicates that there is a great variety in the sequence of the application of salvation and discussion as to whether the sequence is logical, temporal or natural. The temporal ordering is not important apart from the question of the precedence of regeneration and the fact that any sequence is grounded in calling and union with Christ. cf. J. V. Fesko, 'Sanctification and Union with Christ: a Reformed Perspective', *Evangelical Quarterly*, 82.3 (2010), pp. 198–207.

48. Gaffin, art. cit., p. 276.

49. J. Murray, *Redemption Accomplished and Applied* (London: Banner of Truth 1961 [1955]), p. 161.

50. Horton, op. cit., pp. 256–66, 300 – 'we never leave the forensic domain even when we are addressing other topics in the *ordo* besides justification proper.' Justification, says Horton, does not *include* its effects, it *generates* them. 'Justification is exclusively juridical, yet it is the forensic origin of our union with Christ, from which all our covenantal blessings flow.', ibid., p. 139.

sanctification is a consequent phase in which union with Christ is progressively worked out, in the already/not yet present of the lives of believers, leading to glorification.

The current qualifiers used for sanctification, 'definitive' (or positional) and 'progressive' are susceptible to misunderstanding. The former seems to contradict the experience of believers, whereas the latter raises the issue of how to measure progress. Is sanctification a definitive reality or simply a progressive experience? If exegesis must ultimately decide,[51] the New Testament metaphors for union with Christ incline in favour of definitive sanctification. Ingrafting in the vine suggests that once in Christ, His life constantly abides and flows into the believer like sap in a graft. Perhaps in contrast with the 'false' vine (Ps. 80; Ezek. 15:2-4), Jesus says, 'already you are clean because of the word I have spoken to you' (John 15:3). The analogy of the union of husband and wife indicates that the pledge of troth issues in an unbroken relation. Christ as the foundational stone implies that the living stones integrated in Him form a new building, the temple of the Spirit. In each case an initial act of union constitutes a new state, definitive sanctification, and subsequently issues into a dynamic relation, that is, transformative sanctification. Even the image of adoption into the family of God hints at the fact that once we are members of the family, we receive both a new name and the rights of sons.

If, as we have proposed, Jesus is the first and only holy person, and if His resurrection from the dead attests His righteousness and holiness (His justification and sanctification),[52] then our human nature is sanctified in Him, for our sake. Once united to Him, what is His is ours. As S. Ferguson states, 'The whole of Christ's life, death, resurrection and exaltation have, by God's gracious design, provided the living deposit of his sanctified life, from which all our

---

51. On the exegesis, see the following, contra the J. Murray view of progressive sanctification, Fesko, art. cit., pp. 207–214 and the reply by R. Cunnington, 'Definitive sanctification. A response to John Fesko', *Evangelical Quarterly*, 84.3 (2012), pp. 234–52.

52. R. B. Gaffin, *Resurrection and Redemption. A Study in Paul's Soteriology* (Phillipsburg: P & R Publishing 2012).

needs can be supplied. Because of our union with him we come to share his resources.'[53] So His is ours, with all that belongs to Him, in a real sense, and this constitutes the believer's *status*. Sanctification in union with Christ is definitive as our identity, not because it is definitive *in us*, but because it is *in Him*. Christ *is* our sanctification, completely, entirely and definitively, and union with Him makes His status ours through calling and faith. 'They, who are once effectually called, and regenerated, having a new heart, and a new spirit created in them, are further sanctified, really and personally, through the virtue of Christ's death and resurrection, by His Word and Spirit dwelling in them.'[54] The emphasis here is on the saving work of God applied to believers through the Holy Spirit.

Sanctification is certainly subject of dynamic development in spiritual transformation after conversion, but 'in the New Testament it primarily refers to God's way of taking possession of us in Christ, setting us apart to belong to him and to fulfil his purpose for us.'[55] In this definitive sense, Kuyper can say, 'Christ is my complete holiness before God, just as much as my perfect righteousness ... the holy works which Christ has done for us are just as positively an *imputed* holiness, as we stand right before God by an imputed righteousness. Nothing can be added to it. It is whole, perfect, and complete in every respect.'[56]

---

53. S. Ferguson, 'The Reformed View', in D. L. Alexander (ed.) *Christian Spirituality. Five Views of Sanctification* (Downers Grove: InterVarsity Press 1988), p. 50.

54. *Westminster Confession of Faith*, XIII, i. If 'further' here is taken to mean 'also' in a logical sense and not 'subsequently' in a temporal sense, then the Confession appears to be teaching definitive sanctification; cf. Cunnington, art. cit., section II, for a discussion of the historical sources of definitive sanctification before Murray.

55. Peterson, op. cit., p. 27.

56. Kuyper, op. cit., p. 454. Cunnington, art. cit., p. 247, states: 'The category of the forensic (which simply means legal) includes justification but is not exhausted by it. Adoption and redemption are also forensic categories in the sense that they are predicated upon a change of legal status. Thus it is quite possible for the forensic to be present in sanctification without abandoning the traditional distinction between the forensic category of justification and the transformative category of sanctification.' In this sense, Kuyper's use of 'imputation' is not wrong. Horton, op. cit., p. 292, affirms that 'to the very last, the forensic Word of justification reverberates through the entire *ordo*.'

What are the parameters of definitive sanctification? Four biblical aspects suggest that it is a function of union with Christ. Firstly, a past aspect indicates that sanctification is already obtained completely in Christ. It is manifest in the present in union with Christ in His death and resurrection. Furthermore, the power of sin has been definitively neutralised. Finally, the believer, a new man in Christ, is now part of the new creation. We will look briefly at each of these features of definitive sanctification in the lives of believers.

4.1 The past aspect, in Christ

Sanctification (*hagiazo*) often refers to a decisive change that took place in the past in union with Christ. In 1 Corinthians 1:2, 'those sanctified in Christ' is generally taken to refer to positional rather than transformative sanctification. Later, at the end of the same chapter (1:30), Christ is said to have been made 'our righteousness, our sanctification and redemption' by God. George Whitefield took this to be a reference to God's past decision in Christ and declared, 'Would to God this point of doctrine was considered more, and people were more studious of the covenant of redemption between the Father and the Son!'[57] Even should it be taken to refer to the outcome of Christ's historical work, redemption as eschatological salvation, preceded in the wisdom of God by justification and sanctification, the reference is still being made to something complete in Christ. In Christ, God's people are given a new and consecrated status which establishes a distinct and new relationship.[58]

In a further passage, 1 Corinthians 6:11, three metaphors are used (through using verbs in the aorist passive) to describe the results of Christ's past work. 'But' (*alla*, 3 times, in contrast with

---

57. Sermon 44, *The Works of the Reverend George Whitefield* (London 1771–2).

58. Peterson, op. cit., pp. 42–4, although Peterson refers redemption to the liberation from sinful slavery and not the eschatological redemption of the body, Rom. 8:23; Eph. 4:30. Bavinck, op. cit., IV, p. 250, points out that Christ is our *hagiasmos*, sanctification, not our holiness, *hagiosune/hagiotes*, an important distinction; we are not in ourselves holy, but consecrated in Christ.

what the Corinthians had been), 'you were washed, you were justified, you were sanctified, in the name of the Lord Jesus and by the Spirit of God.' It is through the redemptive work of the Son that believers are separated from an unholy life, and the Spirit brings to bear on them the results of Christ's work.[59] Murray states that the references in 2 Timothy 2:21 and Ephesians 5:25f. have the same sense and that the substantive 'sanctification' has a similar connotation as a once-for-all definitive act, determining the identity of the people of God in Christ[60] (cf., Acts 20:32, 26.18).

4.2 Present experience

Secondly, the present experience of believers reflects their once-and-for-all sanctification though union with Christ's death and resurrection. The key passage here is the complex text in Romans 6:1-14. If 1 Corinthians 1:30 presents a shorthand for the double grace of justification and sanctification in union with Christ, Romans 5 and 6 give a longer version. Christ could die and live for us because He entered our mode of existence in a way that was redemptive for us, presented in Romans 6 in terms of dying and rising with Him. 'With him' and 'for us' indicate the corporate nature of union 'in' Christ and the church's objective state of salvation in Him. What took place in Him is applicable to us, as all that happened to Christ happened to us with Him.[61] M. Garcia comments on Calvin's view that to have Christ for justification without newness of life would be to 'tear Christ apart'. Christ's death and resurrection, represented by baptism (6:4), indicate that we are engrafted into Christ to be one with Him in a real death to sin in Christ's death, the efficacy of which is seen in rising to new life with Him. So we 'pass from our nature

---

59.   ibid., pp. 44–6.

60.   J. Murray, 'Definitive Sanctification', *Collected Writings*, II (Edinburgh: Banner of Truth 1977), pp. 277f. The terms for purification in Acts 15:9, Eph. 5:26 and Titus 2:14 have the same import, according to Murray.

61.   H. Ridderbos, *Paul. An Outline of his Theology* (Grand Rapids: Eerdmans 1975), pp. 57–60.

to his'.[62] Ferguson adds that Paul's logic here (6:8-11) is impeccable, summing up in six points rooted in the historical transition that took place in Christ:

1. We receive forgiveness of sins through Christ

2. Receiving Christ involves being united to Him

3. The Christ to whom we are united died to sin

4. Since we are united to Him, we also have died to sin

5. If we have died to sin, we cannot continue living in it

6. Therefore we cannot continue in sin that grace may increase[63]

Verse 7, 'one who has died has been set free from sin', has therefore nothing to do with a perfectionistic move to a higher sphere beyond the clutches of sin, nor to a positive self-image. Baptism pictures something that has taken place outside of our experience, and identifies us with that epoch-changing event: Christ died to sin and with Him we died to it, and that is the basis of sanctification.[64] 'All who sustain the relation to him that baptism signifies likewise died, were buried, and rose again to a new life patterned after his resurrection life.'[65] In Christ we enter a new realm of influence other than that of the rule of sin and death (5:21; 6:12, 14, 17, 20). Our human condition in Adam was 'crucified together' (6:6, *sunestaurothe*) with Christ on the cross. Baptism also signifies that what took place outside us has been mirrored in our experience, as J. Stott states: 'what was crucified with Christ was not a part of me called my old nature, but the whole of me before I was converted.'[66]

---

62. M. Garcia, *Life in Christ. Union with Christ and the Twofold Grace in Calvin's Theology* (Milton Keynes: Paternoster 2008), pp. 125–8. On justification and sanctification in Calvin, see also P. Lillback, *The Binding of God. Calvin's Role in the Development of Covenant Theology* (Carlisle: Paternoster Press 2001), ch. 9.

63. Ferguson, art. cit., p. 54.

64. Peterson, op. cit., pp. 96–8.

65. Murray, op. cit., II, p. 286.

66. J. Stott, *Men Made New. An Exposition of Romans 5–8* (London: InterVarsity Fellowship 1966), p. 45.

So sanctification is the radical new spiritual habitat of those raised with Christ. To have a Christ-and-life-wish is as *natural* to believers, because they live in thrall to the dominion of Christ's new realm, as was the sin-and-death-wish when they were in Adam. This portrays sanctification in union with Christ as a definite break with the old existence.

4.3 The power of sin broken

Thirdly, and following on from this, in definitive sanctification the power of sin is broken. Romans 6:6-7 affirms 'we know that our old self was crucified with him in order that the body of sin might be brought to nothing, so that we would no longer be enslaved to sin. For one who has died has been set free (*dedikaiotai*) from sin.' If the final affirmation is incontestable, how is it to be understood as throwing light on the body of sin being brought to nothing and being set free? One interpretation is that the accusing power of sin, demonstrating guilt and leading to death, has been brought down and we are, in Christ *justified* from sin as guilt.[67] However the issue here is not the guilt of sin, but its dominion. Even though sin is still present, the one who is justified from sin is no longer a slave to its constraining mastery. Further on, in verse 18, the apostle states that this freeing from sin (*eleutherothentes*) issues in a new bondage to righteousness (*dikaiosune*). Christ not only subjected Himself to the reign of sin but also to death, and in His resurrection He was vindicated or justified (*edikaiothe*) by the Spirit (1 Tim 3:16). In Christ, sin is no longer our boss, because in Christ we live to God as He did (Rom. 6:10). Deliverance from sin's dominion 'is the fundamental and universal principle of sanctification for every Christian. Indeed, it is so true of each and every Christian as to be virtually definitive of being a Christian . . . Therefore we are to act as . . . dead men brought to life'[68] (6:13). Christ came

---

67. On the non-technical use of 'justified', referring to sanctification not justification in this context, see the discussion in Cunnington, art. cit., pp. 245–52.

68. Ferguson, art. cit., p. 57. Ferguson's exposition of this question is masterly, as is the whole of his article.

under the reign of sin and death, but was not defeated by them, and His resurrection broke their power. This is part of definitive sanctification because in relation to 'both sin and to God, the determining factor of my existence is *no longer my past. It is Christ's past.* [69] With Christ 'our sinful self was hung on the cross so that the body as a helpless tool of sin might be definitively defeated.'[70]

4.4 New creation in Christ

Finally, the believer is a new person in Christ, now part of the new creation; this new-age perspective undergirds the preceding arguments. Well-intended believers are often troubled by statements such as Hebrews 12:14: 'strive for the holiness without which no one will see the Lord' and the repeated biblical injunction 'you shall be holy, for I am holy' (1 Pet.1:15f). They either feel disqualified by the high standard, or they redefine holiness with less stringent demands and the result is invariably passivism or activism. In fact the whole Roman Catholic doctrine of grace and purification in this life and the next, with its restrictive notion of saintliness, is a reply to this problem.[71]

However, definitive sanctification, while in no way limiting the exhortations to holiness of such texts, points to the fact that those united to Christ are already where is He, 'raised up with him and seated with him in the heavenly places in Christ Jesus' (Eph. 2:6). The 'future ages' (2:7) have already begun. Faith in Christ procures a radical change of status, and His holiness is ours because of corporate identity. In this respect, the glorification of Romans 8:30 is not simply future, but a present

---

69. Ferguson, art. cit., p. 57, Ferguson's italics.

70. D. J. Moo, *Romans 1–8* (Chicago: Moody 1991), p. 393. Peterson (99–103) interprets the freedom from sin in the context of the tension of Paul's thought and the eschatological promise of final liberation. If this aspect is important, the past action of Christ is the overriding consideration and the power of sin is already broken in Him, Romans 6:14.

71. The doctrines of created grace or the 'treasure of the Church' in the purification of sin by the holiness of saints, Mary, etc. *Catechism of the Catholic Church* (1992), §1474–7.

reality in Christ.[72] We are united not only to the whole Christ, but also to *all* His work on our behalf. 'You have died' is not in discontinuity but in continuity with 'when Christ appears, then you will also appear with him', because Christ is 'your life' (Col. 2:11f., 3:1-3). In Christ we 'receive a kingdom that cannot be shaken' (Heb. 12:27). Because sanctification is real in the new life given by the Lord, it is no less definitive than justification.[73] The believer is not an old self and a new living side by side, but is defined by the age to come, and for this reason seeks to 'offer to God acceptable worship, with reverence and awe, for our God is a consuming fire' (12.28).

Two aspects of this surprising situation can be indicated. In Galatians 2:20 the apostle states 'I have been crucified with Christ. It is no longer I who live but Christ who lives in me. And the life I now live in the flesh I live by faith in the Son of God who loved me and gave himself for me.' Two paradoxes are striking. The 'ego' has been 'crucified' but Paul himself lives; he lives, not him, but Christ in him. A two-sided unity is expressed: he is with Christ and Christ is in him. This unity is a new pneumatic fellowship, because it is real by faith in the Son. 'By this faith – which is directed toward Christ in his loving self-surrender – Christ dwells and rules in him and no longer his own old 'I'.'[74] Paul writes this in the context of a vigorous defence of justification, which illustrates that sanctification in the definitive sense is by faith as much as justification, through the new life of the Spirit. This obviously refers to the personal contrast of before and after faith, and conversion.[75]

More emphatic in the apostle's emphasis is a second perspective. The old man belongs to the world of Adam, the

---

72. Bavinck, op. cit., IV, p. 253, glorified 'in the very same moment' as they are justified. cf. W. Marshall, *The Gospel Mystery of Sanctification,* (Fig-books.com [2012] 1692), p. 266 – 'Sanctification in Christ is glorification begun, as glorification is sanctification perfected.'

73. Horton, op. cit., pp. 253f.

74. Ridderbos, op. cit., p. 232.

75. As Stott indicates, n.66 above.

flesh, sin, death and judgment. Christ through His resurrection introduces a new age, a new humanity and a new realm, one characterised by the Spirit, righteousness, life and redemption. Through faith the apostle sees himself as really belonging to this new age and possessing an irrevocable identity because of union with Christ. Life and holiness go with righteousness in Christ. If Paul still has to deal with the flesh, because he is still physically 'in' it until death in Christ, by faith he belongs to a new reality, one which is the foundation of a life of sanctification. Christ imparts and guarantees the Spirit He obtained forever. When we appear before God, it is in Christ and Christ Himself is our holiness. Once in Christ we can never come out of Him, because our 'ego' has been detached from the principles governing the realm of the old man (*palaios anthropos*); it is no longer identified with him, but opposed to him. The believer has become wholly a new man, not partly as if he were a hybrid running on one substance at one moment and on another at another.[76]

This new cosmic context of our lives is almost too much for us to handle, but it is principal for sanctification. We may not feel it, we may have ups and downs, times of spiritual numbness, and we may even plummet into serious sin that calls for self-examination and repentance, but we cannot determine ourselves by experience. What Scripture says is determinative of spiritual life and it encourages us to keep centred on Christ.

When did believers die and rise again in Christ? It can only be in the historic past, when Christ did. However, this once-for-all change is made continuously in the life of the people of God, when they enter into Christ's reality, as is symbolised by baptism itself.[77] Definitive sanctification is both in Christ, with whom we died and rose, and an event we experience simultaneously with effectual calling and regeneration, when we join the people of God and are transferred from the kingdom of Satan to the kingdom of the Son. Believers are sanctified passively and

---

76. Kuyper, op. cit., pp. 481–2; Ferguson, art. cit., pp. 58–60.
77. Murray, op. cit., II, pp. 289f.

definitively in Christ, just as they are passive in regeneration, and only consequently is sanctification active in transformative sanctification. Furthermore, as Bavinck states,

> Evangelical sanctification is just as distinct from legalistic sanctification as the righteousness that is of faith differs from that which is obtained by works. For it consists in the reality that in Christ God grants us, along with righteousness, also complete holiness, and does not just impute it but also inwardly imparts it by the regenerating and renewing work of the Holy Spirit, until we have been fully conformed to the image of his Son.[78]

This means that sanctification has nothing to do with the law and the obedience it demands. Christ is our holiness. Sanctification is His work for us and in us. Jesus Himself has fulfilled the law in a way that it was never fulfilled for blessing in the Adamic administration, or in the old Mosaic covenant in Israel. That law no longer regulates the holiness-relation between God and His people. 'Now Christ has come in the place of the law; in and through him God regulates the relationship between him and his people... Jesus sanctifies his people by the Spirit, who as such is now called the Holy Spirit and is the prime agent in sanctification.'[79] This shuts the door on all legalistic forms of self-made holiness, which remove sanctification from the realm of grace and faith making it the moralism of 'nice people' who happen to go to church on Sunday. This has probably hurt evangelicalism a lot more than we can begin to imagine. It has made us respectable and middle class.

5. Transformation in Conformity to Christ as Lifestyle

It is normal that the process of sanctification should preoccupy us, because growth is generally a sign that an organism is healthy. However progress is a slippery concept in the spiritual realm if

78. Bavinck, op. cit., IV, p. 248.
79. ibid., p. 252.

it is taken to mean achievement and tangible results. For one thing we are too susceptible to self-satisfaction to be lucid about ourselves. We have an unhealthy tendency to compare ourselves favourably with others in order to prove our *bona fide* holiness. The other extreme is no healthier either, saying that we can do little to further sanctification. If, in justification, faith is passive and receptive, in sanctification it becomes active, and God remains the source and the giver in both cases.

'The term sanctification identifies the process of a new believer's gradual transformation from his sin-fallen condition to the perfect, holy and righteous image of Christ.'[80] In the context of union with Christ, transformation is increasing conformity to Christ, because we are one with Him, united in one body by the Holy Spirit. There are three ways in which sanctification can be spoken of as transformation in union with Christ: firstly, as Christ's continuing work in us; secondly, this work is carried on by a replication of His work in the suffering/glory pattern; finally, the result is increasing conformity to Christ in renewal. In each of these, our lives are made over in Christ and patterned after His life.[81]

5.1 Christ's continuing work in believers

Sanctification in Christ is a day-by-day process, His continuing work in us. The distinction between definitive and progressive is artificial and limited; both forms of sanctification are the fruit of Christ's work and His holiness. We are one with Him in an uninterrupted union because of the agency of the Holy Spirit. The Christian cannot abuse the body sexually because 'he who is joined to the Lord is one spirit with him . . . your body is the temple of the Holy Spirit within you' (1 Cor. 6:17, 19). The Spirit the Lord Jesus Himself received for living and dying, the Spirit that raised Him from the dead, unites believers with Him. The

---

80. J. V. Fesko, *Growing in Holiness. Understanding Sanctification* (Fearn: Christian Focus 2012), p. 1, commenting the *Westminster Shorter Catechism*, q.35.

81. Garcia, op. cit., p. 140, on sanctification as a replication (not imitation) of the pattern of Christ in Calvin's thought.

end of His incarnation was to prepare the holy nature of the new creation in Himself and for us; having atoned for our sins, He freed Himself from sin and death, destroying the body of sin. As the last Adam, He was raised a spiritual body and became 'a life-giving spirit ... the second man from heaven ... and as is the man from heaven, so are those who are of heaven ... we shall bear the image of the man of heaven' (1 Cor. 15:45-49). If Paul primarily envisages the future resurrection image of humanity in Christ, in the present believers receive the Spirit as a down-payment on their future inheritance. One with Christ, the believer is endowed with the power of the indwelling Spirit of holiness.

New life in Christ is life in the Spirit, making believers one with the Lord, animated by Christ's Spirit and alive because of it. Already part of the new creation, they are bound by the Spirit of life to Christ and His resurrection life. This is the beginning in the present world of tension and strife, even though spiritual oneness with Christ is the prime focus of the Christian life. 'In our pilgrimage, we are not, strictly speaking, growing in *our* holiness, but we are bearing the fruit of our union with Christ and his holiness.'[82] In other words, the new nature and holiness are first in Christ and then by the Spirit in us, by a principle of derivation from Him to us. As believers we do not work sanctification on our own, or even together with Christ, but *we actively take His holiness to ourselves*; sanctification is fellowship with Christ.[83] We apply Christ to ourselves not only for believing in salvation, but also for sanctification. In both cases, and observing that order, Christ Himself is received in our hearts by faith, so transformation is the result of intimate personal fellowship with the risen Christ. Believing on, resting in, and walking in trust carries with it the assurance of saving faith. We must certainly persuade ourselves continually that it is so, neutralising doubts

---

82. Horton, op. cit., pp. 248, and 248–56.

83. W. Marshall, op. cit., pp. 33f. In these paragraphs I refer indirectly several times to Marshall's *The Gospel Mystery of Sanctification*, one of the best on the subject, according to John Murray.

by mentally re-appropriating the promises of God to faith and making them our spiritual nourishment.[84] Living consciously in Christ will bring in its wake comfort, peace of mind, confidence and enjoyment of life – what it means to be well satisfied with Jesus. This alone will help us to overcome the ingratitude, dissatisfaction and complaining nature that well up from sinful dispositions, and to reformat our lives in a growing stability that is so different to the roller-coaster rides of 'mountain and valley' experiences.

Living in Christ is the opposite of wavering, doubting, fearing and staggering (Rom. 4:20) that arise when our eyes are fixed on the world around and not on Christ. 'The way to avoid these evils is to get assurance, and to maintain it, and renew it upon all occasions by the direct act of faith, by trusting assuredly on the name of the Lord, and staying yourself on your God, when you walk in darkness and see no light in any of your own qualifications.'[85]

So it is that Christ dwells in believers' hearts through faith, when they are 'rooted and grounded' and know 'the love of Christ that surpasses knowledge, filled with the fullness of God.' (Eph. 3:17-19) W. Marshall points out that fellowship with Christ is indicated by three biblical metaphors, which all imply the closeness of being 'one spirit' with Christ and growing into Him: the vine and branches, the head and the body, and the bread and the eater. Regarding the nourishment symbolised by the Lord's Supper he states:

> Though Christ is in heaven and we on earth, yet He can join our souls and bodies to His at such a distance without any substantial change of either, by the same infinite Spirit dwelling in Him and us; and so our flesh will become His, when it is quickened by His Spirit, and is flesh ours, as truly as if we ate his flesh and drank his blood. And he will be in us Himself by His Spirit, who is one with Him, and who can unite more closely to Christ than any

---

84.   Marshall, op. cit., pp. 130ff.
85.   ibid., p. 156.

material substance can do, or who can make a more close and intimate union between Christ and us.[86]

So we grow spiritually by living off the life of Christ who dwells in us by faith through the efficacy of the Spirit. Union with the benefactor, knowing Christ and communing with Him, is always more precious than any of His benefits. The person is greater than the gifts and is Himself the giver. It is important not to major in minors, as has often been the case in the history of the church, and remains a temptation today. The continuation of Christ's work in us depends not on experiences, but on real and close communion in the body of Christ.

5.2 Replication of the work of Christ

Secondly, transformation is carried forward by a replication of Christ's suffering/glory pattern in the life of the church and of believers, part of what Calvin called self-denial, of which bearing the cross is a part.[87] The main aspects of Christian living he indicates – self-denial, carrying one's cross, relativising the present life and meditating on eternity – are not major items on the spiritual wish list of evangelical Christians today. In fact, a consistent ministry on this might well turn some punters off.

Calvin, like Luther, saw the Christian life in terms of the theology of the cross and not as a theology of glory. Even a cursory reading of the New Testament (think of the dozen or so references to suffering in 1 Peter!) validates this approach, to say nothing of the theology of martyrdom that developed in early Christianity. Not only that, suffering with Christ was seen as the travail of the body of Christ in a situation of cosmic conflict with the forces of evil.[88] Doing 'all to the glory of God'

---

86. ibid., p. 35. Marshall's view implies a Calvinist doctrine of the real presence in the Supper. Any discussion of sanctification and union with Christ ought to include also the external means of union, the Word, the Church as body of Christ and the sacraments, which space does not permit here. cf. Ferguson, art. cit., pp. 67–74.

87. Calvin, in 'The golden book of the Christian life', *Institutes*, III.vi–x.

88. cf. P. Middleton, *Radical Martyrdom and Cosmic Conflict in Early Christianity* (Edinburgh: T & T Clark 2006).

is the keynote in the opposition and struggle with evil, and the apostle Paul urges the Corinthians to 'be imitators of me, as I am of Christ' (1 Cor. 11:1; 4:16). The context of suffering is becoming one with the head in the body of Christ and growing away from the world into Him. So in Romans 8, the great chapter on union with Christ, personal, soteriological and cosmic, the apostle states that we are children and heirs of God, *fellow heirs with* Christ, 'provided we suffer with him in order that we may also be glorified with him.' Sufferings are little in the light of the 'glory to be revealed' (Rom. 8:17f.; 5:3).

This glory which invariably provides the hope-backdrop of suffering, is no doubt the resurrection glory of Christ's kingly rule, as in Philippians 3:10. To live according to the righteousness of God that depends on faith is 'to know him and the power of his resurrection, and to share his sufferings, becoming like him in his death, (to) obtain the resurrection from the dead.' 'The fiery trial' of suffering is not a surprising thing, as it is 'sharing Christ's suffering . . . as a Christian' (1 Pet. 4:12-16). What then is the nature of this suffering and how is it an aspect of sanctification in union with Christ? Was Pascal right when he said, 'Jesus will be in agony even to the end of the world. We must not sleep during that time'?[89]

Replication of the Christ-model in the Christian's suffering is neither a repetition, an imitation or a continuation of Christ's earthly suffering, simply because of the decisive event of the resurrection. 'The believer's engrafting to the resurrected Christ (organic) originates or produces the (sequential) pattern of suffering then glory, or obedience then eschatological life. . . . The organic character of this union ensures that the pattern that was true for Christ in history is true for those united to him.'[90] Participation in suffering following Christ is as essential to the Christian's calling as justification is, a *sine qua non* of authenticity in belonging to Christ. The bond of participation in Christ is the

---

89. B. Pascal, *Pensées* (Harmondsworth: Penguin Books 1966), p. 313.

90. Garcia, op. cit., pp. 143f.

Holy Spirit, the same eternal Spirit at work in Christ's obedience and self-offering, who 'purifies our conscience . . . to serve the living God' (Heb. 9:14). This sequential suffering is in no way redemptive, a point which brings us to the unavoidable statement in Colossians 1:24, where Paul states: 'I rejoice in my sufferings for your sake, and in my flesh I am filling up what is lacking in Christ's affliction for the sake of his body, that is the church.' Commenting on this, Calvin says:

> There is so great a unity between Christ and his members, that the name of 'Christ' sometimes includes the whole body, as in 1 Corinthians 12:12 ... (for) in Christ the same thing holds as in the human body. As, therefore, Christ has suffered 'once' in his own person, so he suffers 'daily' in his members, and in this way there are 'filled up' those sufferings which the Father hath appointed for his body by his decree.[91]

C. F. D. Moule indicates two strands in the interpretation of this verse, which he collates. Firstly, the participational: those who are in Christ share in His suffering, like the apostle, and complete 'what is lacking' in the community of faith. Alternatively, the eschatological: the 'what is lacking' refers to the messianic woes, the period of eschatological distress before the end comes, through which the church must pass and in so doing hasten the coming end. Moule collates the two by summing up that Paul contributes to the quota of sufferings which the whole church must undergo in the working out of God's designs.[92]

So Pascal was right, in a non-redemptive sense. If Christ is not suffering *for* the church any longer, final redemption awaits eschatological completion, and during the interim between resurrection and return, He continues to suffer *with* those who belong to His body in their trials. Because of the image of the body, Christ's agony is in His members and His suffering is His

---

91. Calvin, *Commentary on Colossians* at http://www.studylight.org/commentaries/cal: Col. 1:23. cf. *Institutes*, III.v.3–4.

92. C. F. D. Moule, *The Epistles of Paul the Apostle to the Colossians and to Philemon* (Cambridge: CUP 1962), p. 74.

compassion for them (Heb. 2:18). What is lacking for salvation to be complete is the revelation of the man of sin, the final opposition to Christ and the time of suffering through which His people must go before their final salvation. Christ participates with them in this trial in the opposition between Christ and antichrist. Suffering therefore plays a part in the final salvation of the body of Christ. The mystical union between the Lord and those who are His includes His fellowship in their suffering, spiritually, morally and physically. In His eternal humanity, Christ is united with our humanity and suffers compassionately with us.

Suffering is therefore part of union with Christ and plays a part in sanctification, whether it be in facing the contradiction of sinners, injustice, persecution, learning radical obedience, counting all things loss for the sake of Christ (Phil. 3:8), physical illness, and even death in Christ. All these are modelled in the sense of 'becoming like him in his death' (3:10). The glory of the cross lies in Christ's complete and willing submission to doing the will of the Father. The body of Christ, the Spirit-filled church, can trace no other furrow than the one made by the Master.[93]

The suffering-glory pattern contributes to sanctification, because suffering binds us to Christ as its hermeneutical matrix, and binds Christ to us as our hope in the concrete sufferings we endure. This produces spiritual and moral victories in the face of adversity 'by keeping sweet, peaceful, patient, obedient and hopeful, under sustained and seemingly intolerable pressures and frustrations'.[94] Suffering with Christ, for His name, is no

---

93. Most recent literature on the subject of suffering treats it as a problem of theodicy and apologetics and addresses the world's problems (*The Problem of . . .*), rather than questions which edify the body of Christ in terms of mystical union and sanctification. For this reason, perhaps, without ignoring the complexities of the subject, in my experience few Christians seem to learn anything from their sufferings, and tend to come back continually to the same old sterile question: 'Why does the Lord allow . . . ?' An exception (in French) is Pierre Ch. Marcel's *Souffrir . . . Mais Pour Quoi?* (Lausanne: L'Age d'Homme 1994).

94. J. I. Packer, on commenting the struggles of the Puritans 'who lost, more or less, every public battle that they fought', *Among God's Giants. Aspects of Puritan Christianity* (Eastbourne: Kingsway 1991), p. 25.

reason for doubt and alienation, but a proof of sonship and paradoxically, for us as human beings, a reason for rejoicing and joy. 'Suffering for believers is a means by which God fixes our hearts more firmly on "the glory about to be revealed to us".'[95] What the apostle Paul stated theoretically in Romans 5:3-5, that suffering produces endurance, character and hope 'because God's love has been poured into our hearts through the Holy Spirit', he demonstrated concretely in the prison-joy of his captivity epistles. Christians have a much better hope than a more efficient NHS!

5.3 Increasing conformity to Christ

Thirdly and finally, the result of transformative sanctification is increasing conformity to Christ in the liberation and renewal of our humanity. In union with Christ, by the Spirit, our earthly humanity is joined with Christ's heavenly and perfect humanity and, by faith, Christ lives in us. This does not mean that by some form of suggestion we develop a 'what would Jesus do?' mentality. It does mean we are transformed in thought and action in conformity to the Lordship of Christ. 'Having the mind of Christ' is having a new critical stance that is different from a mind set on the things of the world (Rom. 8:5, 7).

The apostle Paul makes mind-renewal the lynchpin for Christian living: 'Do not be conformed to the world, but be transformed by the renewing of your mind' (Rom. 12:2). The word transformed (*metamorpheo*) is also used in Mark 9:2 for the transfiguration of Jesus and in 2 Corinthians 3:18: 'We beholding the glory of the Lord, are being transformed into the same image, from one degree of glory to another.'

The renewal of the mind in Christ is as radical as the pre-resurrection glory of Jesus' transfiguration, and is a vehicle for carrying the image of Christ, in contrast with the Adamic image. The new birth brings us into a spiritual standing with the living God and this never happens without a change of mind. The

---

95.   Peterson, op. cit., p. 118.

mind is an agent in ongoing transformation. Our feelings roller-coaster and our will wobbles like jelly, but our union with Christ will become more marked, as divine truth cuts deeper into our lives and sanctifies them.

Sin has disastrous consequences on the contents of our minds because in their sinful state, our minds thrash about, at enmity with God (Eph. 2:11ff). Through the renewal of the mind, what was sin-dominated is restored to some semblance of normality, although the final big change of mind awaits the resurrection body. Faith in Christ is a change of mind. Before we believed, our self was everything, God nothing; we didn't even know it and lived for ourselves (1 Cor. 2:14). Once united to Christ, living in Him becomes everything to us; we start to want to please Him and our values change.

The apostle Paul gives two exhortations to get our minds on the right track in union with Christ as a vehicle of sanctification. In 2 Corinthians 10:3-5 he encourages us to 'take every thought captive to obey Christ' and in Colossians 2:8 he says, 'See to it that no one takes you captive by philosophy and empty deceit . . . and not according to Christ.' This does not happen by some kind of osmosis. Communion with Christ trains our minds in three complementary ways. First of all, we learn, little by little, to fix our thoughts on Him and live in Him. We fill our minds with fine thoughts of the beauty of His saving greatness. He shows us what true humanity is and, as we meditate on His life, we are metamorphosed into His likeness. The image of the Lord Jesus is formed in us, through love of the truth (Eph. 4:24; Col. 3:10). What is the mental content of the image? It is the Lord Jesus Himself, His person and work.

The motor of progressive sanctification takes place in a mind renewed by the truth that becomes biblically critical of this-worldly vanities. Jesus is Lord over all and we look at everything critically from that perspective – to make Him Lord of our lives. We work to take distance from what we were like before we knew what was wrong with us.

A renewed intelligence is a mind directed by God and informed by His Word. This leads us to healthy self-examination and criticism of our motives, goals and standards, to bring them into line with what serving Christ demands. In practice, what God approves, we seek to do; what He loves we seek to love; what is against His truth is our mortal enemy. If the opposite of error is truth, the Christian strives to line his life up with God's truth and to discern what is right and wrong by God's standards.

The Christian mind strives for transformation into a Christ-like mind. This implies godliness in all areas of life in a broad perspective and deepening trust in Christ in a deep perspective, because of what His Word demands. The result is ever-greater conformity to Christ, according to the nature of His humanity and therefore transformation of the old into new forms of obedience and service. Romans 12:1-2 is a reversal of Romans 1:18-32; no different form of life can be envisaged in the consecrated sacrifice of ourselves, without a radical renewal of the mind.[96] We should be wary of denigration of the mind, as this is not according to Christ:

> Perhaps the current mood (cultivated in some Christian groups) of anti-intellectualism begins now to be seen as the serious evil it is. It is not true piety at all but part of the fashion of the world and therefore a form of worldliness. To denigrate the mind is to undermine foundational Christian doctrines. Has God created us rational beings, and shall we deny our humanity which he has given us? Has God spoken to us and shall we not listen to his words? Has God not renewed our mind through Christ, and shall we not think with it? Is God going to judge us by his Word, and shall we not be wise and build our house upon this rock?[97]

To sum up: sanctification is the expression of the holiness of the renewed humanity of the Lord Jesus Christ in communion with Him, in which His qualities become increasingly ours through

---

96. ibid., pp. 127–9.

97. J. Stott, *Your Mind Matters. The Place of the Mind in the Christian Life* (London: InterVarsity Press 1972), p. 26.

the Holy Spirit in renewal, transformation and growth. The whole process is a continuous and daily conformity to Christ, until it reaches its terminus in glorification.

6. Tension in the Struggle for Sanctification

The overlap between this present age and the age to come, the fact that salvation is already and also not yet, the contrast between union with Christ and living in the world, all contribute to the fact that sanctification in the life of the Christian is an experience of constant tension. This double perspective is an aspect of the cosmic process in which the creation itself waits for liberation and the revelation of the children of God. The believer also longs for personal liberation and groans, waiting to be 'clothed upon' by the redemption of the body (Rom. 8:18-25). For that reason, many things in the present life smack of 'futility' to those who look to the future glory. 'Imperfect sanctification' seems a sad compromise, and in our more lucid moments we long for the arrival home that follows a tiring journey.

For this reason, there have been many attempts of one form or another in the history of the church to transcend this tension – in the vision of God, perfect love, entire sanctification, freedom from conscious sin, perfection or a simple denial of the world and a despising of the body, either in asceticism or its opposite. These aspirations often find expression in a crisis experience by which the believer finds freedom from sin and lives on a higher plane as a result of it.

6.1 Perfectionisms

Warfield analysed recent holiness movements in the articles which make up volumes VII and VIII, entitled 'Perfectionism' in his collected *Works*. It is claimed that this modern search for complete holiness is new, related to a new consciousness of the Holy Spirit in the latter day, and that whereas Athanasius was the pioneer in Christology and Luther in justification, Wesley led the way in holiness. Warfield considers that these holiness movements invariably separate justification from sanctification and propose complete sanctification rather than total freedom from sin, which would go against all our experience. A crisis moment marks progress with a different experience of faith (complete surrender to Christ as Lord) from that which is known in justification (Christ as Saviour). Distinctions are consequently drawn between categories of Christians: 'mere', surrendered or victorious types of believer. Surrender is a human step leading to victory and though the carnal nature remains, the new nature gives the victory over it, in a 'liberation of the Spirit', often resulting in psychological or physical healing.

Warfield indicates that the synergistic mentality exists in many instances and the fact that if the experience claims a new level in the work of the Spirit, it depends on a human decision and the aspiration to move from one level to the superior one. A kind of consistency is at work, because when human decision is determinative in receiving salvation, it reappears as a necessary condition in sanctification. At the end of his article on the 'victorious life' Warfield makes a hard judgment on various forms of free-willism (the 'you can have it, it's up to you' mentality):

> [I]t is something far worse than Pelagianism, something the affinities of which are with magic rather than religion, which supposes that the activities of God can be commanded by acts of men, even if these acts be acts of faith. It is the essence of magic as distinguished from religion that places supernatural powers at the disposal of men for working effects of their own choosing ... This stands things on their head, and in doing so degrades God into merely the instrument which man employs to secure his objects.[98]

Enough said; many of us have witnessed such things or lived through them. Even though those involved in different forms of 'crisis holiness' will not be so lucid about it, experience-based sanctification often makes man the kingpin and the actor of his

---

98. Warfield, op. cit., VIII, p. 609. cf. Bavinck, op. cit., IV, pp. 260–6.

own sanctification, even if the whole process is dressed up in the language of consecration, piety or giftedness. Berkouwer, however, points out that this is not the case: 'Progress in sanctification never means working out one's own salvation under one's own auspices; it means working out salvation with a rising dependency on God's grace.'[99]

The question that must be answered concerns our expectations of sanctification in the context of tension and conflict. Five issues dealing with living the tension may be broached, as follows: firstly, spiritual warfare; secondly, the old man and the new; thirdly, the mortification of the flesh; further, questions raised by Romans 7 and finally, the role of the law in Christian life and good works.

6.2 Spiritual warfare

What some Christians seem to lack is a sanctified realism or common sense about sanctification. The basic New Testament model for reaching heaven is spiritual warfare in the context of pilgrimage. It is realistic to think that we will never get beyond this state. This is not an unspiritual view of life in Christ. On the contrary: the conflict comes precisely from renewal in grace and the presence of the Holy Spirit uniting us to Christ, as we continue to deal with the three enemies – the world, the flesh and the devil. They are enough for any believer to take on, without becoming our own worst enemy by cultivating unrealistic expectations of what we can achieve. Our self-knowledge is unreliable and only Scripture can correct our false expectations about holiness in this life. The situation is uncomfortable and the process painful, because as we are raised from the dead in Christ, we are living in the graveyard of the old man until this life is over.

Spiritual conflict is the normal situation of all Christians and there are no exceptions, no people who achieve 'peace and quiet' by transcending it. The exhortations of Ephesians 6:10ff, to be 'strong in the Lord and the power of his might', are issued in the context of the cosmic struggle against the devil and the powers

---

99.   Berkouwer, op. cit., p. 112.

of the present darkness; conflict is an aspect of union with Christ in which we 'stand firm in the evil day'. The armour of the Christian, as described in W. Gurnall's magnificent *Christian in Complete Armour*,[100] is both defensive and offensive. If the sword is the Word of God, the body protection is provided by righteousness, the gospel of peace, faith (probably subjective faith) and salvation, all of which are focussed in union with Christ. If prayer itself is not part of the armoury, perhaps that's because our communion with Christ in sanctification is by the external means of 'the Word of God and prayer'.

One thing that 'victory Christianity' overlooks is that the victory is not a subjective experience in the context of our sin, a conquest by our overcoming, but it is *already* in Christ Himself. Though we can never leave the battlefield until life's end, we know that the outcome is sure, because we are united to the triumphant Christ who has reduced sin, death and the devil to powerlessness, under His Lordship. Only those who have left the battlefield have ceased conflict, the saints of Hebrews 11. We must continue to struggle in situations of great adversity and hope for the certain outcome based on the divine promise.

Is it legitimate to have expectations other than the reality described by 'treasure in jars of clay'? Is it not realistic to accept that in this life our fate will not be better than the apostle's: afflicted, perplexed, persecuted and struck down, all this being described as a 'light momentary affliction'? Yet the life of Jesus is manifested; in spite of affliction we are not crushed, despairing, forsaken or destroyed (2 Cor. 4:7-18). So why lose heart when 'the surpassing power that belongs to God' is at work? Strength made perfect in weakness is not a form of moral weakness but courage, because it is the weakness of recognised dependence on the power of God.

6.3 The old man and the new

The struggle is not only going on outside and around us, but also in us spiritually, in the presence of the old and the new man and

---

100. cf. D. M. Lloyd-Jones, *The Christian Warfare* (Edinburgh: Banner of Truth 1976).

in the remains of the old alongside the new reality. 'The conflict is not only external and objective; it is internal and subjective – with the flesh as well as with the world and the devil. All that is true *for me* in Christ has not yet been accomplished *in me* by the Spirit.'[101] If *for me* the old self was crucified with Christ (Rom. 6:6) and the believer shares by regeneration in the new humanity and the new creation in Christ (2 Cor. 5:17) what is true in principle must be carried out in practice *in me*. We were born in the old man, but if we belong to Christ our self is in principle detached from the old man, no longer identified with him and even opposed to him, but the debris still litters our existence.[102] We are wholly the new man in Christ, not partially. By mystic union with Christ every believer possesses the entire new man, but does not yet fully enjoy it. Sanctification must mortify what sin has quickened in our Adamic nature. Christ bore our sins that we 'might die to sin and live to righteousness' (1 Pet. 2:24). If we 'have put off the old man with its practices and put on the new which is being renewed' (Col. 3:9f.), this definitive death to sin must be manifested ever anew. So 'God's child remains the old man's gravedigger until the hour of his own departure.'[103]

At this juncture, reference to union with Christ in sanctification is vital, because if we are born in Adam, it is not we who get out of him; the death of the old man is the fruit of the cross of Christ in us, as Christ lives in us. The Holy Spirit, by whom we live in Christ, is the instrument of this dying, imparting to us new personal dispositions. The deflection of our inclinations and affections from the old to the new is the fruit of the work of the cross in us. This is a direct effect of union with Christ in us, as the life of Christ flows into us through the indwelling Spirit, carrying forward the work of renewal and the increasing sanctification of our persons. So 'the dominion of the whole body of sin (of the regenerate) is destroyed and the several lusts

101. Ferguson, art. cit., p. 62.

102. I am following some elements from Kuyper's presentation, op. cit., pp. 468–84.

103. ibid., p. 484.

thereof are more and more weakened and mortified; and they are more and more quickened and strengthened in all saving graces to the practice of true holiness.'[104]

Imperfect sanctification is 'perfect in parts, imperfect in degrees', to use an old expression.[105] This notion corresponds to a biblical conception of sin. Depravity in all the parts and faculties of sinful man is not complete sinfulness anywhere, thanks to God's restraining grace; remainders of the image of God, are still evident. Likewise sanctification is present everywhere, in every aspect of the new life, but it is never complete. Nobody reaches fullness of stature in Christ. The believer must grow up into Christ. Growth is inward strength and increasing assurance, being 'strengthened in the inner man'. As it is 'perfect in parts', the entire sinful disposition of the old man comes under attack in an action against each individual sin, which is one reason for the lists drawn up under the exhortations 'put to death' or 'do not gratify' (Col. 3:5ff.; Gal. 5:16).

No person united to Christ can escape from a divided existence in the present, described by the words *sarx* and *pneuma*. The flesh and the Spirit are held in constant antithesis in the New Testament writers, and nowhere more concisely than in Romans 8:5-8, where two mindsets are presented:

The flesh cannot please God: The Spirit:

- death
- hostility to God
- rejection of God's law

- life and peace

The struggle between the flesh and the Spirit 'explains much of the spiritual angst and conflict that Paul sets forth in detail in Romans 6:1; 8:1-17, Galatians 5:15-26 and Ephesians 4:17-24.'[106] The desires of the flesh rear their ugly head and war against the

104. *Westminster Confession of Faith*, XIII, i.

105. Kuyper, op. cit., pp. 468–72.

106. Fesko, art. cit., p. 204.

Spirit and the result is 'to keep you from doing what you want to do' (Gal. 5:17). This is the realism of someone who knows what they are talking about, in the struggle for sanctification. It is the universal tension opposing the present evil age and the world to come that is being played out in the microcosm of the believer's experience. That is precisely what we feel every time we pass that place where the tempter calls our name, when we are fighting an evil thought that comes out of the blue, when we are drawn to the sin that gratifies our lusts, or when the narrative of sin seems more desirable than holiness. 'Faith is different in degrees, weak or strong (including oscillation in our life-histories) and weakened, but gets the victory: growing up in many to the attainment of a full assurance, through Christ . . .'[107] 'Keeping in step with the Spirit' will undermine our most insidious and disagreeable traits: pride, conceit and jealousy should be the first bastions of the flesh to fall (Gal. 5:25f.) but all too often get away with it because of our rationalisations, self-justifications and defence mechanisms that protect them with the excuse, 'that is just what I'm like'.

6.4 Mortification and vivification

Pilgrimage in the struggle against the flesh follows the path of the descent of the old man and the rising of the new, described in terms of mortification and vivification, which together constitute the deep structure of new life in Christ. In the conclusion to Romans 8:1-11, where the apostle contrasts life in the flesh with life in the Spirit, the apostle introduces the theme of the mortification of sin. The body (*soma*) is dead because of sin – it is through our physical life that we belong to this present world, but the resurrection-Spirit of Jesus who dwells in believers gives life to those mortal bodies that are dead (v. 11). In consequence (*ara oun*, v. 12) believers owe nothing to their physical inheritance of sin, but they owe everything to the Spirit to live according to the Spirit. It is the flesh, the principle of sin reigning in the present age that takes over the body and brings physical existence to death. Those in Christ are not to live according to the flesh principle (*kata sarka*). Their duty is to put to death the

---

107. *Westminster Confession of Faith*, XIV, iii.

acts of the body (*soma*) to live. In Greek the words *put to death* and *will live* are side by side at the end of verse 13 (*thanatoute zesesthe*), making the strongest possible contrast. Note that this action can only be undertaken by the Spirit (*pneumati*), because the Spirit is the resurrection power that ends death, in Jesus's physical body and in those who belong to Him, and in whom the Spirit dwells. This is a great sign of sonship (v. 14) and recognition by the Father. In the struggle against sin, the present experience of the believer in union with Christ in His death and resurrection is a beautiful example of trinitarian action in sanctification and the centrality of the mediation of Christ between Father and Spirit.

So mortification of sin by the work of the Spirit is of a piece with vivification, part of the new resurrection life in Christ as it unfolds in the believer. Mortification is an ongoing action which progressively takes away the power of sin and neutralises its vigour. W. Marshall in his classic *The Gospel Mystery of Sanctification* states that mortifying the deeds of the body is the way of putting off the old man. He addresses the fact that it is an act that *we* do ('if you put to death') in the Spirit, by saying that if no natural resolution of our own is valid, Christ died to crucify the old man and we resolve to trust in Christ to subdue our natural inclinations. The way of mortifying the flesh is not by purging it, but by putting it off and getting above it, growing into Christ by faith and walking in the new nature by Him: 'we must trust in Christ to enable us above the strength of our own natural power, by virtue of the new nature which we have in Christ and by His Spirit dwelling and working in us.'[108] It is crystal clear here how mortification is part of sanctification in union with Christ, brought about by Him living in us through the Spirit. The reverse side of trust in Christ is cultivating self-critical examination and guarding against indwelling and habitual sin, identifying it and determining to eradicate it.[109]

---

108. Marshall, op. cit., pp. 198–200.

109. John Owen, in his classic, *On the Mortification of Sin in Believers*, in *Works*, VII (London: Banner of Truth 1965), pp. 377–84, identifies the symptoms of unchecked sin. On mortification in Owen see S. B. Ferguson, *John Owen on the Christian Life* (Edinburgh: Banner of Truth 1987), pp. 145–53.

This, states the apostle, is not an option, but a necessity for the believer, because apart from it we die, whereas trust in Christ brings with it the promise 'you will live'. Life in this case is not only the eternal hope, although it is that in contrast with death; it is also life free from the slavery of sin (Rom. 8:15). Life which is the result of mortification will be a life in which love for Christ and others is expressed, fulfilling the great commandment of love, which is the opposite of life in sin, ruled by the principle of egoism and the satisfaction of one's own desires, which make us dead to God. The new nature mortifies sin both directly in opposition to the works of the flesh and indirectly by positive love and obedience to God, which strengthen the new man and advance sanctification. Holiness is a fruit of sanctification, derived from it and distinguished from sanctification itself, as a conformity to the image of Jesus Christ and the reflection of His glory in our lives, present in a little measure now, and complete in His presence in heaven. Both are in Christ, through His Spirit.[110]

Vivification is the unfolding of the life of the new man, the age to come and the life of the Lord Jesus Himself in the lives of believers. As union with Christ unites us to His humanity, what we 'put on' in Christ are the attributes that characterised the incarnate life of Jesus, true righteousness and holiness (Eph. 4:24). The new nature is not simply a matter of battling with sin but is present in the positive aspects of a new lifestyle that take its place. Holiness is in the heart, a holy disposition by which the believer hates and flees all sin without exception, and delights and exercises all virtues without exception, an expression of conformity with God. We could list in this respect as imaging the holiness of Jesus: love and communion with the Father in the Son, obedience to doing the will of God, compassion toward others, and zeal for God's Word and service. Jesus lived out

---

110. W. à Brackel, *The Christian's Reasonable Service*, III (Pittsburgh: Soli Deo Gloria Publications 1994), pp. 9–16, has a useful section on the functioning of the old man in the believer, mortification and vivification.

His own Psalms: 'I have sworn an oath and I will perform it, to keep your righteous rules . . . I incline my heart to perform your statues for ever, to the end' (Ps. 119:106, 112). To do this, Jesus showed enormous spiritual courage and suffered all His life long, most of all in His death on the cross.[111] Holiness belongs to faith; it is a conformity to God's rule that aligns heart and conduct (Rom. 7:12). It has a holy objective, the glory of God in its end, heavenly perfection. These are attained by union with Christ as His holiness is worked out in our lives, in the courage to be Christ-like, different from the world around us, actualised in freedom, obedience and love.[112]

Forgetfulness and coldness of heart are our big enemies, and we need to be warmed by the gospel again and again so that our joy is found in remembering Christ's sacrificial love, holiness and example. The imperative for sanctified living comes from the indicative of the Spirit of holiness dwelling in us, uniting us to Christ, and expressing that unity in a continuing communion in His new life, because 'to whomever Christ is imputed and granted, he is imputed and granted totally'.[113] As Ferguson comments: 'Grace demands mortification. Without it there is no holiness. John Owen writes graphically: "Let not that man think he makes any progress in true holiness who walks not over the bellies of his lusts".'[114]

6.5 The 'wretched man' of Romans 7:14-25

Does the sketch of the war of flesh and spirit, mortification and vivification and the freedom from the slavery of sin in Christ given above correspond to Paul's 'wretched man' or not? Past reformed interpretation in the Augustinian tradition, represented by John Murray's more recent commentary, has

---

111. *Heidelberg Catechism*, q.36.

112. Webster, op. cit., pp. 92–8.

113. Bavinck, op. cit., IV, p. 263; Peterson, op. cit., pp. 111–113.

114. Ferguson, op. cit., p. 64, quoting Owen, *Works*, VI, 14.

proposed that this is the case,[115] and even that Paul in this text portrays someone who, advancing in sanctification, becomes more aware of the holiness of God and their own unworthiness. However, several recent reformed commentators, inspired by H. Ridderbos's redemptive-historical interpretation or not,[116] have held the view that an unconverted and frustrated Jewish seeker after righteousness is described here. Some go as far as to affirm that the description of these verses does not tally with other descriptions of Christian experience in the New Testament.[117] In the following comments we will suppose that the classic view is correct. The fundamental question is whether Romans 7 is compatible with union with Christ or not.

Prima face, apart from the fact that first-century Christians in Rome would be naturally inclined to think, without Ridderbos present to help them see otherwise, someone speaking in the first person singular in the present tense is most likely speaking about their own experience. Moreover, what the text actually says is not contrary to the New Testament understanding of the Christian experience, but the opposite can be plausibly argued in the light of what it teaches elsewhere about the impossibility of righteousness by the law.[118] Romans 7 in no way contradicts what is said of the flesh and the spirit in Romans 8 or the fact

---

115. J. Murray, *Romans* (Grand Rapids: Eerdmans 1965), ch. XII.

116. Ridderbos, op. cit., pp. 126–130. Paul, says Ridderbos, is speaking of the one who stands on the highest plan attainable by pre-Christian man, the man who gives himself to the law with all his strength, p. 129. It is not to be taken in a biographical sense as Paul's pre-conversion experience, as Romans 7 is concerned with redemptive-historical contrasts and not individual experiences. Dennis E. Johnson also proposes that the 'I' of Romans 7:13-25 presents 'Israel's corporate experience in the covenant with God reflected in the experience of the conscientious individual Jew who sought to keep the Torah' in 'The Function of Romans 7:13-25 in Paul's Argument for the Law's Impotence and the Spirit's Power, and Its Bearing on the Identity of the Schizophrenic "I"', in Lane G. Tipton and Jeffrey C. Waddington, (eds.) *Resurrection and Eschatology, Essays in Honor of Richard B. Gaffin,* (Phillipsburg: P & R Publishing, 2008), p. 57.

117. See, for example, D. M. Lloyd-Jones, *Romans 7:1 to 8:4: The Law, Its Functions and Limits* (Edinburgh: Banner of Truth 1973).

118. Section 2 of this article on the difference between righteousness and holiness.

that the desires of the flesh stop us doing what we want to do (Gal. 5:17), which is rather close to 'I do not do the good I want' in Romans 7:19f. So Packer proposes that in Romans 7 Paul describes his own experience of the law before his conversion in 7:7-13 and subsequently (vv. 14-25) at the time of writing as one who in Christ realises the full dimension of the problem of the law. The final verse 'Thanks be to God' leads into the 'rhapsodic setting forth of the content of Christian assurance, expanding the themes of 5:1-11, which fills all thirty-nine verses of Romans 8.'[119] If believers are new creatures in Christ, sin still remains in their hearts, and the remnants of the old nature that need mortifying are precisely what the flesh vivifies (7:18, 20, 23, 35). Sanctification and assurance are not by law-performance, but by union with Christ.

Finally, what kind of exclamation is 'O wretched man that I am! Who will deliver me from this body of death?'? It is hardly something that would have crossed the lips of a Pharisee, or an expression fitting for the unregenerate, who are rather satisfied by and in their sin (8:5a), nor the frustration of pre-Christian seekers, Jews or otherwise, as they have no insights into the 'flesh', nor the despair of one who cannot pass from a lower stage to a higher Christian life, as the apostle knows of no two-stage experience. For this reason, the classic reformed interpretation seems the most adequate, in spite of the intrinsic difficulties of the text. Peterson concludes that 'it is a groaning of the Spirit-led person for the fullness of redemption that will take place when our bodies are resurrected (cf. 8:11, 23). Only then will we be free from endless warfare with sin, death, flesh and the law.'[120]

In this perspective the cry of the wretched man is neither incompatible with union with Christ, nor with sanctification, but is the presupposition of a Spirit-motivated confidence in God and the outworking of His saving plan

---

119. Packer, op. cit., pp. 128f.

120. Peterson, op. cit., p. 109. Peterson's overall presentation of the Christian and God's law in Romans 7 is generally most satisfying, pp. 103–9.

6.6 The role of the law

The role of the law in the Christian life has been a longstanding thorn in the flesh of evangelical and reformed theology. In spite of the influence of Calvin's teaching on the 'third use of the law',[121] embedded in confessional documents, they have rarely been exempt from the temptations of both legalism and antinomianism. The former is often more a question of attitudes and practices, rather than full-blown theory, but antinomianism is always at the door, and has gained a widespread following in 'love only' or 'under grace alone' theologies. Luther's more extreme statements about law in contrast to gospel[122] and false interpretations of the role of the law in the Mosaic covenant are the usual suspects. The question of law concerns us only from one angle: if sanctification is by communion with Christ in the Spirit in the body of Christ, and by direct trust in Him in a living relationship, does the law have a role to play in Christian sanctification, and if so, in what respect? This question is complex and multifaceted and only the briefest reply is sketched here.[123]

In theory, and at the most fundamental level, if Christ did not abolish the law but fulfilled it (Matt. 5:17), then believers are united to Him in that fulfilment, which implies an attitude to the law analogous to the one found in their Head. The guilt and condemnation of the law have been removed in Christ because He fulfilled the condition of the covenant in their place. His active obedience, His life by example and His teaching, validated the law as precept. Sanctification in unity with Him will therefore be in terms of God's law lived out by Christ, and then lived out by believers in Him and after Him. The love of Christ Himself will be present in them as the Spirit works faith through love

---

121. Calvin, *Institutes*, II.vii.12.

122. cf. Hypercalvinist legalism and controversies around Edward Fisher's *Marrow of Modern Divinity* (1645). Fisher is sometimes accused of being too cosy with antinomianism. See M. Jones, *Antinomianism. Reformed Theology's Unwelcome Guest* (Phillipsburg: P & R Publishing 2013), pp. 13–18. Antinomianism in evangelical circles has often been due to the influence of dispensationalist theology.

123. cf. Peterson, op. cit., pp. 143–9.

in sanctifying obedience to the law.[124] This disposition does not stand apart from Christ, but is an aspect of conformity to life as He lived it. The law is upheld in Christ, only its condemnation is abolished; works are dispensed with only in terms of merit. The 'third use of the law' is not contrary to grace in Christ, but leads constantly back to Him.

This is a rather abstract argument, but the function of the law in the structure of the history of salvation can serve to underpin it. The interpretation of Romans 8:15 ('you did not receive a spirit of bondage to fall back into fear, but you have received the Spirit of adoption') has been a crux in interpretation in the light of 7:7-13. The pattern of Christian experience, bondage to sin followed by liberation by the gospel, is projected back on to the history of salvation, and creates a false discontinuity and dichotomy. The Mosaic covenant and the law are thought of as being done away with and replaced by an opposed principle of freedom in Christ.

However, in what respect was the law an instrument of bondage? Not in this stark form of opposition, but in a more complex way, in the context of God's promise. The Mosaic law integrates the 'do this and you shall live' condition of the Adamic covenant into the post-exodus situation. This rule for life, which defines man in relation to God and His sovereignty as a condition for communion in righteousness, does not disappear because of Adam's disobedience, but remains as a fundamental covenantal structure in the relationship between God and man.[125] If the condition remains, it is impossible for man to meet it, as holiness has been forfeited by Adam. The law is incorporated in the Mosaic covenant even if it is a gracious arrangement made by God with His people, who have been saved from bondage as a result of the gratuitous promise to Abraham. The Mosaic

---

124. cf. Murray on the 'pattern of sanctification', op. cit., ch. 24. Murray says that 'the law of God, the revealed will of God, and the example of our Lord are the criteria and patterns according to which sanctification proceeds', p. 307.

125. Vos, art. cit., p. 244.

covenant is therefore a 'mixed' arrangement, combining the Adamic works condition and the grace-salvation promise of the Abrahamic covenant.[126] In this perspective, the law has a historical function, awaiting final fulfilment of God's promise of grace to Abraham, in Christ. As the 'guardian' of Galatians 3:24, it shows the impossibility of righteousness by the law for salvation, which can only be by divine grace and God fulfilling His promise.

In His life and death Christ replied to both the condition of the covenant of works and the law of the Mosaic covenant, and established the righteousness by grace through faith that was promised to Abraham. In this respect Christ is the 'end (*telos*, completion) of the law for righteousness to everyone who believes' (Rom. 10:4).[127] As mediator, Christ fulfilled the Mosaic law: its ceremonies, commands and penalty. The believer is free from obedience *for* salvation, in each of these areas. Christ revealed the true spiritual nature of the law as holy obedience to God.

In the new covenant, the law is not abolished, but given its proper place in human life. It 'is holy, and the commandment holy and righteous and good' and sin, not the law, 'produces death through what is good' in the sinner (Rom. 7:12f). In the new covenant the law is written on the heart in regeneration (Jer. 31:33; 2 Cor. 3:3). The believer is united to the law-fulfilling Christ. In union with Him through faith 'the righteous requirement of the law' is 'fulfilled in us, who walk according to the Spirit' and 'set their minds on the things of the Spirit' (Rom. 8:4f). Union with Christ makes new obedience possible, because we are one with Christ, and the law in its 'third use' is a guide to obedience. This is illustrated by the fact that in the New Testament the Ten Commandments are all confirmed, in one way or another; they are interpreted spiritually in the Sermon on the Mount, and they are reiterated in a different form in exhortations

---

126. M. Horton, *Introducing Covenant Theology* (Grand Rapids: Baker 2006), ch. 3.

127. cf. T. Schreiner, *The Law and Its Fulfilment. A Pauline Theology of the Law* (Grand Rapids: Baker 1993).

and encouragements. In fact it can be said that 'because of the greater indicatives of the new covenant, the imperatives are not relaxed but strengthened.'[128]

6.7 Good works

What then of good works? When the rich young man asked Jesus about what good deed to *do* to inherit eternal life, Jesus replied, 'there is only one who is good' (Matt. 19:16f.). To this He added that keeping all the commandments is necessary, in other words a perfect righteousness in terms of obedience to the law for holiness and acceptance. But this road is closed as Jesus demonstrated practically, and the young man went away sorrowful. No work or works can be good and perfect before God.

However, 'because of justification the defilement of good works does not prevent their being accepted and rewarded by God' through His grace.[129] Turretin makes the distinction between good works that are not necessary *to effect* salvation, but are present in believers as *a means* of possessing salvation in Christ.[130] Obedience to the law, which is the only criteria for good works, mirrors the perfect obedience of Christ in us by faith, working righteousness and sanctification in the life of the believer.

Kuyper makes a contrast that might seem to go too far: 'Sanctification is a work of God; good works are of men. Sanctification works internally; good words are external. Sanctification imparts something to man; good works take something out of him. Sanctification forces the root into the ground; to do good works forces the fruit out of the fruitful tree.'[131] Sanctification is the seed which produces the blossom and fruit of good works, God's work in us, when we are united to Christ in

---

128. Jones, op. cit., p. 37.

129. Horton, *Covenant and Salvation*, pp. 263–6, quoting W. Ames, *The Marrow of Theology* (Grand Rapids: Baker 1977), p. 171, proposition 35.

130. Turretin, op.cit., II, p. 702.

131. Kuyper, op. cit., p. 485.

His holiness. So Kuyper says that 'good works are the ripe fruit from the tree which God has planted in sanctification.'[132] What Kuyper wishes to describe is a double reality. Any and all works outside Christ or considered apart from His sanctifying sphere, though they may appear 'good', are sinful before God's holiness. In Christ, who alone is holy, works are called good concessively and by default, not because of the works themselves, but because they express the sanctifying work of the Spirit of Christ.

Works result from sanctification, and should they be called 'holy', it is only derivatively so, as the result of sanctification. As God works in us, we work, and consequently express *Christ's* holiness in our lives. So the New Testament calls the works of believers 'holy' and exhorts them to holiness (or godliness) on many occasions. Good works in and of themselves are not sanctifying, but reveal the presence of the sanctifying Spirit of Christ in the lives of believers. If they come from sanctification they always refer back to sanctification in Christ, as its fruit.[133] So Kuyper's rather abrupt statements are acceptable. Works as such are a by-product of union with Christ. The *Westminster Confession of Faith* says of believers, along similar lines:

> The corruption of nature, during this life, does remain in those that are regenerated; and although it be, through Christ, pardoned, and mortified; yet both itself, and all the motions thereof, are truly and properly sin . . .

> Our best works ... as they are good, proceed from (God's) Spirit, and as they are wrought by us, they are defiled, and mixed with so much weakness and imperfection, that they cannot endure the severity of God's judgment ...

> Notwithstanding, the persons of believers being accepted though Christ, their good works also are accepted in him ...

---

132. Kuyper, op. cit., p. 496.

133. Maybe this is what Owen has in mind when he says 'There is *no duty of holiness whatever*, but there is a disposition in a sanctified heart unto it.' Duties are consistent with the new nature. Ferguson, op. cit., p. 68, quoting from Owen's *Works*, III, p. 458.

God looking upon them in his Son, is pleased to accept and reward that which is sincere, although accompanied with many weaknesses and imperfections.[134]

Nearly all the moral exhortations in the book of Titus, for example, refer to qualities that can be called good works as a result of sanctification. The works of believers are good when they are pure; believers show they know God by presenting a model of good works; they adorn the doctrine of God by being zealous for good works. Believers are to be ready for every good work and fruitful by devoting themselves to them (Titus 1:15f.; 2:7, 10, 14; 3:1, 8, 14). Nor is this a form of meritorious moralism; it is quite the opposite of Greek moral virtues that make men like gods. To avoid any misunderstanding, the apostle states that we are not saved 'because of works done by us in righteousness, but by the washing of regeneration and renewal of the Holy Spirit, through Jesus our Saviour' (3:5).

Sanctification is a work of God enacted in union with Christ through the Spirit. God also commands that good works be done to the glory of His name. So holiness is expressed on both sides of the covenant, in the divine requirement and by man, in an analogous way, in the covenant response: 'As he who has called you is holy, so be holy in all manner of conversation' (1 Pet. 1:15; 2 Pet. 3:11).

Conclusions

Drawing together various strands from this presentation, the following modest conclusions are suggested:

1. Sanctification in union with Christ that came to the fore in the Reformation presents a form of spirituality that is different from previous models – the vision of God by union, the imitation of Christ, saintliness as perfection, asceticism or the cloister life. It placed sanctification in a covenant context, in the body of Christ and the priesthood of all believers and

---

134. *Westminster Confession of Faith*, VI. v, XVI. v and vi. See Frame's analysis, op. cit., pp. 865–71, 1102–4.

was therefore a kind of 'democratisation' of holiness, the daily life-calling of all who are in Christ.

2. Holiness and righteousness are distinct concepts, both bearing relation to God who is alone holy and righteous. When Adam fell he lost both holiness and righteousness, which are restored only in Christ. Out of Christ man neither is, nor can be, one or the other before God.

3. Sanctification is rooted in the work of Christ, in His death and resurrection as He consecrates a second-Adam humanity and begins the new creation.

4. The mediatorial work of Christ is for us; all that is in Christ in the accomplishment of salvation is ours through union with Christ.

5. Sanctification is participation in Christ; His holiness is ours as derived holiness. It begins with regeneration, as believers are bound to Him by faith, through the work of the Spirit, the agent of sanctification.

6. In Christ believers already belong to the reality of the new creation. Sanctification is already complete in Him; believers are 'saints' because of wisdom, righteousness, sanctification and redemption in Him. Glorification is future, but also a present reality in union with Christ.

7. The sphere of sanctification is our lives, which are transformed and increasingly conformed to Jesus Christ. Renewal, transformation and growth (more than 'progression') are operative aspects of sanctification in union with Christ.

8. Implanted in Christ, believers are restored in the image of God. Growth in grace is through pilgrimage and conflict, the mortification of the flesh which removes the pollution of sin, and vivification, the presence of new dispositions to holiness. Obedience and faithfulness are according to the image of

Christ and holiness is the new lifestyle of the Christian and includes good works. Sanctification therefore has both a divine and human aspect.

9. Union with Christ in sanctification underlines the fact that it is the work of Christ in us, and encourages dependence on Christ and trust in Him, an attitude of continually looking to Christ in all things. It undermines the false idea that perfection can be obtained in this life or that performance or experience help grow in grace.

10. Communion with Christ and fellowship with Him are central in sanctification and for this reason faith is as important in sanctification as in justification, even if it is passive in justification and active in sanctification. In both Christ is all in all, as Luther said, *Nos nihil sumus; Christus solus est omnia.*

QUESTIONS FOR DISCUSSION

1. Are there imbalances in this presentation of sanctification? What correctives are necessary?

2. Christians, particularly evangelicals, have a reputation of being 'holier than thou', proud, judgmental, etc. Is this the case in your church experience? How might reformed theology encourage true humility and holiness in our churches?

3. What are the biblical weaknesses of 'holiness/higher life/charismatic' spiritualities and how could a reformed theology of sanctification serve as a corrective?

4. How are justification and sanctification distinct but complementary in the *ordo salutis*?

5. How can the position presented in this paper contribute to our preaching/teaching about sanctification? What elements might be lacking in our ministry and what might be more developed?

6. Does union with Christ in sanctification bring with it assurance of salvation? How? If not, what needs adding in this area?

7. 'God imputes to me the perfect satisfaction, righteousness and holiness of Christ' (*Heidelberg Catechism*, q.60). Note how not only righteousness but also holiness is said to be imputed. Is this theologically correct? What are the implications of this for sanctification?

8. What is the importance of the order/distinction: righteousness/holiness? How can a better understanding of justification and sanctification affect our teaching?

9. Is the John Murray view (presented in modified version here) of definitive sanctification biblical? What are its positive and negative implications for Christian life?

10. How, in the light of union with Christ, would you counsel (i) someone who thinks they are not holy enough, (ii) someone who has little desire for biblical sanctification or (iii) someone who has an over-inflated view of their own level of holiness?

CHAPTER SEVEN

'Union with Christ': Towards a Biblical and Systematic Theological Framework for Practical Living

Stephen Clark

Introduction[1]

In the course of a sermon preached in the autumn of 1958 the late Dr Martyn Lloyd-Jones lamented the fact that it was almost impossible to find in the church's hymn book – or in other hymn books, for that matter – hymns which dealt with the subject of union with Christ.[2] The previous week he had made the charge that many failed to see and appreciate the prominence given to this great doctrine in Romans chapter 6, the reason for this failure being a preoccupation with the reference to baptism that is found in the opening verses of that chapter.[3]

It would not be an overstatement to say that things have changed considerably since those days. For example, a hymn book which was first published in 1977 – the popularity of which amongst evangelical churches in England and Wales was such

---

1. Unless otherwise indicated biblical quotations are from the New International Version (NIV).

2. D. M. Lloyd-Jones, *Romans. An Exposition of Chapter 6: The New Man* (Edinburgh: Banner of Truth Trust 1972), pp. 43-4.

3. ibid., p. 30.

that it went through a considerable number of reprints before a second, revised edition was published in 1985, and a new edition in 2004 – has a whole section of twenty-eight hymns devoted exclusively to the theme of union with Christ.[4] This is seen to be all the more significant when one realises that the same hymn book devotes but twelve hymns to divine calling and new birth, and thirty hymns altogether to the themes of repentance, faith and justification. Union with Christ was evidently something which figured prominently in the minds of the editors of that volume and clearly it was something about which they wanted churches to sing.[5] It is not, therefore, merely a doctrine to dissect and analyse but that which should both nourish the souls of God's people and lead to praise of our great and glorious God and Saviour Jesus Christ. It is perhaps not without significance that Dr Lloyd-Jones searched for this theme in that part of his church's hymn book which dealt with the Christian Church,[6] whereas *Christian Hymns* – the volume which has corrected this lack of emphasis – locates the doctrine of union with Christ in the large section headed, 'The Christian Life'. It belongs, of course, to both: for, while every believer is personally and individually united to Jesus Christ (did He not say, 'I am the vine; you are the branches',[7] not, 'you make one large branch'?), it is also the case that together we form a communal and corporate whole (the body of Christ,[8] the bride of Christ[9]), a fact which needs to be re-emphasised at a time when the church in the West is in

---

4.   Paul E. G. Cook, Graham Harrison (eds.), *Christian Hymns* (Bridgend: Evangelical Movement of Wales 1977).

5.   Since writing this paragraph, I have learned that it was at Dr Lloyd-Jones's suggestion that the editors devoted a distinct section to 'union with Christ'. (Personal communication from Philip Williams, a retired minister and member of the church I serve as pastor. Mr Williams was a member of the Westminster Fellowship and distinctly remembers Lloyd-Jones saying this at one of the meetings of the Fellowship.)

6.   Lloyd-Jones, op. cit., p. 43.

7.   John 15:5.

8.   1 Cor. 12:27; Eph. 4:15-16.

9.   Eph. 5:25-7; Rev. 21:2.

increasing danger of succumbing to the rampant individualism and consumerism which is so prevalent in the society in which we are placed and to which we are called to bear witness. As the late Professor John Murray observed: 'Union with Christ is really the central truth of the whole doctrine of salvation not only in its application but also in its once-for-all accomplishment in the finished work of Christ.'[10]

But what *is* union with Christ? What do the words 'union with Christ' actually mean and to what reality do they refer? The phrase, like the word 'Trinity', is nowhere to be found in the Bible; as with the term Trinity, however, the reality to which it relates permeates so much of Scripture, and it is explicitly set forth in certain specific passages. The phrase is a convenient theological shorthand for a rich vein of truth which runs through the Bible. It is to the biblical teaching that we now turn, before considering how this teaching has been organised into a coherent, systematic framework, and, briefly, how certain aspects of it – in particular, the place of union with Christ in the *ordo salutis* – have been worked out historically. Finally, some of the pastoral implications of the believer's and the Church's union with Christ will be addressed.

1. Biblical Teaching

Old Testament

Although the present volume focuses on the New Testament material,[11] with particular emphasis falling upon the Johannine and Pauline literature, it is important to stress that the doctrine of

---

10. John Murray, *Redemption Accomplished and Applied* (Edinburgh: Banner of Truth Trust 1961), p. 161.

11. The chapters were originally papers given and discussed at the biennial Affinity Theological Study Conference in 2015. A conference of this kind had to be severely selective in the choice of subjects to be considered under the overall theme of union with Christ. The present chapter seeks, in measure, to make good some of the deficiencies necessarily inherent in the range of material covered in such a conference.

union with Christ is something which can be traced throughout the whole of the Bible. The doctrine is found, in embryonic form, very early in the book of Genesis. The judgment pronounced upon Satan in Genesis 3:15 includes a number of glorious promises which were made within the hearing of our first parents. Satan[12] is told that there will be enmity between him and the woman, and that this is something which will be instigated by the LORD Himself and will result from divine initiative. Since the woman had effectively placed herself on the side of Satan and against the LORD in succumbing to temptation, the enmity which will be placed between her and Satan inevitably means that the LORD will reverse this situation. There is, therefore, a promise of reconciliation between her and the LORD and between the LORD and her. Implicit in this is the fact that she will be delivered from divine wrath (that is, there will be a change of her state before God), and her inner condition will be changed (she will no longer be characterised by rebellion against God).

These promises, however, do not terminate exclusively with the woman's state and condition. The serpent is told that this

---

12. Constraints of space preclude me from discussing the significance of 'the serpent' in the narrative. The interpretative options include the following: it was only a talking serpent, and nothing more; Satan had transformed himself into a serpent (cf. 2 Cor. 11:14) and therefore the serpent *was* Satan; Satan had 'possessed' the serpent, and spoke through him; the serpent is a literary device by which Satan is represented (cf. 'Go tell Herod, that fox . . .'). 'Close reading' of the text indicates that far more is going on than only that of an animal using human language. (For example, the reference in verse 7 to their eyes being opened is clearly not to be understood in a naively, literalistic way: such a reading would entail and imply that hitherto their physical eyes had been closed, something which would not only be nonsensical but which is also flatly contradicted by v. 6.) Moreover, a 'canonical reading' of the text, which, although treating the text in its own terms and in its immediate context, seeks to treat it as part of the whole canon of Holy Scripture, must take account of the following: in John 8:44, which alludes fairly clearly to Genesis 3 and 4, Jesus speaks quite openly of the devil; more significantly, Revelation 20:2 specifically identifies the ancient serpent as Satan. This being so, the first interpretative possibility – that it was only a serpent speaking to the woman – must be decisively rejected. This baldly literalistic interpretation moves the account into the realm of fable. The argument that I am building on Genesis 3:15 is unaffected by whichever of the other interpretations of the serpent one adopts.

divinely instigated state of hostility between him and the woman will extend to their respective seed. Constraints of space will not allow for the canvassing of all the exegetical options with respect to how these words are to be understood or for laying out the reasons in support of the view that I shall present. Suffice it to say that the 'seed of the serpent' can hardly refer to other demonic beings but, rather, to those who, though biologically descended from the woman, will be the spiritual descendants of the devil: they will be like him, will practise his works and be hostile to the spiritual seed of the woman. Thus, Jesus can refer to those who were of their father the devil and who did the works that he did.[13] Similarly, John identifies Cain, the first person that Scripture says that the woman bore, as belonging to the evil one and as being spiritually different from his righteous brother Abel.[14] If the seed of the serpent denotes those who belong to Satan, those in whom he is at work, and who, like Adam and the woman in the immediate post-Fall period, are under divine wrath,[15] then the seed of the woman must refer *not* to all those who are biologically descended from her but, rather, to those who will, as a result of the divine initiative, be reconciled to God, delivered from His wrath, and inwardly changed in their attitude and spirit with respect to God and to Satan. 'Seed', therefore, whether in reference to the seed of the serpent or of the woman, is a 'corporate' reality. The focus of this conflict between the two seeds crystallises with one ('he') who will strike the serpent's head and who will, in turn, be struck in the heel by the serpent. We may gather these data together to formulate the biblical teaching found in what has been called the *protoevangelium* as follows: there will be two groups, and only two groups, of people in this world, and they will be corporate entities, one group being but the biological descendants of the woman (and, of course of the man) who will be the 'seed' of the serpent, and another being the

---

13. John 8:44.

14. 1 John 3:12.

15. Eph. 2:2-3.

'spiritual' descendants of the woman (that is to say, being like the woman *after* she has been set at enmity with Satan), who will be united to the one who will strike Satan's head.

The 'seed' motif is one that is worked out through Genesis, particularly with respect to the line of Abra(ha)m.[16] The significance of Isaac, the child of promise, and of Jacob being the ones in whom God's saving purposes are to be worked out is something which is thoroughly developed in the New Testament, especially by Paul in Romans and Galatians. It is important to bear in mind, however, that the kind of reasoning which Paul employs in these two letters is, as we shall later see, anticipated by John the Baptist and by Jesus Himself, and is but the outworking of the Old Testament teaching. Although the children of Israel are formed into a nation with whom God enters into covenant at Sinai, there are clear indications within the Old Testament that not all the children of Israel were the 'spiritual' seed of Abraham, and that not every Israelite was part of the corporate people who make up the seed of the woman in union with the one who would strike the serpent's head. In New Testament language this truth is expressed by the words: 'For not all who are descended from Israel are Israel.'[17] After rehearsing the blessings and cursings of the covenant, and prophesying that the people would be banished to distant lands, Moses looks forward to the LORD restoring the fortunes of His people, one of the great blessings at that time being that He would circumcise their hearts.[18]

Reference to the LORD circumcising the hearts of the people is a theme that is taken up by Jeremiah in his promise of the new covenant, a covenant which would involve the writing of the law upon the people's hearts and minds.[19] Earlier, Isaiah had spoken of Israel as the servant of the LORD, but as a servant who was failing and who would continue to fail. This section of Isaiah's great

---

16. See, e.g., 12:7; 13:15.

17. Rom. 9:6.

18. Deut. 30:6.

19. Jer. 31:31-4.

prophecy contains what are known as 'the Servant Songs'. One of the things which make this section of Scripture so fascinating is the way in which there is an oscillation between 'the one' and 'the many': at some points it is clear that the servant is Israel but in other places the servant can only be understood as one very special person, indeed someone who is utterly unique. What is found in embryonic form in Genesis 3:15 – that is to say, the idea of a corporate body of people who are represented by one who is united to them and thus part of this corporate entity – is worked out in much more detail in the Servant Songs and comes to a climax in the great fifty-third chapter. We read here of the immense sufferings of the Servant, sufferings which are inflicted by the LORD Himself. But these sufferings are for the sake of the people who have gone astray so badly. It is by the suffering and death of the Servant that the people are healed and justified. The Servant's sufferings are penal, vicarious, substitutionary and representative. But they can only be so because He and the people He represents and for whom He suffered so greatly are one people, one body.

The teaching in Matthew and Luke

Matthew identifies the great reality of union with Christ in the opening chapters of his Gospel. At the very outset he tells us that Jesus Christ is the son of David, the son of Abraham: here is the Davidic king who will both reign over and represent His people; here is the seed of Abraham in whom all nations of the earth will be blessed. A little later we learn that Jesus will 'save his people from their sins':[20] it is *His people* whom He will save. The fact that He is the Davidic king, the true Messiah, and, as such, named 'king of the Jews',[21] could lead one to think that 'his people' will be the Jewish nation. But various Old Testament passages[22] prepare us

---

20. Matt. 1:21.

21. Matt. 2:2.

22. e.g., Gen. 12:3b; Ps. 2:7-12; 110:4: as 'a priest for ever, in the order of Melchizedek', it is clear that this is not a priesthood based on Jewish descent, and the change of priesthood would inevitably involve a change of the law: cf. Heb. 7:11-12; Isa. 49:5-7; etc.

for what Matthew will later spell out so clearly, namely that this will be the Messiah for all nations.[23] Fulfilment themes are plentiful in Matthew's Gospel, not least in the opening chapters.[24] One of the most fascinating of these is to be found in 2:15. The quotation comes from a part of Hosea's prophecy in which the prophet clearly appears to be referring to Israel as God's son[25] and being called out of Egypt at the time of the Exodus. As this Gospel unfolds, however, it becomes clear that Matthew is showing how Jesus 'recapitulates' and lives out the history of Israel as the true Son of God. As the son of Abraham, He is the true Israel, and this is made evident in Matthew's account of the temptation in the wilderness.[26] Where Israel had failed so badly, Jesus the Messiah, the true Israel, triumphed gloriously. But this triumph was not for Himself and His own benefit. Hints of the doctrine of union with Christ which will be worked out so fully by Paul are to be found in a verse like 10:40: to receive one of the Twelve was to receive Christ, and to receive Christ was to receive the One who sent Him, namely His Father.[27] Jesus and His Father, therefore, are intimately identified with each other, and Jesus and those whom He sends are also closely identified. Those who do the will of His Father are His

---

23. This theme is introduced by the visit of the Magi in Matthew 2:1-12, and forms the conclusion of the book, 28:18-20, where Jesus' total sovereignty - and, therefore, universal reign - is the basis for making disciples 'of all nations'. Thus the Gospel begins with its reference to Jesus being the son of Abraham - with the blessing to the nations which this reference implicitly evokes (Gen. 12:3b) - and ends by explicitly stating that those who will be Jesus' people will be drawn from all nations. These are 'his people', whom He will save from their sins.

24. e.g., 1:22; 2:15, 17-18, 23; 3:3; 4:14-16.

25. Hosea 11:1; cf. Exod. 4:22-3.

26. Matt. 4:1-11. The fasting for forty days (v. 2) is reminiscent of the forty days during which Moses was on Mount Sinai, when the Israelites failed so miserably to worship God (cf. v. 10). The number forty also evokes the forty years in the wilderness. Jesus' quotation of Deuteronomy 8:3 in v. 4 calls to mind the feeding of the children of Israel with manna in the desert, and the quotation from Deuteronomy 6:16 reminds one of Israel tempting the LORD at Massah (cf. Ps. 95:9).

27. References to Christ as the Son of God (16:16-17) and the Parable of the Tenants (21:33-44) make it clear that it was God the Father who had sent Jesus (21:37), and it was to Him that Jesus was referring in 10:40.

family,[28] and the nature of His relationship with them is so close that He calls them His brothers: what is done or is not done to His brothers is done or not done to Him.[29] It is a sobering reminder that, on the Last Day, the evidence that we are those for whom the Father has prepared the kingdom will be the way that we treated Christ, and the way that we treated Christ will be demonstrated by the way that we treated His people.

Luke's perspective is somewhat different from Matthew's. If Matthew begins his Gospel by telling us that Jesus is the true Davidic king and the seed of Abraham, Luke, in his genealogy, begins with Jesus and traces his ancestry all the way back to Adam, who was the son of God.[30] Unlike Matthew's genealogy, which opens his Gospel and which clearly has the Exile as one of its main motifs,[31] Luke's genealogy is sandwiched between the account of Jesus' baptism (the climax of which is the Father's voice from heaven proclaiming Jesus to be His Son in whom He is well pleased) and the temptation in the wilderness. In Matthew Jesus recapitulates in Himself Israel's history and He triumphs where she had failed, whereas in Luke Jesus is presented as another Adam, another son of God, who will triumph where Adam failed. Although writing from different perspectives, both of these gospel writers present a unified picture of Jesus and His mission. Both inform us early on that natural descent from Abraham is not what makes one to be truly a member of God's covenant community: in that physical sense, God is able to raise descendants of Abraham from the very stones.[32] Indeed, the coming of the kingdom of heaven signalled a time of great eschatological upheaval, when every unfruitful tree would be uprooted and cast into the fire.[33] The context of these verses makes it abundantly clear that John the Baptist was referring to those physical descendants of Abraham who would continue to be spiritually unfruitful. By contrast,

---

28. 12:48-9.

29. 25:40, 45.

30. Luke 3:38.

31. Matt. 1:11, 12, 17; 2:15, 17-18.

32. Matt. 3:9; Luke 3:8.

33. Matt. 3:10; Luke 3:9.

Gentiles would be admitted to the kingdom of God alongside those physical descendants of Abraham who were also his spiritual seed, thereby being one people.[34] These, who would truly do the will of God, would be Jesus' true family,[35] His brothers,[36] and would be drawn from all nations.[37]

Other New Testament Material

Although aspects of the believer's union with Christ may be inferred from the Gospels of Matthew and Luke, things are spelled out much more clearly in John's Gospel. As Cor Bennema demonstrates in his chapter on John's writings, material concerning union with Christ is particularly concentrated in the Upper Room Discourse, found in chapters 13 to 17 of the Fourth Gospel, and the themes of indwelling/abiding and oneness are especially emphasised in the Johannine literature. The nature of the reality conveyed by John's language, as well as the nature of the language which conveys that reality, is something to which we shall return later.

It is, however, in the Pauline corpus, in particular, that the theme of union with Christ is especially prominent. Indeed, it is a commonplace of New Testament studies to observe that although the doctrine of justification by faith has been linked in an especial way with the apostle Paul, the phrase 'in Christ' is used by him far more than the phrase 'justified by faith'. For example, the 'in' language dominates the early verses of Ephesians,[38] as

---

34. Matt. 8:11-12.

35. Matt. 12:48-9.

36. Matt. 25:40, 45.

37. Matt. 25:32.

38. The Greek preposition *en* is used repeatedly in vv. 1-10: the recipients of the letter are the faithful 'in Christ Jesus' (v. 1); God has blessed us 'in' every spiritual blessing 'in' the heavenly realms 'in Christ' (v. 3); having chosen us 'in Christ' (v. 4); God the Father has given us grace 'in the beloved' (v. 6), 'in whom' we have redemption through His blood (v. 7); God's will according to His good pleasure was purposed 'in him' (v. 9); 'in whom' we were also chosen, having been predestined (v. 11); we were the first to hope 'in Christ' (v. 12); 'in whom' you also were included, 'in whom' also, having believed, you were sealed (v. 13); your faith 'in the Lord Jesus' (v. 15). (I have translated more literally, retaining both the personal pronoun and the relative pronoun where sometimes the NIV substitutes the name 'Christ'.)

well as being found many times throughout Paul's writings.[39] And this phraseology is not confined to the Pauline writings.[40] But it would be a mistake to think that it is only this phrase that denotes union with Christ. Paul employs a range of language to refer to this spiritual reality. Thus, in Romans 6:3 we have been baptised 'into' (*eis*) Christ's death, while v. 4 informs us that 'we were buried **with** him through baptism **into** death'.[41] Similar language is used in Colossians 3:1-3, where, referring both to what has happened to his readers and to what will happen when Christ appears, Paul uses the preposition 'with' three times as well as once using the preposition 'in'.[42]

Of course, we must beware of seeking to deduce this doctrine simply from certain linguistic expressions or only from the use of certain prepositions; rather, we must understand this language not only in its immediate context but also against the background of the whole teaching of Scripture. We have already seen how the Old Testament writers thought in corporate terms when speaking of the relationship of the Messiah-yet-to-come to His people, while the familial language employed by Jesus to describe the nature of His relationship to His disciples, and the use made by the gospel writers of Old Testament realities being fulfilled in Christ indicate that the doctrine of union with Christ is set forth in Scripture by a variety of literary material.

---

39. The following is but a brief, almost random, sample: Rom. 16:3, 7, 9, 10, 11-13 ('in the Lord' x 4); 1 Cor. 1:2, 30; 6:11 (here the phrase is, 'in the name of the Lord Jesus Christ'); 2 Cor. 5:17, 19, 21. (Some understand the reference in v. 19 in a causal, instrumental way, although the 'instrument' is a person: thus, reconciling the world to Himself '*by* Christ'. The fact that only two verses earlier Paul speaks of those 'in Christ' as a new creation, and only two verses later refers to those who are 'in him' as becoming the righteousness of God might well be a reason for retaining the understanding 'in Christ' in v. 19); Phil. 1:1; 2:1; 3:3, 9 ('in him'); 4:21; Col. 1:2, 4; 3:3 ('in God'); 4:17 ('in the Lord'); 2 Thess. 1:1 ('the church . . . in God our Father and the Lord Jesus Christ'); etc.

40. See, e.g., 1 Pet. 5:10.

41. Paul uses a compound verb: instead of the verb *thaptō*, he uses the verb prefixed by the preposition *syn*, which means 'with'.

42. 'You have been raised *with* Christ' (v. 1); 'your life is now hidden *with* Christ *in* God' (v. 3); 'you also will appear *with* him in glory' (v. 3).

Furthermore, as Tim Ward demonstrates in his chapter, much more sense is made of Paul's letter to the Galatians when one appreciates the major part played by the theme of union with Christ in the overall structure and argument of the letter. One could, of course, focus on some of the pictures which are given elsewhere in Paul's writings – as well as in other parts of the New Testament – to demonstrate how important union with Christ really is to the thought world of the New Testament writers. One thinks of the head and body language in Ephesians 5:23, 28-32, as well as the picture, found in a number of places in 1 Corinthians, of the church as a body.[43] The 'body' metaphor suggests an organic, living relationship and the very closest possible union. Similarly, the likening of the relationship of the church to Christ to that of a bride and her husband also indicates that this is a living relationship, which is capable of growth and development.[44] In a fascinating way the last book of the Bible, true to its tendency to present pictures which change rapidly in almost kaleidoscopic fashion,[45] describes God's people as a 'holy city . . . prepared as a bride beautifully dressed for her husband'.[46] This mixing of metaphors brings together different pictures which are found throughout Scripture. Thus, if Paul calls the church the bride of Christ in Ephesians,[47] he also refers to God's people as God's household and a holy temple 'in the Lord', in which God lives by His Spirit.[48] Similarly, if he can refer, in 1 Corinthians, to the church as the body of Christ,[49] it is no less the case that, in the same letter, he can remind the Corinthian Christians that they are God's temple in whom God's Spirit lives.[50]

---

43. 6:13-17; 10:17; 12:27.

44. Rom. 7:1-4; 2 Cor. 11:2-3; Eph. 5:22-33; Rev. 21:2.

45. For example, in chapter 5 Jesus is presented as the Lion of the tribe of Judah in v. 5, only for John to see, in the very next verse, Jesus as a Lamb, as if it had been slain.

46. 21:2.

47. See the reference in note 44, above.

48. Eph. 2:19-22.

49. 1 Cor. 12:27; cf. 6:15-17; Eph. 5:23.

50. 1 Cor. 3:16. The 'you are' and 'in you' are plural.

2. What *is* union with Christ?

We have seen, therefore, that various metaphors or models of the relationship between Christ and his church are set forth in Scripture, some of which are fundamental to the doctrine of union with Christ. Jesus is the vine and His disciples are the branches;[51] the church is His body, of which He is the head;[52] He is the husband and His church is His bride.[53] While each of these pictures refers to a different aspect of the relationship which exists between Christ and His people, what they all have in common – as distinct from the teaching that the church is a temple[54] – is that of life: the vine is living and the branches share in the life of the vine; the body is living and there is an essential relationship between each of its members and between the whole body and the head; the bride is a living person. In other words, spiritual life is possessed by the church. Metaphors such as that of the vine and the branches, and of the body and the head make it quite clear that this spiritual life only exists by virtue of the union between Christ and the church. The very existence of the church and her possession of the spiritual blessings which she enjoys is possible only because she is 'in Christ'. This observation has huge theological and pastoral implications, to which we shall return later in this chapter.

The use of the terms 'model' and 'metaphor' may give rise to concern that certain spiritual realities are thereby being downgraded. Two points need to be emphasised in response to such a concern. First, these are *divinely authorised*

---

51. John 15:5.

52. Eph. 5:23.

53. Eph. 5:25-7.

54. 1 Cor. 3:16; Eph. 2:21-2; 1 Pet. 2:4-5. It should be noted, however, that Peter compares God's people to 'living stones' (v. 5) who 'come to him', i.e., Christ. So even when using the simile of a building, which is an inanimate object, Peter makes clear that this is no ordinary building, since it consists of 'living stones'.

metaphors, not merely human ideas. It is God Himself who has chosen to reveal aspects of the truth concerning the union which exists between Christ and His church by employing these metaphors. This being so, we have no right to jettison them in favour of metaphors or models which we might, in our arrogance and folly, presume to be more meaningful or relevant to our day and age. Although the relationship between Christ and the church is presented in many different ways – vine and branches, head and body, groom and bride, living Stone and living stones – which must partake of the nature of metaphor, these are the divinely sanctioned metaphors and should not, therefore, be viewed as mere human understandings of the nature of the union between Christ and his church.

The second response is to be found in Bennema's thought-provoking and stimulating chapter in this volume: to say that something is metaphorical is not to deny its reality. To take an extreme example, the portrayal of the Lord Jesus Christ as both a lion and a lamb in Revelation 5 is not intended to convey that He is at one and the same time both a carnivore and a herbivore! One is in the realm of apocalyptic literature, where the references to lion and lamb are intended to convey something of His majestic supremacy and kingship, and the sacrificial nature of His death. In the same way the employment of the language of vine and branches, of body and head, and of bride and groom is intended to convey certain vital truths concerning the nature of union with Christ. One may wish to refine somewhat, or even disagree with, certain aspects of Bennema's analysis of the relationship between metaphorical and literal language. For example, the bald contrast between literal and metaphorical, on the one hand, and the continuum from weak metaphor through strong metaphor to nonsense, on the other hand, might be regarded as unnecessary and unhelpful, while the idea that some metaphors may be 'quasi-literal' begs the question as to what *quasi-literal* actually *means*.[55] These observations notwithstanding, Bennema's main argument with respect to metaphor is surely beyond dispute. Metaphorical language is that which refers to a literal reality but the reality is not a literalised understanding of the metaphor.[56]

We return, however, to the question, what does union with Christ *mean*? What is the literal reality conveyed by the metaphors which Scripture employs? If we take the phrase 'in Christ' as being the convenient shorthand which summarises this reality, it is clear that what is conveyed by that phrase is used in a number of ways. Three different aspects may be distinguished. In Ephesians 1:4 Paul writes: 'For he chose us in him before the

---

55. Bennema's example of the difference between having a wife or colleagues and having a bunch of keys – the former not denoting possession but the latter most definitely doing so – is less an example of a continuum of the category of metaphor than of the semantic range of the verb 'to have'. A linguistic analysis of the sentence, 'I have a wife', could restate the same semantic content by saying, 'I am a man and I am married to a woman'. This is what 'I have a wife' *means*. In this example the verb 'to have' has been substituted by the verb 'to be' in order to convey the same semantic content. In the case of having a bunch of keys, one could also substitute the verb 'to be' for the verb 'to have', and convey the same semantic content. Thus, 'I am the owner of a bunch of keys' or (since 'having', strictly speaking, does not necessarily entail ownership but merely possession), 'I am in possession of a bunch of keys'. Restating the sentence by the substitution of the verb 'to be' for the verb 'to have' clarifies the entirely different semantic content between 'having' when used in the phrase, 'having a wife' or 'having colleagues' and when used in the phrase, 'having a bunch of keys'. Indeed, 'I have a bunch of keys' is somewhat ambiguous: the sentence does not convey whether I own them, have stolen them, or merely have been allowed the use of them for a limited period of time. Strictly speaking, 'I have a wife' could be viewed as ambiguous and is not as specific as, 'I am a man and am married to a woman'. A kidnapper, or a terrorist might say, 'I have a wife', when he means that he has a married woman in his custody: it does not necessarily mean that the woman is *his* wife. Bennema's example is not so much a demonstration of the continuum of metaphor, from weak through strong to nonsense, as an illustration of the range and flexibility of the verb 'to have'.

56. On metaphorical language in general and the philosophical issues involved in the use of metaphor, see Monroe C. Beardsley, 'Metaphor' in Paul Edwards (ed.) *The Encyclopaedia of Philosophy*, vol. 5 (New York: Macmillan Company & The Free Press 1967).

creation of the world to be holy and blameless in his sight.'
Here is a clear pre-temporal[57] aspect to union with Christ. Other
passages, however, appear to indicate the effects of our union
with Christ in time but before we came upon the scene. Thus,
Romans 6:3 uses the 'into' (*eis*) preposition, while vv. 4-8 use the
preposition 'with' (*syn*) and a number of compound verbs with
this preposition to speak of our union with Christ in His death
and resurrection. Colossians 3:1-4 also uses the preposition 'with'

---

57. I am mindful that to speak of something which is eternal as being 'pre-temporal'
     might be regarded as a kind of 'category error' and even as nonsense: for if one
     accepts Augustine's observation that God did not create 'in time' but 'with time',
     it follows that time itself is then part of the created order. Indeed, since the work
     of Minkowski and of Einstein, physicists routinely think of the dimensions of
     space and time together, *space-time*. Within this framework of understanding, time
     is as much part of the creation as is space. This being so, one cannot meaningfully
     have sentences that contain the words 'before God created the universe' because
     the word 'before' refers to a 'flow of time'; but if time is part of this created
     universe, it follows that there could be no 'flow of time' apart from creation.
     Hawking cites Augustine as one who understood this well when, in reply to the
     question as to what God was doing before He created the universe, he stated that
     since time is a property of the universe that God has created, time did not exist
     before the creation of the universe (Stephen W. Hawking, *A Brief History of Time:
     From the Big Bang to Black Holes* ([London: Bantam Press 1988], p. 8.) According to
     this view one cannot use the word 'before', in any meaningful way, outside of the
     realm of creation. It has been likened to the North Pole: once one has reached
     it, one can no longer go north. However, one may go up and leave the earth,
     thereby being 'outside' it and thus transcend it. Applying this to the relationship
     of eternity to time and of God to time one might say that God is *outside* time and
     that eternity is *outside* time, not that it existed before time and will continue after
     time. These observations notwithstanding, the Bible clearly uses the language
     of time in the context of eternity: thus, in Ephesians 1:4 Paul writes: 'For he
     chose us in him before the creation of the world . . .' Whether this is an example
     of God accommodating Himself to us in our limited, finite understanding, of
     what Calvin refers to as God 'lisping with us as children', or whether there is
     a sense in which *from our standpoint* there is an 'eternity past' and an 'eternity
     future' need not concern us now. What does concern us is the fact that the Bible
     speaks of God electing people in Christ *before* the creation of world. This being
     the case, my reference to something eternal which is 'pre-temporal' cannot be
     dismissed by those who accept the authority of Scripture as being nonsensical.
     (For a stimulating treatment of God's relationship to time, a treatment which
     stands both within the classical doctrine of God and which is philosophically
     rigorous and sophisticated, see Paul Helm, *Eternal God* [Oxford: Clarendon Press
     1988]).

to convey the same message. The point here is that we were mysteriously involved in Christ's death and resurrection: since He died and rose at a particular point in time and space, it follows that, since His people also died and rose *with* Him, they were – in a way yet to be explained – *there*[58] with Him. Although Paul can thus speak of a pre-temporal union with Christ and a being-in-Him in time but before we came to faith, other material in Paul's writings clearly indicates that there is an existential coming to be in Him, which occurs at the moment of faith in Christ. Thus, in Romans 16:7 Paul writes of relatives of his who 'were in Christ before I was'.[59] Similarly, the Ephesian Christians are told that 'they were included in Christ when you heard the word of truth' (Eph. 1:13).

How does one 'theologise' this and get to the heart of what it all means? David McKay has helpfully drawn attention to the importance of the category of 'covenant' in Scripture. While not denying that the study of Ancient Near Eastern (ANE) covenants may help us to understand what the Old Testament means by covenant,[60] he rightly points out that which is so obvious but

---

58. As well as the biblical passages to which we have referred, many great hymns of the church celebrate this profound reality. John Elias, a great Welsh preacher of the last decade of the eighteenth century and of the early nineteenth century, and the architect of the Confession of Faith of the Welsh Calvinistic Methodists – a confession which has a particularly full statement on union with Christ – wrote a hymn in Welsh on Christ's death. The fourth verse of Noel Gibbard's translation of this hymn reads: 'For in His death our death / Died with him on the tree, / And a great number by his blood / Will go to heaven made free'. For the full English translation see hymn number 199 in *Christian Hymns* or 231 in *New Christian Hymns* (Paul E. G. Cook, et al. [eds.], (Bridgend, Evangelical Movement of Wales and the Christian Hymns Committee, Welwyn Garden City, 2004). In the latter book the third line of the quoted verse is slightly different, and reads: 'and great the number by his blood'.)

59. In a discussion session at the Affinity Study Conference, at which the chapters in this book were first presented as papers, Tim Ward helpfully drew attention to these three different aspects of union with Christ, particularly referencing Romans 16:7 as an example of the 'existential' element to coming into union with Christ. I am indebted to him for drawing the conference's attention to this.

60. One thinks here of the similarities, which have often been remarked upon, between the structure of the book of Deuteronomy and ANE suzerainty covenants.

which we can easily miss: namely, that we should consider how *the Bible* employs the concept of covenant. What is particularly helpful about McKay's treatment of this category is the way in which he demonstrates that much of the biblical material concerning covenant is *not* modelled on that of a commercial contract. The obvious covenant which takes us into a different thought world from that of commerce is the marriage covenant. Love must lie at the heart of it; and love entails and implies warmth, affection, and devotion. But this does not deny that there are also covenant responsibilities, responsibilities which are the outworking of that love which lies at the heart of the marriage covenant. Covenant, therefore, does not necessarily entail a cold, mechanical, and commercial approach to the divine-human relationship, although there have, no doubt, been those who have falsely assumed this to be the case. There is, of course, an abundance of material in Scripture which likens the relationship of the LORD to Israel and of Christ to His church to that of a husband to his bride or wife.[61] Being chosen in Christ before the foundation of the world must surely refer, therefore, to a covenant relationship which God entered into with people 'in Christ' before time began. This covenant relationship was based upon a particular covenant love which God had for them in Christ. In this connection the language of 'foreknowledge' is all-important. This refers *not* to something which God knew about certain people before they were born – namely, that these would be those who would believe, and on that basis God chose them; for in that case it was not the people whom He foreknew but some facts about them which He foreknew. Rather, taking 'to know' as terminology which is used in the Old Testament to refer to the intimate knowledge which a husband has of his wife,[62] and of the covenant relationship of love which the LORD

---

61. The sheer wealth of material is such that it will not be referenced here. As a sample of Old Testament passages, one might consult Isa. 50:1-3; 54:4-8; Jer. 3:1-2; Ezek. 16; numerous passages in Hosea. In the New Testament, 2 Cor. 11:2; Eph. 5:22-33; Rev. 19:7-9; 21:2.

62. In Genesis 4:1, the Hebrew is quite clear that it was because Adam 'knew' his wife that she conceived a son.

had with His people,[63] foreknowledge must refer to an eternal covenant love which God has had for His people in Christ. This foreknowledge undergirds God's choice of His people[64] and His predestining of them to be conformed to the image of His Son and to be glorified.[65] Significantly, Paul tells us that one of the results of God's people being predestined to be conformed to the image of His Son is that His Son might be 'the firstborn among many brothers' – the language of union which we noted in Matthew's Gospel.

This is the background, therefore, to those passages which teach that Christ already had a people when upon earth, even if they had not yet come to Him.[66] These are the ones who had been 'given to him'.[67] Christ's mission to save them is, therefore, a mission to save a covenant people. In the words of Samuel Stone's well-known hymn: 'From heaven he came and sought her to be his holy bride; with his own blood he bought her, and for her life he died.'[68] This inevitably raises the question as to whether there is such a thing as a 'covenant of redemption' between the Father and the Son. Opinions have differed within the Reformed evangelical community over this. Robert Letham has, for a number of reasons, expressed unease with the idea, not least of his concerns being related to the fact that the very nature of covenant suggests a Binitarian, rather than a Trinitarian,

---

63. Amos 3:2, where the LORD says of Israel: 'You only I have known of all the families of the earth.' Clearly this does not mean that an omniscient God did not know about the other nations; rather, it refers to a love which led to covenant commitment on God's part to Israel. Thus, the NIV renders the Hebrew, 'You only have I *chosen*' (emphasis mine). Stuart notes that the verb may be rendered 'chosen' because the Hebrew term 'can denote covenantal commitment and not merely cognitive perception.' (D. Stuart, *Hosea – Jonah*. Word Biblical Commentary, vol. 31 [Waco: Word Books 1987], p. 321, note 2a).

64. 1 Pet. 1:1-2.

65. Rom. 8:29-30.

66. e.g., John 10:16.

67. John 6:37; 17:2.

68. *The Church's One Foundation*, Samuel Stone (1839–1900): Hymn number 343 in *Christian Hymns*.

phenomenon: it is akin to a committee of three persons where
the Holy Spirit is absent at lunch![69] McKay is alert to this danger;
indeed, there have not been wanting among theologians who
placed great stress on covenant theology those who emphasised
the Trinitarian nature of this great eternal *pactum salutis*.[70] To stress
the necessarily different nature of the inter-relationship of three
co-equal Persons who are one in the divine essence in the great
plan of salvation from a covenant between the one God and
His creatures, some theologians have preferred to speak of 'the
council of redemption'.[71] Whatever terminology one uses, the
biblical data clearly indicate that the three persons were involved
in the plan to save a particular people and to bring them into
a covenant bond with Jesus Christ.[72]

The eternal, pre-temporal union that exists between Christ and
His church is, therefore, to be understood in terms of the fact
that the Father gave a people to His Son before the foundation of
the world. But what does it mean to say that *in time* Christ's people
were 'in him' and died and rose with Him years before their coming
to faith and even before they have come into existence? Surely no
more and no less than this: that since Christ's people were given
to Him in eternity and since He represented them in time, there

---

69. This is how Letham described it in a paper on 'Covenant' that he gave at the 2009
     Affinity Study Conference. The papers for that conference were not published.

70. A fine example of this is Hugh Martin, *The Atonement: In its Relations to the Covenant,
     the Priesthood, the Intercession of Our Lord* (Edinburgh: Knox Press 1976).

71. See, for example, R. B. Kuiper, *God Centred Evangelism* (London: Banner of Truth
     Trust 1966).

72. e.g., Ps. 2:8; Isa. 53:12; Matt. 28:18-20; John 6:37, 45-46; Acts 2:33; Rom. 1:4; Heb.
     9:14. Although the emphasis falls upon the Father giving a people to His Son, the
     pouring out of the Spirit is to be seen as part of the reward given to Christ for
     His obedience and as an essential element in bringing the elect to faith in Christ.
     Indeed, the Holy Spirit may be seen as 'the executive agent' of the Father and
     of the Son in the drawing work which is not only attributed to the Father (John.
     6:45-46) but also to the Son (John. 12:32). The activity of the Spirit in sustaining
     the Son in His great work, and the role of the Spirit in bringing people to faith
     in Christ must be viewed in the context of an eternal plan; otherwise, it would
     mean that the Spirit is acting without reference to the Father and the Son, and this
     cannot be.

is a sense in which *in time but before they come to conscious faith or even before they come into existence*, they are, nevertheless 'his'. This means that all that He did for them, He did as their representative. In this sense, precisely because His work was a representative work and his people were being represented by Christ, they were there *then*, just as they are in the heavenly places *now* – though not yet there ontologically – precisely because the One who represents His people *is* there now as their representative. This is what covenant representation means.

An illustration may help to elucidate this point. A treaty may be signed between two countries whereby one country confers considerable benefits upon all the citizens of the other country. Let us say that the treaty was signed a hundred years ago but is still in force. Let us imagine two people who become citizens of this country on the same day: one is born a citizen and the other, an immigrant, acquires citizenship. When were the benefits to which these citizens are entitled under the treaty conferred upon them? In one sense, it was when the treaty was made, though clearly the two people needed to become citizens in order to have title to these benefits. Despite the limitations of the illustration, this is precisely the case with union with Christ: as our representative, Christ won all the blessings of salvation for His people when He died and rose for them, yet in another sense these blessings only become theirs when they are born again and exercise faith in Christ. The 1823 Confession of Faith of the Welsh Calvinistic Methodists expresses this point helpfully and clearly in its very full statement on union with Christ. The relevant part of the paragraph dealing with union with Christ reads as follows:

> Those who are effectually called are brought into a mystical union with Christ. Though they were elected in Christ from eternity, and represented by Him in the eternal covenant, nevertheless they are by nature the children of wrath, even as others, enemies of God, and far from Christ until the Holy Ghost is sent to convince them of sin, show them their state of misery, reveal Christ to them, draw them to Him, and create

them in Him; then they will be members of His mystical body, and will be in Him as the branches are in the vine; then Christ and His salvation becomes theirs;[73]

The importance of the teaching contained in this statement will be seen when we come to consider the place of union with Christ in the order of salvation, the *ordo salutis*.

Jesus Christ was, therefore, appointed as the covenant head of His people, a people who were given to Him even before they were born, let alone before they come to conscious faith. In this sense, union with Christ is eternal. But what Christ did for His people was done in time. In this respect the comparisons and contrasts between Adam and Christ that Paul draws in Romans 5:12-19 and in 1 Corinthians 15:21, 44-9 are of great importance and are deeply instructive for the light which they throw upon the meaning of union with Christ. An exegesis of these verses would take us beyond the scope of this chapter. Suffice it to say that careful reading of the text indicates that the human race is 'one' with Adam and one in him. His fall into sin is ours;[74] his death brings us death.[75] It is usual to speak of this as Adam's federal headship and of our covenant solidarity with him. We are 'in Adam': he represented all descended from him, with the exception of Jesus Christ, Christ's miraculous conception being such that, although He is truly human, He is the covenant head of a new humanity. Thus, we may also speak of Christ's covenant headship of His people. Might more, however, be said?

The nature of the union between Christ and His church has frequently been denoted by the phrase 'the mystical union'. Mysticism has been pilloried as being alien to authentic Christianity, beginning with 'mist', having 'I' at its centre, and ending in 'schism'![76] Mysticism, in this pejorative sense of the word, however, refers to something which is non-cognitive, something which bypasses the mind and which has affinities with the non-rational 'spiritualities' which Paul

---

73. Para. 23: 'Of Union with Christ'.

74. Rom. 5:12-14, 19.

75. Rom. 5:14-18; 1 Cor. 15:22.

76. Dr Gaius Davies made this observation in a paper entitled *George Fox: A Radical Spirit* that was given at the Westminster Conference of 1996.

castigates in 1 Corinthians and Colossians. There is, however, another sense of the word, found, for example, in the 1662 Prayer Book marriage service, which states that human marriage sets forth 'the mystical union between Christ and his church'. This service and these words go back to Cranmer in the sixteenth century; and Cranmer was no mystic, if by mystic we understand a non-rational, non-cognitive approach to matters of faith. Mystic, in this connection, surely refers to something which is so sublime that human language is inadequate to express or convey it. We are not unfamiliar with the idea that things which are anything but irrational may not be able to be expressed in human language. One thinks, for example, of certain mathematical equations, which may express certain realities of the physical universe far more elegantly and meaningfully than verbal language. Again, 'body language' may, at times, be more expressive and communicative than that which is verbal. In this context, the biblical language of Adam *knowing* his wife is surely instructive: there was a 'knowing' which occurred in the sexual act, an act which both sealed the one-flesh union and which expressed it. Adam's knowledge of his wife was experienced, quite literally, by 'body language' of a very particular kind![77] Of course, more than the physical act of sexual intercourse is meant here. An animal that mates does not thereby 'know' the other animal; Adam and Eve were persons made in the image of God, and this means that more than the physical act was involved. Nevertheless, it cannot be doubted that a very important aspect of the 'one flesh' union that exists between husband and wife is 'cemented', sealed, or consummated in the sexual act. And this *is* something which

---

77. Thomas Howard makes the following keen observation: 'This is piquant irony: here we are with all our high notions of ourselves as intellectual and spiritual beings, and the most profound form of knowledge for us is the plain business of skin on skin . . . When two members of this godlike, cerebral species approach the heights of communion with themselves, what do they do? Think? Speculate? Meditate? No, they take off their clothes. Do they want to get their *brains* together? No. It is the most appalling of ironies: their search for union takes them quite literally in a direction away from where their brains are.' T. Howard, *Hallowed be this House* (Harold Shaw 1979), pp. 115f., quoted in G. Lloyd Carr, *The Song of Solomon: An Introduction and Commentary* (Leicester: InterVarsity Press 1984), p. 35, note 2.

is mystical: mystical, *not* in the sense in which the ancient fertility religions sought to achieve union with the divine through so-called sacred hierodules or prostitutes, but in the sense that the oneness between husband and wife is something beyond human language. There is a mystery to it.[78]

This inevitably raises the question, however, as to whether there *is* anything *that* mysterious about the idea of covenant headship. I have already employed an illustration of how, for example, a citizen born into a particular nation state may have certain privileges – and obligations – as a result of a treaty arrangement made by the government of that country long before he was born. Is this kind of arrangement that mysterious? Surely such a state of affairs can hardly be called 'mystical'. This being so, the question may be posed as to whether the idea of federal headship *exhausts* the meaning of union with Christ. The analogy of marriage helps us at this point. Just as the one-flesh union between husband and wife is a great mystery, which goes beyond the promises of love to each other made in the mutual covenant engagement, so it may be argued that there *is* a mystical union between Christ and His church, a union which is never less than a covenant union but which, within that covenant bond, involves a great mystery. The language of the vine and the branches, of abiding in Christ, of being 'in the Spirit' and the Spirit being in us: it may well be the case that the realities conveyed by these phrases are not fully plumbed by referring to covenant headship. Indeed, while we are not physically descended from Christ, mankind is made in God's image and Christ *is* that image.[79] In Christ, that image in which we were created – damaged but not eradicated by the Fall – is being restored.[80] If language means anything, we are here in the realm of something that is full of deep mystery – mystical! It is surely significant that the paragraph on union with Christ which is found in the Confession of Faith of the Welsh Calvinistic Methodists, and from which I have already quoted, although acknowledging that those who are effectually

---

78. In discussion of his paper at the conference, Bennema helpfully elucidated the concept of 'mystical' as applied to union with Christ, as referring to that which is mysterious and beyond human language.

79. Col. 1:15.

80. James 3:9; Col. 3:10.

called were 'elected in Christ from eternity' and 'represented by Him in the eternal covenant', nevertheless states: 'Those who are effectually called *are brought into a **mystical union with Christ*** – that is, when the Spirit works in them, bringing them to faith in Christ – 'then will they be members of His mystical body'[81] (italics and emphasis mine). In other words, the mystical union or becoming members of His 'mystical body' is something which comes into existence *not* when God's people are elected in Christ nor when Christ, as their covenant head and representative procured salvation for His people by His death, resurrection, and ascension but, rather, when the Spirit applies the benefits of Christ's work and brings the elect sinner into vital union with Christ. The implications of this for the *ordo salutis* as well as the pastoral implications will be worked out later in this chapter.

3. Union with Christ and the Lord's Supper

In connection with the words 'mystery' and 'mystical union', Calvin's doctrine of the Real Presence in the Lord's Supper is surely important. Robert Letham has helpfully elucidated Calvin's teaching in his chapter on *Union with Christ in John Calvin*. Some have struggled with Calvin's ideas, preferring a merely memorialist view, a view which is identified with Zwingli's teaching. One of the reasons for these struggles may well be difficulty in 'pinning down' precisely what Calvin is saying.[82] Again, however, the difficulty does not so much arise from an inability on Calvin's part to express his thought as, rather, from the profundity of what he was expressing. The point to grasp is surely this: baptism and the Lord's Supper are given to the church precisely because more than verbal communication is needed. One is right to be on one's guard against a sacramentalism that is destructive of the gospel of God's grace: the opening four chapters of Romans, as well as other biblical material in both the Old and the New Testaments, clearly teach that there is that in human nature which is, alas, all too ready to place confidence in an outward rite and ceremony. Authentic evangelicalism is always something of a protest against this.[83] Justification by faith

---

81. Para. 23, 'Of Union with Christ'.

82. Certainly, in the small group discussion to which the writer belonged at the Conference, some expressed the difficulty they had in understanding Calvin's teaching.

83. Paul's words in 1 Corinthians 1:17 are not without importance and significance at this point.

means that one is justified by faith alone in Christ alone, not by faith *plus* the sacraments, nor even by faith *expressed* in the sacraments. This having been said, the abuse of something is not an argument for keeping a low view of it. Some people, after all, have fallen into bibliolatry, a worship of the Bible, rather than a worship of the God of the Bible. This does not mean that we must have a low view of Scripture as a necessary safeguard against such a thing. Likewise, some have undoubtedly worshipped preaching, rather than the Christ who is preached. Worse, as is clear from the opening chapter of 1 Corinthians, some have even worshipped preachers. None of this means, however, that we should adopt a 'low' view of preaching or of the preaching office. In the same way, abuse of the sacraments is no reason for adopting a 'low' view of them. The Great Commission recorded at the end of Matthew's Gospel and the account in the book of Acts of the early church's practice make it abundantly clear that baptism is something which is closely tied to discipleship, and so is observance of the Lord's Supper. Although we are not justified by faith expressed in observing the sacraments, it is undoubtedly the case that those who have been justified by faith should express and nourish their faith by observing the sacraments.

The point here is that many Christians have testified to the great blessing, the great grace which they have received in observing these *means of grace*: for that is what they are – means of grace to us, where God gives grace to us. Baptism – whether of the credo- or paedo-variety – is not *only* a dedicating of the believer or, in the case of paedobaptism, the believer's parent(s) (though it *is* this); it is also to be a 'sealing' ordinance, by which God blesses His child(ren).[84] One fears that too often in Baptist circles baptism is seen as nothing other than an act of testimony to others, rather than also being a means of grace to the believer being baptised. Likewise, in paedobaptist circles the rite can easily degenerate into a kind of 'rite of passage'. In the same way, we can fail to realise that the teaching found in 1 Corinthians 10 indicates that our celebration of the Lord's Supper is *more* than our act

---

84. For his experience at his baptism, see C. H. Spurgeon, *Autobiography Volume 1: The Early Years 1834–1859* (rev. edn published in two volumes) (London: Banner of Truth Trust 1962), pp. 149-50. See also Packer's discussion of Thomas Goodwin's sacramental theology, in J. I. Packer, *Among God's Giants: Aspects of Puritan Christianity* (Eastbourne: Kingsway Publications 1991), pp. 242-5.

of remembrance: it is a means of grace by which Christ draws near to His people.[85] It is an act of communion: our union with Christ is meant to be known, enjoyed and felt. And one of the ways in which this is done is through the sacraments. This inevitably has a bearing upon assurance of salvation; yet, sadly, it is not unknown for books dealing with assurance to make no mention of the sacraments. But it is precisely because of the mystical nature of our union with Christ that these 'extra verbal' signs and seals are given by Christ to His church: I say 'extra verbal' because, as Calvin is at pains to say on numerous occasions, the sacrament without the Word is empty.

4. John Owen on union with Christ and his use of the Song of Solomon

John Fesko has treated the subject of union with Christ in the teaching of John Owen. His locating of Owen within his historical context is particularly helpful, as is his treatment of Owen's controversy with William Sherlock. Sherlock, of course, was an Anglican. But the fact that the 1662 Prayer Book marriage service refers to the 'mystical union between Christ and his church' demonstrates that the nature of this union is something which goes well beyond that for which Sherlock contended. Sherlock has to be seen as something of a 'maverick', especially when one considers the 'catholic' nature of this doctrine, and the sources on which Owen drew. Fesko has placed us heavily in his debt by clarifying Owen's teaching.

Owen's treatment of union with Christ draws heavily at points upon the Song of Solomon. Indeed, historically much has been made of the way in which this somewhat unique book of the Bible sets forth the union of Christ with the church and the believer. More recent treatments of the Song have tended to see it as being exclusively a love song which celebrates human love. Numerous questions arise at this point. If the exegesis of Owen – and of others who have found this book to be a treasure trove of 'high' spirituality – is rejected, will this mean that the rich vein of spiritual teaching concerning the mutual love of Christ and His people (a vein of teaching which has characterised the church

---

85. See Iain H. Murray, *David Martyn Lloyd-Jones: The Fight of Faith 1939–1981* (Edinburgh: Banner of Truth Trust 1990), p. 84.

in her brightest periods) will have to be dismissed as something fanciful, notwithstanding the eminence of those who espoused this understanding of the Song? Or might it be the case that the kind of spiritual rhapsodies experienced by someone like Samuel Rutherford are still possible for God's people but are not to be found mirrored or encouraged by the Song of Solomon? Are there other passages of Scripture which might hold forth the possibility of rich intimate communion with Christ? Or may it be the case that we are not faced with a simple either/or choice in our interpretation of the Song? Might it be possible to say that it is first a song which celebrates human love, but, given the comparison Paul draws between human marriage and that of Christ and the church in Ephesians 5:22-33, might the Song not be used to illustrate this reality? This, however, generates another question: was it part of the divine author's intention that the book have this illustrative meaning and content? In other words, did God intend the book to operate on these two levels or is it merely another interpretative dimension which is being added to the interpretation of the book? And this leads on to another question, which is this: is one then able to interpret *every* marriage in the Bible in this way? Are the marriages of Abraham and Sarah, Isaac and Rebekah, Moses and Zipporah, Priscilla and Aquila, all to be regarded as illustrative material of the relationship between Christ and the church? Might this not be too much of a good thing – or bad thing, depending on your perspective? And given the messianic typology of David, might one not then say that his marriage is illustrative of the relationship between Christ and the church? But one must then ask, which of his marriages? Surely not to Bathsheba. The problem is compounded when one considers the messianic significance of the phrase 'son of David'. One could hardly regard Solomon as illustrating Christ *in the area of marriage* and therefore of Christ's relationship to the church. All of which raises the question, why is it particularly the couple in the Song who are believed to represent Christ and the church, rather than other couples? And this brings us full circle to the original issue. Is there something to be said for regarding the book as something other than a human love song?[86] All the time

---

86. Mike Reeves, in his introduction to the Banner of Truth Trust's reprint of Richard Sibbes's *Bowels Opened*, under the title *The Love of Christ* (Edinburgh, 2011), identifies some fascinating parallels and similarities in the descriptions of the beloved and that of the tabernacle in the Pentateuch and of the beloved and Israel also in the Pentateuch and in Isaiah. He also draws attention to a very interesting similarity between descriptions of the LORD in Exodus and the lover coming up from the wilderness like a pillar of smoke. In addition, therefore, to the general hermeneutical principle which sees human marriage as pointing to the marriage between Christ and His church, Reeves draws attention to inter-textual links between the parties in the Song and the LORD and His people in the Old Testament, thereby deriving the lessons relating to the union and communion of the Lord and His people from a reading of the text as part of the canon of Holy Scripture: i.e., a canonical reading of the text. Reeves's approach has the great merit of identifying the Song as a rich seam of spiritual teaching without having to resort to an unprincipled or fanciful exegesis of the text. This having been said, he possibly overdoes this when, noting that 4:9 identifies the beloved as the lover's sister, he goes on to say that the taboo on marrying one's sister (Lev. 18:9) means that the Song could hardly be describing an ordinary Jewish romance. As Carr points out, ANE love poetry routinely used sibling terminology metaphorically to denote the object of one's affections, just as the language of royalty is used figuratively in ANE love poetry to speak of one's beloved (op. cit., p. 121 and note 1 on p. 121). (In the modern West, reference by a young woman to her beloved as her 'prince charming' is not meant to be taken literally, any more than cars displaying the sign, 'Princess on board' means that William and Kate's daughter is an occupant of the car!) In the interpretation of the Song, therefore, one needs to consider *both* its canonical context *and* its historico-geographical literary context: in so doing one discovers that the Song uses language and allusions which are employed in Scripture to denote the relationship of the LORD and His people *and* uses language common in ANE love poetry to denote the relationship of a man and a woman deeply in love. A biblical and thoroughly evangelical doctrine of Scripture demands that we take seriously both the divine and the human involvement in the writing of Scripture: the Bible is not the same as the Qu'ran! This approach enables one to read the Song primarily as a love song, sharing many features with other love songs of the ANE. At the same time, one is able to see that the LORD employs this genre to give rich teaching on the nature of His relationship with His people, just as the book of Hosea does something similar. This then means that it is part of the divine author's intention that we learn lessons both about human love and about the love of the LORD for His people and of His people for Him. This explains why this marriage, like that of the first man to the first woman, and that of Hosea and his wife, was always intended by God to be illustrative of the LORD and His people, whereas this need not and may not be so for other marriages in Scripture. At the same time, precisely because this is first a human love song, the book is not, therefore, an allegory. Furthermore, since not every detail of a marriage is to be pressed as illustrating the relationship of the LORD and His people, so an allegorical interpretation of the book must be ruled out of court.

we need to keep in mind the differences between a typological book and a typological interpretation of a non-typological book, and between an allegory and an allegorical interpretation of a non-allegorical book. The raising of these questions does not, of course, answer any of them; nor does the framing of them in the way in which I have done so suggest that only certain answers are acceptable. What does need to be emphasised is that the way one understands Scripture necessarily has a bearing upon the nature of one's spirituality.

5. Union with Christ and the 'ordo salutis'

The immediately preceding two chapters of this book consider union with Christ and justification, and union with Christ and sanctification. Inevitably questions of the *ordo salutis*, or the order of salvation, arise in connection with the realities which these chapters consider. Indeed, the chapter on union with Christ in Calvin's teaching touches upon these issues.

That there is an *ordo salutis* should be obvious to anyone who is sensitive to the already/not yet tension or motifs found in the New Testament. While we are already saved, we do not yet have full salvation.[87] Looking at the matter from a different perspective, we were chosen in Christ before the creation of the world[88] but this does not negate the fact that, *in time,* some are in Christ before others.[89] This much may be granted. But some may wonder if questions as to whether union with Christ precedes justification and if justification precedes sanctification are rather sterile questions, questions which owe more to our modern western concern for conceptual categorisation than to a straightforward reading of God's holy Word. To put the same point slightly differently, some may feel that this is to impose the categories of a system – systematic theology – onto Scripture rather than reading something out of it. A little reflection, however, upon

---

87.   Rom. 8:23-5; Col. 3:3-4; 1 John 3:2.

88.   Eph. 1:4.

89.   Rom. 16:7.

a very small sample of biblical material soon demonstrates that this is not the case. Before considering the relationship of union with Christ to justification and to sanctification, it will be useful to demonstrate that there most certainly *is* an *ordo salutis* within Scripture.

In His conversation with Nicodemus, Jesus makes it quite clear that new birth is necessary for someone to be able to see the kingdom of God and to enter that kingdom.[90] This, of course, does not necessarily mean that there is an order of chronology; what is clear is that there is an order of nature. Paul says something similar in Romans 10:13-14. In verse 13 we are told that everyone who calls on the name of the Lord will be saved. Paul immediately follows this statement with his question as to how someone who has not believed in the Lord is able to call on Him. Clearly, therefore, there is an order of nature here: belief in Christ – in His being the Saviour and in His ability to save – logically comes before the calling upon Him to become one's Saviour. And this inevitably necessitates the questions as to how people can believe in the One of whom they have not heard, and how they can hear unless one preach. Moreover, in chapter 8:28-30 Paul had already laid out something of an *ordo salutis*. It is those God has predestined whom He called – not the other way around; it is those He has called whom He justified – not the other way around; it is those He justified that He glorified – not the other way around. If these passages of Scripture clearly indicate an order of nature in the matter of salvation, then a passage such as Titus 3:4-7 distinguishes very clearly different elements in the total 'package' of salvation. The word 'Saviour' is used twice, and the word 'saved' is used twice: this is, therefore, the overarching category in this passage. *What* does salvation involve, and which specific blessings does it entail? Paul clearly distinguished regeneration from justification. Regeneration, therefore, is one of the blessings of salvation, as is justification, but neither can be defined in terms of the other, nor can either exhaust the meaning of the overarching term 'salvation'.

---

90. John 3:3, 5.

The question which now needs to be addressed is this: Which blessing comes first in the *ordo salutis*? A number of important points and necessary distinctions need to be kept in mind. The 'pre-temporal' union with Christ denoted by the words, 'For he chose us in him before the creation of the world',[91] clearly precedes the existential union with Christ denoted by the words, 'they were in Christ before I was'.[92] Similarly, this pre-temporal aspect to union with Christ precedes justification and sanctification. It is true that some have sought to argue for 'justification from eternity' or 'eternal justification'.[93] Since, however, the Scriptures repeatedly emphasise that we are justified by faith,[94] and since faith is something which *we* exercise, this is something therefore which is exercised in real time; and since God's justifying verdict is consequent to our exercise of faith, it follows that justification cannot occur in eternity.[95] What, however, of the relative place of *existential* union with Christ, and of justification and of sanctification within the *ordo salutis*? Does existential union precede justification? Does justification precede sanctification?

---

91. Eph. 1:4.

92. Rom. 16:7.

93. e.g., in the eighteenth century John Brine, *A Defence of The Doctrine of Eternal Justification From Some Exceptions made to it By Mr Bragge, and others* (Printed and sold by A. Ward at the King's Arms in Little-Britain and H. Whitridge, at the Corner of Castle-Alley, near the Royal Exchange, 1732). Obtainable at http://www.mountzionpbc.org/Index/index03.htm, and, from a different perspective, Abraham Kuyper, *The Work of the Holy Spirit* (Grand Rapids: Eerdmans 1900). On this, see Kuyper, op. cit., pp. 367-71. Chapter XI, para. IV of the *Westminster Confession of Faith* specifically denies the teaching of eternal justification, distinguishing the decree to justify from the actual verdict of justification.

94. e.g., Rom. 3:28, 30.

95. It might be thought that since justification is something which occurs *coram Deo* – before God – and since God inhabits eternity, justification is effected in eternity. We are here again faced with similar kinds of issues to those referred to in note 57, issues which concern how an eternal God relates to creatures who exist in time. These kinds of issues cannot be divorced from questions concerning the nature of the relationship of a God who is immense and transcendent to creatures who exist within space. The fact remains, however, that since justification is by faith and since faith is a spiritual act of the sinner, an act which the sinner exercises in time, it follows that faith on the part of the sinner is antecedent to God's justifying of the sinner.

Such questions should not be regarded as theoretical questions which belong only in the 'ivory towers' of academic theology but which have no relevance for Christian living in the church and Christian witness to the world. A little thought should demonstrate just how vital such questions are. Justification is concerned with one's legal or judicial status or standing before God. If, for the moment, we understand sanctification as a progressive reality, as the process by which one becomes increasingly conformed to the image of God's dear Son,[96] then it follows that to place sanctification *before* justification will inevitably make our standing before God to be grounded in, and based and dependent upon, God's work *in* us by His Spirit rather than on God's work *for* us by His Son. As David McKay points out, this is essentially the error of the Roman Catholic Church, and it is a fatal error, which strikes at the very heart of the gospel: for no matter how conformed to the image of God's Son a believer may become in this life, the fact remains that sin will still be present in him and, therefore, he can never be accepted by God on this basis. In other words, this would not be as good news from a far country nor as water to the thirsty; rather, it would be a message which would cut out the very heart of the gospel and which would either lead to spiritual pride and self-righteousness or to a doubting despair which makes assurance of salvation an impossibility. The moment we forget that God justifies *the ungodly*,[97] we lose an essential aspect – and one of the most glorious aspects – of the message of salvation: it is as ungodly people that sinners are justified, it is as God's enemies that we are reconciled to Him, and justification is essential and central to this reconciliation.[98] All holy

---

96. Thus, in 1 Thess. 4:3, the words which follow the statement, 'It is God's will that you should be sanctified', clearly indicate that Paul is dealing with the ongoing work of spiritual and moral transformation in God's people. This is clearly different from the 'definitive sanctification', as John Murray calls it (*Collected Writings of John Murray, Volume 2: Select Lectures In Systematic Theology* [Edinburgh: Banner of Truth Trust 1977], pp. 277-84), to which Paul refers in 1 Cor. 1:2 and 6:11.

97. Rom. 4:5.

98. Rom. 5:10 states that it was when we were God's enemies that we were reconciled to Him through the death of His Son. It is clear, however, that Paul is expanding upon his statement in 5:9 that we were justified by His blood – 'blood' being a clear reference to Christ's sacrificial death. This means that justification is essential and central to reconciliation.

living proceeds from this status of justification and it is only justified people who can so live. Although we have seen that the Bible does not teach a doctrine of eternal justification, it is clear that what lay behind Abraham Kuyper's advocacy of such a doctrine[99] was not the kind of Hyper-Calvinism discernible in John Brine's promotion of justification from eternity[100] nor a desire to minimise the importance of faith; rather, Kuyper had a jealous concern to stress that *the person* of the sinner must be accepted by God as righteous before the process of holiness can begin. Kuyper's theological and pastoral instincts were right at this point, but his formulation of biblical doctrine was clearly fallacious and the biblical support for it was non-existent.[101]

There is, however, another way of understanding sanctification, and in this sense one may speak of sanctification preceding justification. If one understands the implanting of the new spiritual life which occurs at regeneration as the beginning of the work of sanctification – that by which, in Berkhof's definition of regeneration, 'the governing disposition of the soul is made holy'[102] – it is this implantation of spiritual life which enables the sinner to exercise saving faith; and since the first exercise of faith *precedes* the verdict of justification which God passes upon the sinner, it follows that, *in this very limited sense*, sanctification precedes justification.

Great care and discrimination are needed in the articulation of this point. The implanting of this principle of spiritual life is in no way the *ground* or *basis* of the sinner's justification. Until the justifying verdict is passed by God, the sinner stands before Him in a state of guilt and condemnation. The faith which can be seen

---

99. See note 93.

100. Ibid.

101. Ibid. It is surely significant that in his chapter on eternal justification, apart from one verse at the head of the chapter – a verse which is not adduced by Kuyper in support of eternal justification – there *is not one verse of Scripture cited*. Instead Kuyper seeks to reason illustratively and from first theological principles. The result is the appearance of Scripture being forced into a logical system rather than teaching being derived from the text of Scripture.

102. Louis Berkhof, *Systematic Theology* (London: Banner of Truth 1958), p. 469.

as the first exercise of the regenerate soul, much as the cry of the new-born babe indicates that it is truly possessed of physical life, is the instrumental means by which the sinner lays hold of Christ. As the sinner lays hold of Christ in self-abandoning despair, resting on Christ alone for salvation, God justifies the sinner *not* on the basis or ground of the sinner's faith but, rather, on the ground of Christ's obedience. As David McKay so helpfully demonstrates, this obedience comprises both Christ's active and His passive obedience, or, as it may be expressed – since Christ was tremendously active in offering Himself and bearing the sins of many – His obedience in obeying the precepts of God's law and His obedience in receiving the punishment demanded by that law. This is the basis for the great and wondrous exchange whereby our sins are reckoned or imputed to Christ and His righteousness imputed to us.[103] Thus, although faith can only be exercised by those who have received new spiritual life from God, it is nevertheless the case that this saving faith is in 'God who justifies the wicked'.[104] This is the great truth to which Luther referred when he spoke of the 'alien righteousness' that we receive: nothing that we do or feel or think – not even our faith – contributes anything, not even the merest atom, to the righteousness by which we are justified.

What has been argued for is that although justification and sanctification are *distinct*, they are not separated. In everyone who is justified, the process of sanctification has been begun: this is the clear import of Paul's teaching in Romans 6, when he responds to the objection that justification leads to the view that the more one sins, the more grace will abound. The essence of his response to this objection is precisely to demonstrate that grace breaks the power of sin and it does so by uniting us to Christ in His death and resurrection.[105] It is surely not without significance that Paul's teaching in these verses is to relate justification and

---

103. 2 Cor. 5:21.

104. Rom. 4:5.

105. Rom. 6:2-11.

sanctification to union with Christ. The spine of the argument which runs through Romans 6 is that those who have been justified are 'in Christ', and 'in Christ' they have died with Him and risen to new life in Him. In the same way, in Galatians 2:15-16 Paul twice refers to justification being 'by faith', while in verse 17 he writes: 'If while we seek to be justified in Christ . . .'

It may be thought that our death and rising to new life in Christ to which Paul refers in Romans 6 are something which happened to us when Christ died and rose; such an understanding, however, betrays a lack of sensitivity to the argument which Paul is deploying in these verses. He is responding to an objection which arises with respect to justified people, an objection which relates to those who have already exercised faith. Although it is true to say that all those who are yet to believe upon Christ down to the end of time were united with Him in His death and resurrection, it only becomes true of them when they believe. Again, while it is true that those who had been given by the Father to the Son were, in eternity, His people and, as such, Jesus could refer to them when He was on earth as being *then, at that time* as His people,[106] the fact remains that He stressed that they would need to be brought *existentially* to Him:[107] their coming to faith in Him would not be an empty charade. What a verse such as John 10:16 does make clear is that since those who had been given to Him were already, in one sense, His people, what He did in His life, death, and resurrection was done for them as their representative. The fact that Jesus could teach that His death would secure the coming to life of people[108] and that His death would draw all people unto Him[109] – the 'all people' here to be understood as all people without distinction, rather than

---

106. e.g., John.10:16: 'I *have* other sheep that are not of this sheep pen. I must bring them also.'

107. See note 106. The important words in this connection are, 'I must bring them also.'

108. John 12:23-4: Jesus' death, compared to a seed falling into the ground and dying, would produce many seeds.

109. John 12:32.

all people without exception – indicates a clear link between His saving work and the imparting of spiritual life and the coming to faith of His people. In a very real sense, one may say that Christ purchased all the blessings of salvation for those whom He represented, regeneration and faith being two of those great blessings.[110]

How does justification relate to existential union with Christ in the *ordo salutis*? A consideration of Galatians 2:15-21 and of 2 Corinthians 5:21 will help us to answer this question. In Paul's tightly woven argument in the Galatians passage, twice he refers to justification by faith in v. 16: 'knowing that a man is . . . justified . . . by faith in Jesus Christ . . . we, too, have put our faith in Christ Jesus that we may be justified by faith in Christ.' However, when in verse 17 Paul refers to this same reality, he writes: 'If, while we seek to be justified in Christ . . .' Therefore, being justified by faith = being justified in Christ. This must mean that faith is the bond by which, in the realm of experience, we come to be 'in Christ'. In verse 21 Paul makes it clear that righteousness does not come through the law but through the death of Christ. In the flow of the whole argument in this section of the letter the benefits of that righteousness which comes by Christ's death become ours by faith-union with Christ. Such justifying righteousness can only come by faith in Christ; equally, as Galatians 2:17 and 2 Corinthians 5:21 make clear, it comes only by being 'in Christ'.

Which is first, faith or union with Christ? The debate about this can become somewhat sterile and is not dissimilar to the question as to whether true gospel repentance precedes, in order of nature, saving faith or if it is consequent upon it. As John Murray pointed out, the question as to which is prior 'is an unnecessary question and the insistence that one is prior to the other is futile. There is no priority.'[111] They are Siamese twins: all

---

110. This is a point made by John Owen in his great work, *The Death of Death in the Death of Christ*.

111. John Murray, *Redemption Accomplished and Applied* (Edinburgh: Banner of Truth Trust 1961), p. 113.

true gospel repentance is *believing* repentance, and all true faith is *penitent* and *repentant* faith. Likewise there is no believing in Jesus without union with Christ being effected, and there is no union with Christ apart from faith. Without in any way trying to erect a theology based upon the use of certain prepositions, the fact remains that belief *in* ('en') Christ, *into* ('eis') Christ, and *on* or *upon* ('epi') Him is a belief which joins the sinner to Christ and places him 'in Christ'. Likewise it is impossible to exercise faith in Christ if one is still in Adam, if one is still 'in the flesh'. Believing upon Christ and being in union with Him are two sides of the same coin.

To understand the nature of the relationship between faith in Christ and existential union with Him, it may be helpful to observe how the status of those who are not in Christ can be viewed from differing, complementary angles, and then go on to see how the same applies to those who are in Christ. In 1 Corinthians 15:21-22 – verses which bear striking similarities to Romans 5:12-21 – Paul refers to those who are 'in Adam' and to those who are 'in Christ'. In Romans 8:8 he refers to those who are 'in the flesh' and contrasts them with those who are 'in the Spirit'. Those who are in the flesh, he tells us in verse 8, cannot please God. Although the letter to the Hebrews was written by a different human author from the letter to the Romans, the divine author of Holy Scripture is one and the same. This being so, Hebrews 11:6 is surely saying the same kind of thing as that which Romans 8:8 asserts: without faith it is impossible to please God. Therefore to be in Adam is to be in the flesh and this is to be without faith and thus it is impossible to please God. By analogy, we may say that to be in Christ is to be in the Spirit and this is to possess faith and to be pleasing to God.

It may be thought that Paul's words in Ephesians 2:5, that God 'made us alive *with Christ*', indicate that our being made alive only occurred in union with Him; and since this quickening or vivifying work of God *precedes*, in order of nature, the exercise of faith, we are 'in Christ' before we are regenerate and before we believe. As we have already seen, in one sense this is true: we are told in 1:4 that we were chosen in Christ before the foundation of the world; and it is true that *in one sense* we were with Christ in His death and resurrection *when He died and rose again*. However, this is a union which only becomes ours *in experience* when we believe. It is for this reason that Paul can write in verse 3: 'Like the rest, we were by nature objects of wrath.' In judicial terms the elect are under wrath until they are justified. But, as Paul goes on to say in verse 4, it is precisely 'because of his great love for us' – this love being His special love for His elect, not His general love for all mankind – that God, who is rich in mercy, 'made us alive with Christ'. This vivifying act of God proceeds from God's sovereign electing love and thereby enables those whom God has made alive to believe and thus to enter into all the blessings of the new covenant. Now, thus united to Christ, we are raised up with Him and made to sit in the heavenly realms 'in Christ Jesus' (v. 6). So, in one sense union with Christ *precedes* regeneration and in another sense it is consequent upon it and upon the first exercise of faith.

Regeneration, of course, may be more broadly conceived. John Murray has helpfully demonstrated how some passages of Scripture use the language of new birth in the narrow sense of the *immediate* work of God upon the soul in implanting new life, while other passages demand a broader understanding of this terminology, where new birth includes the agency of the Word of God *calling the newly implanted life into expression*.[112] in these latter passages new birth is virtually synonymous with conversion and operates at the conscious level, and includes a *mediate* element, in that the Word of God is instrumental *not* in the implanting of the new life but, rather, in the calling of that life into expression. In this connection a distinction needs to be drawn between the Spirit imparting the new life which secures the response of faith, and the giving of the Spirit which is consequent upon the exercise of faith. In Galatians 3:2 Paul poses the question as to whether his

---

112. Murray, *Collected Writings*, vol. 2, pp. 195-8.

readers had received the Spirit by the works of the law or by the hearing of faith? The question clearly implies that the reception of the Spirit came *after* believing into or upon Christ.

From the foregoing we may briefly summarise the biblical teaching on the relation of union with Christ, faith, justification and sanctification within the *ordo salutis* in the following way. Those who were chosen in Christ before the foundation of the world were given by the Father to the Son. The Son came into the world to redeem those who were, in one sense, already His. Therefore, in His life, death, resurrection, and ascension He represented them and His life was *their life*, His death was *their* death, and His resurrection was *their* resurrection. In His work for His people He purchased all the blessings of salvation for them, their regeneration and faith being amongst those blessings. His death for His people once for all time secured their coming to Him in due course. Those who are thus 'in Christ' are quickened into spiritual life and place their faith in Christ and are experientially in Him; as such, on the basis of Christ's work for them they are justified and, in consequence of their union with Christ in His death and resurrection, begin to live a new life.[113]

6. Practical lessons

Theology is meant to affect life; if it does not do so, then it becomes sterile and lifeless, and we turn one of God's blessings into something of a curse. Union with Christ is a fact for all of God's people, however well-taught or otherwise they may be with respect to this great reality. And it is this union which is the context in which our whole salvation takes place and exists: from our election in Christ before the creation of the world

---

113. The late Professor John Macleod has a fascinating discussion of the differences with respect to the precedence of regeneration to justification or of justification to regeneration as found in the writings of the great Thomas Halyburton (who placed regeneration first) and Alexander Comrie and his later admirer Abraham Kuyper (who placed justification before regeneration): see John Macleod, *Scottish Theology In Relation To Church History Since The Reformation* (Edinburgh: Banner of Truth Trust 1974), pp. 124-33.

right through to the coming of the Lord at the end. If Paul can tell the Ephesians of election in Christ, he can write to the Thessalonians of 'the dead in Christ' rising at the coming of the Lord.[114] The words 'the dead in Christ' clearly refer to the bodies of those believers who had died because Paul speaks of them 'rising': this must, therefore, be understood of the bodies that have mouldered in the graves. The reference to these having fallen asleep is not to some kind of 'soul sleep'[115] but to their bodies. How comforting that the body of the believer remains united to Christ, no matter how many years it lies in the grave! Indeed, even if the body is vaporized in a nuclear blast or eaten by wild animals or by the fish of the sea, in some mysterious way that entity is still united to Christ. The answer to Question 37 of the Westminster Shorter Catechism expresses this truth with sublime simplicity and succinctness: '. . . their bodies, being still united to Christ, do rest in their graves till the resurrection.' Of course, this is because the whole person is united to Christ and, unlike the marriage bond (with which the relationship between Christ and the church is likened in Scripture), this is a union which not even death can break: '. . . your life is now hidden with Christ in God. When Christ, who is your life, appears, then you also will appear with him in glory.'[116]

Although it is true to say, then, that union with Christ is a reality for all God's people, whatever their knowledge or ignorance of this, the fact remains that, all other things being equal, our understanding of this great truth and of its implications should have enormous consequences for the way that we live our Christian lives. It is to this truth that Paul appeals in order to steer Christians away from the opposite dangers of licence and legalism. Thus, in Romans 6:3, in response to the question, 'Shall

---

114. 1 Thess. 4:16.

115. The erroneous idea of 'soul sleep' is not a novel idea invented by the Jehovah's Witnesses, as may be seen by the fact that Calvin wrote against it in his little work entitled *Psychopannychia*.

116. Col. 3:3-4.

we go on sinning, so that grace may increase?' Paul appeals to his readers' knowledge of their union with Christ, and goes on to work out its implications in this very practical realm: 'Don't you know that all of us who were baptised into Christ Jesus were baptised into his death?' In 1 Corinthians 6:15-17 Paul makes a startling application of this great truth when dealing with the issue of Corinthian Christians who were still, it seems, consorting with prostitutes of the city. Rarely has such high theology been brought to bear upon an issue so sordid. The fact that those who were members of Christ became one flesh with a prostitute suggests a grotesque reality which was intended to shock and alarm Paul's readers and to jolt them into a godlier way of living. Underpinning Paul's exhortation is his appeal to what they already knew concerning their union with Christ: 'Do you not know that your bodies are members of Christ himself?'[117]

If licence is one great enemy of authentic Christian living, it is no less the case that legalism can do just as much damage to the child of God, perhaps more so because it may be less easily recognisable. As Tim Ward demonstrates in his chapter on Galatians, Paul's whole polemic against the legalistic teaching which was threatening the Galatian churches is grounded in the doctrine of union with Christ, chapter 2:19-21 being something of a climactic *locus classicus* with respect to this.

It is probably not an exaggeration to say that much of twentieth-century evangelical Christianity was characterised by a legalistic and 'rule-centred' approach to Christian living, where many of the rules had little, if any, biblical basis. When this approach began to be questioned and broke down, something of a spiritual vacuum resulted and this led to a feelings-orientated Christianity, which was characterised by an unhealthy individualism which paid scant regard to biblical principles and to the responsibility which the believer has to the people of God. I am, of course, painting the spiritual landscape of the twentieth century with a very broad brush, and there were notable exceptions which

---

117. 1 Cor. 6:15.

brightened the landscape considerably. Nevertheless, I think that the picture generally represents some of the disfiguring features of evangelical life in the twentieth century and in the first two decades of this millennium. While the roots of this legalism and the consequent licence were – and are – no doubt many and varied, the virtual absence of an emphasis upon the doctrine of union with Christ goes a long way in explaining one of the fundamental problems. It is cause for thankfulness that three of the most popularly influential theologians of the second half of the twentieth century restored this doctrine to its rightful place and sought to show its relevance to the matter of Christian living[118]. The doctrine is now being 'rehabilitated' and numerous publications have emphasised its importance.[119]

Individualism is, of course, a luxury enjoyed by those in affluent societies or by those who are fortunate enough to be able to live 'comfortably' in less privileged countries. It is, therefore, very much a phenomenon which characterises much of life in the West, and Christians given over to such individualism are usually simply living lives which mirror their culture and society: in other words, to call it by its right name, it is worldliness. By contrast, many of our brothers and sisters are living lives in very different circumstances. The wave of persecution which has been unleashed in some parts of the Islamic world upon Christian people has led to a displacement of believers from their homes which reminds

---

118. The three theologians were Martyn Lloyd-Jones, John Murray and James Packer. Their emphasis on union with Christ is to be found in the following: D. M. Lloyd-Jones, *Romans Chapter 6: The New Man* (Edinburgh: Banner of Truth Trust 1972); D. M. Lloyd-Jones, *Life in the Spirit in Marriage, Home and Work: An Exposition of Ephesians 5:18 to 6:9* (Edinburgh: Banner of Truth Trust 1974); John Murray, *Redemption Accomplished and Applied;* John Murray, *Collected Writings* vol. 2 (Edinburgh: Banner of Truth Trust 1976); J. I. Packer, *Keep in Step with the Spirit* (Leicester: InterVarsity Press 1984).

119. For example, 'popular' treatments are Natalie Brand, *Crazy But True. Connected to Jesus for Life* (Bridgend: Bryntirion Press 2014) and Kevin DeYoung, *The Hole In Our Holiness: Filling the Gap between Gospel Passion and the Pursuit of Godliness* (Wheaton: Crossway 2012). An example of a more scholarly work in this field is Robert Letham, *Union With Christ: In Scripture, History, and Theology* (Phillipsburg: P & R Publishing 2011).

one of the scattering of the Jerusalem church recorded in Acts 8. Few things can be as distressing as to have to leave the area where generations of one's family have lived, thereby abandoning one's possessions and the whole network of those relationships which so enrich life. Truly, such displaced people experience poverty in more ways than one. At such times, it is really only the believer's union with Christ, and the communion which flows from this, which can enable the believer not to go under completely and, even more, to rejoice in such sufferings. It is not the understanding of a piece of theology but the rich communion which Jesus gives that can enable the believer to sing during even the darkest day. 'The fellowship of sharing in his sufferings' is something to which many severely persecuted Christians have testified and this is only possible because of the believer's union with Christ. Moreover, that union leads to union with all God's people, and at such times the reality of union with Christ may be experienced through the love and care of fellow believers. Certainly, it is in the context of the deprivation of His people that Jesus refers to acts of kindness being done to them as being done to Him.[120] Perhaps it is not surprising that it is Paul who gives such emphasis to this reality: the truth was burned into his soul on the Damascus road when he learned that his persecuting of the Lord's people was regarded by the Lord as persecution of Him.[121] It may well be the case that this was how he entered so much into the reality of what it meant to 'fill up in [his] flesh what is still lacking in regard to Christ's afflictions, for the sake of his body, which is the church.'[122] Certainly, many of the saints have testified that few things sweetened their sufferings for Christ so much as to know that, although it was in a non-redemptive sense, Christ's union with them meant that their sufferings were His.

Some, of course, are called upon to lay down their lives for Christ. And, apart from those who will be alive when the Lord

---

120. Matt. 25:40.

121. Acts 9:5.

122. Col. 1:24.

returns, all of us will have to leave these bodies and experience the unnatural separation of body and soul, which is what physical death is. As we have seen, however, our union with Christ will not be broken even by death. Indeed, although still the last enemy, the sting of death has been removed for the Christian and death is therefore described as falling asleep in Jesus. The union which began in eternity goes on into eternity.

Most of this chapter – and, indeed, of the whole book – has been taken up with an understanding of union with Christ from what may be broadly described as a 'Reformed perspective'. But the last word on this shall be left to that great hymn writer of Christian experience, Charles Wesley. Charles Wesley, of course, like his brother John, was not Reformed, and the name of the Wesley brothers is associated with an Arminian understanding of the plan of salvation and of its application to the individual. But union with Christ means that we are united to all of God's people, Calvinists with Arminians, Baptists with paedobaptists, and so on. Indeed, Affinity – under whose auspices the conference at which the papers, which formed the basis for the previous six chapters, were given – is a body of churches and Christian bodies united by the common core of truth known as evangelical, and, as such, accommodates both Calvinist and Arminian. It is fitting, therefore, in a book written by men who are Calvinistic in their understanding that the last word be given to a great Christian who was Arminian. Certainly, his words express a rich experiential enjoyment of communion with Christ. They remind us that union with Christ is to be more than a doctrine to understand, but to be the context of living in the presence of a 'felt Christ'. If the pages of this book lead to a greater realisation and enjoyment of this by God's people, they will not have been written in vain. Here are Wesley's words:

> Thou hidden source of calm repose,
> Thou all-sufficient love divine,
> My help and refuge from my foes,
> Secure I am, if Thou art mine:

And lo! From sin, and grief, and shame,
I hide me, Jesus, in Thy Name.

Thy mighty Name salvation is,
And keeps my happy soul above;
Comfort it brings, and power, and peace,
And joy, and everlasting love:
To me, with Thy dear Name, are given
Pardon, and holiness, and heaven.

Jesus, my all in all Thou art,
My rest in toil, my ease in pain,
The medicine of my broken heart,
In war my peace, in loss my gain,
My smile beneath the tyrant's frown,
In shame my glory and my crown:

In want my plentiful supply,
In weakness my almighty power,
In bonds my perfect liberty,
My light in Satan's darkest hour,
My help and stay whene'er I call,
My life in death, my heaven, my all.[123]

---

123. Charles Wesley (1707–1788): Hymn number 613 in *Christian Hymns*.

Bibliography

Augustine. *Confessions*. Trans. Henry Chadwick. (World's Classics) Oxford: Oxford University Press 1992.

Beardsley, Monroe C. 'Metaphor' in Paul Edwards (ed.) *The Encyclopaedia of Philosophy*. vol. 5. New York/London: Macmillan Company & Free Press/Collier-Macmillan Publishers 1967.

Berkhof, Louis. *Systematic Theology*. London: Banner of Truth Trust 1958.

Brand, Natalie. *Crazy But True. Connected to Jesus for Life*. Bridgend: Bryntirion Press 2014.

Brine, John. *A Defence of The Doctrine of Eternal Justification From Some Exceptions made to it By Mr Bragge, and others*. Printed and sold by A. Ward at the King's Arms in Little-Britain and H. Whitridge, at the Corner of Castle-Alley, near the Royal Exchange, 1732. Obtainable at http://www.mountzionpbc.org/Index/index03.htm

Carr, G. Lloyd. *The Song of Solomon: An Introduction and Commentary*. Leicester: InterVarsity Press 1984.

Cook, Paul E. G. and Harrison, Graham (eds.) *Christian Hymns*. Bridgend: Evangelical Movement of Wales 1977.

Cook, Paul E. G., Harrison, Graham, Clark, David and Strivens, Robert (eds.) *Christian Hymns*. Bridgend/Welwyn Garden City: Evangelical Movement of Wales and the Christian Hymns Committee 2004.

Davies, Gaius. *George Fox: A Radical Spirit*. Report of the Westminster Conference 1996.

DeYoung, Kevin. *The Hole In Our Holiness: Filling the Gap between Gospel Passion and the Pursuit of Godliness*. Wheaton: Crossway 2012.

Hawking, Stephen W. *A Brief History of Time: From the Big Bang to Black Holes*. London: Bantam Press 1988.

Helm, Paul. *Eternal God*. Oxford: Clarendon Press 1988.

Kuiper, R. B. *God Centred Evangelism*. London: Banner of Truth Trust 1966.

Kuyper, Abraham. *The Work of the Holy Spirit*. Grand Rapids: Wm. B. Eerdmans Co. 1900.

Letham, Robert. *Union With Christ: In Scripture, History, and Theology*. Phillipsburg: P & R Publishing 2011.

Lloyd-Jones, D. M. *Romans. An Exposition of Chapter 6: The New Man*. Edinburgh: Banner of Truth Trust 1972.

Lloyd-Jones, D. M. *Life in the Spirit in Marriage, Home and Work: An Exposition of Ephesians 5:18 to 6:9*. Edinburgh: Banner of Truth Trust 1974.

Macleod, John. *Scottish Theology in Relation to Church History since the Reformation*. Edinburgh: Banner of Truth Trust 1974.

Martin, Hugh. *The Atonement: In its Relations to the Covenant, the Priesthood, the Intercession of Our Lord*. Edinburgh: Knox Press 1976.

Murray, Iain H. *David Martyn Lloyd-Jones: The Fight of Faith 1939 -1981*. Edinburgh: Banner of Truth Trust 1990.

Murray, John. *Redemption Accomplished and Applied*. Edinburgh: Banner of Truth Trust 1961.

Murray, John. *Collected Writings of John Murray Volume 2: Select Lectures In Systematic Theology*. Edinburgh: Banner of Truth Trust 1977.

Packer, J. I. *Keep in Step with the Spirit*. Leicester: InterVarsity Press 1984.

Packer, J. I. *Among God's Giants: Aspects of Puritan Christianity*. Eastbourne: Kingsway Publications 1991.

Spurgeon, C. H. *C. H. Spurgeon Autobiography Volume 1: The Early Years 1834-1859 (Revised edition published in two volumes).* London: Banner of Truth Trust 1962.

Stuart, D. *Hosea–Jonah.* Word Biblical Commentary Volume 31. Waco: Word Books 1987.

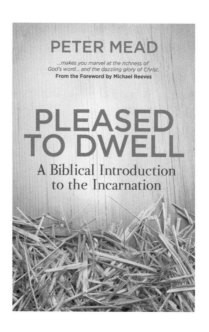

Pleased to Dwell
A Biblical Introduction to the Incarnation
by Peter Mead

At the centre of heaven is Christ, lovingly adored as the forever Lord of all. At the centre of Christmas is Christ, frail and cradled in the tender arms of a young mother. How can the two be put together? Heavenly glory and human frailty? That is the real wonder of Christmas. *Pleased to Dwell* is an energetic biblical introduction to Christmas. It is an invitation to ponder the Incarnation, and a God who was pleased to dwell with us.

ISBN: 978-1-78191-426-7

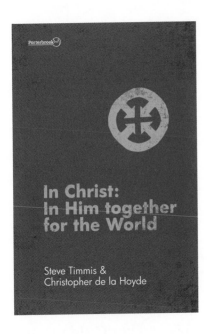

In Christ:
In Him together for the World
by Steve Timmis &
Christopher de la Hoyde

Union with Christ is truly phenomenal and supernatural, but it is not make-believe or mysterious. It is beautifully pertinent to daily experience. *In Christ* focuses on how our union with Christ really does shape and impact not only everything we do and say, but how we say and do it.

ISBN: 978-1-78191-429-8

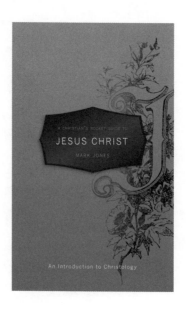

A Christian's Pocket Guide to Jesus Christ

An Introduction to Christology

by Mark Jones

For many of us, the whole concept of Christology is as mystifying as a foreign language, yet Christians down the ages have fought to defend the person and work of Christ – seeing him and what he did quite rightly as a vital element of how we are saved. If we are to understand this subject we need to know the person of Christ; not just what he did (his work) but who he is (his person). Through this book we get to know the Son of God who indeed is God and not just a superman! He is the one who came from above and became fully human having a human body and soul. Being God enabled him to pay the debt owed for sin and being man enabled him to stand on man's behalf for their sin. In straightforward and simple layman terms this book will explain the interconnectivity of the work and person of Jesus Christ and dispel any misconceptions you may have.

ISBN: 978-1-84550-951-4

Systematic Theology
Volume 1
by Douglas F. Kelly

"I have written this first volume, thinking of my heritage as both Reformed and Catholic; gladly appropriating crucial insights of the whole people of God over the last two thousand years – Eastern Orthodox, Western Catholic, and Reformation Protestant – as they sought to live out the foundational truths of the inspired Word of God." **Doug Kelly**

ISBN: 978-1-84550-386-4

Systematic Theology
Volume 2
by Douglas F. Kelly

Douglas F. Kelly returns to the writings of saints and scholars to exemplify the beauty and the wonder of Christ, the Son of God, in this highly-anticipated second volume of systematic theology. Kelly delves through a treasure trove of Patristics, Scholastics, Reformers, Puritans, and Moderns to recover an Augustinian reverence for the beauty of Christ, to illustrate that the Father and the Spirit are most fully revealed through Him, and to make clear that His coming is the restoration of the universe.

ISBN: 978-1-78191-293-5

Christian Focus Publications

Our mission statement –

STAYING FAITHFUL
In dependence upon God we seek to impact the world through literature faithful to His infallible Word, the Bible. Our aim is to ensure that the Lord Jesus Christ is presented as the only hope to obtain forgiveness of sin, live a useful life and look forward to heaven with Him.

Our books are published in four imprints:

CHRISTIAN
FOCUS

Popular works including biographies, commentaries, basic doctrine and Christian living.

CHRISTIAN
HERITAGE

Books representing some of the best material from the rich heritage of the church.

MENTOR

Books written at a level suitable for Bible College and seminary students, pastors, and other serious readers. The imprint includes commentaries, doctrinal studies, examination of current issues and church history.

CF4•K

Children's books for quality Bible teaching and for all age groups: Sunday school curriculum, puzzle and activity books; personal and family devotional titles, biographies and inspirational stories – because you are never too young to know Jesus!

Christian Focus Publications Ltd,
Geanies House, Fearn, Ross-shire,
IV20 1TW, Scotland, United Kingdom.
www.christianfocus.com